Betty Crocker

SMART DINNER

Clever and Versatile Ways to Use What You've Got on Hand

Houghton Mifflin Harcourt

Boston • New York • 2017

GENERAL MILLS

Owned Media and Publishing Director:
Amy Halford

Owned Media and Publishing Manager:
Danielle Andrews

Senior Editor: Cathy Swanson

Recipe Development and Testing: Betty
Crocker Kitchens

Photography: General Mills Photography
Studios and Image Library

HOUGHTON MIFFLIN HARCOURT

Editorial Director: Cindy Kitchel

Executive Editor: Anne Ficklen

Editorial Associate: Molly Ahuja

Managing Editor: Marina Padakis Lowry

Production Editor: Helen Seachrist

Cover Design: Tai Blanche

Interior Design: Tai Blanche

Interior Layout: Kelly Dubeau Smydra,
Rebecca Springer

Senior Production Coordinator:
Kimberly Kiefer

Bisquick® is a registered trademark of
General Mills, Inc.

Inspiring America to Cook at Home™

www.hmhco.com

Library of Congress Cataloging-in-Publication Data is available.

ISBN 978-0-544-95459-5 (trade paper); 978-0-544-95451-9 (ebook)

Manufactured in China

SCP 10 9 8 7 6 5 4 3 2 1

Cover photos: BBQ Chipotle Chicken–Cheddar Sliders (page 47), Creamy
Pulled-Pork Pasta (page 89), Fattoush Salad (page 233), Asian Salmon Sheet
Pan Dinner (page 134)

The Betty Crocker Kitchens seal guarantees
success in your kitchen. Every recipe has been
tested in America's Most Trusted Kitchens™
to meet our high standards of reliability, easy
preparation and great taste.

FIND MORE GREAT IDEAS AT

BettyCrocker.com

DEAR FRIENDS,

What's a smart dinner? It's an easy, no-fuss way to get a meal on the table while using up what you have on hand. Solving the dinnertime crunch while reducing food waste—how awesome is that? From one-pot favorites and meatless meals to even breakfast for dinner, you'll find delicious recipes no matter what your evening has in store. Supper will never be boring with the likes of Roasted Root Veggie Pizza, page 154 (it uses both the beetroot *and* the tops), Chicken "Fridge Sweep" Chowder, page 196 or Spinach-Mushroom Eggs Benedict Enchiladas, page 248.

Take the stress out of meal planning with our Simple Dinner Strategies, page 6. The Quick, Throw-Together Meals, page 8, give easy-to-follow instructions for basic recipes like rice bowls and make-your-own pasta. You customize them by using what you have on hand. And look to the Way to Use tips with most every recipe that give you great ways to use up foods like tortillas, canned beans and fresh herbs.

So inventory your fridge and let's make dinner!

Betty Crocker

Look for recipes with these icons:

QUICK FIX	15 minutes or less prep
ONE POT	Easy to make and clean up
SLOW COOKER	Dinner's ready when you are
MAKE AHEAD	Plan for those rushed nights

CONTENTS

Simple Dinner Strategies 6

Quick, Throw-Together Meals 8

Fresh Veggie Cooking Chart 10

1 **Chicken and Turkey** 12

2 **Beef and Pork** 64

3 **Fish and Shellfish** 112

4 **Meatless** 152

5 **Soups and Sides** 194

6 **Breakfast for Dinner** 246

Metric Conversion Guide 276

Index 277

SIMPLE DINNER STRATEGIES

Getting dinner on the table isn't always easy—busy lives and last-minute changes in plans can make you grab the phone for pizza delivery or head out for takeout. But don't fear: Look here for ways to make it simple to eat at home. It doesn't matter if everyone is eating at different times, if you need to make dinner ahead or if there's no time to cook—you'll find plenty of great solutions to fit your needs. So now you can feel good about serving your family a home-cooked meal while using up what you have on hand—that's a winner, winner, great dinner!

MINIMIZE DINNERTIME STRESS

Use these tips to help the dinner dash go more smoothly:

- On the weekends, look ahead at the week. What nights will cooking dinner be difficult? Look for opportunities to make a meal or two in advance, such as slow cooker soups and chilies. When you're ready for dinner, you've got a big jump on the prep.

- Rely on "planned overs." That is, plan for leftovers. When you know there will be a night that people will be eating at different times, make a larger batch of dinner the night or two before so that the leftovers can be reheated on the hectic night. Store the leftovers in individual microwavable containers to make it easy for everyone to grab and reheat when they are ready.

- Plan to make just one dish, then round out the meal with items you or another family member pick up at the deli.

- Enlist the help of family members to get dinner on the table and clean up afterward. Not only does it spread out the work, but you get to spend more time together!

GRAB-AND-GO CUSTOMIZABLE PANTRY

Keeping your pantry stocked with items you use frequently will help on those nights when you need to whip something together. Below is a general guide: You can adjust it to your needs and family's tastes. As you make meals and find new favorite ingredients, make them staples for your own, customized pantry.

- Meals can be whipped up quickly when you keep packaged goods like pasta and sauce, rice, soup and sauce mixes, broth, dried fruits and nuts on hand.

- Favorite condiments can become secret ingredients to quick meals. Use ketchup, mustard, mayonnaise, Worcestershire sauce, salsa, barbecue sauce or salad dressings as sauce for pasta or rice, or to season meat before cooking. Try mixing a few together to create your own sauce.

- Meats such as ground beef or turkey, pork chops, chicken breasts and shrimp are great to keep in the freezer for quick meals. Leftover cooked meats from the freezer are easy to reheat and add to pasta or rice dishes, burrito bowls, quesadillas or taco salads. Also look for frozen and refrigerated cooked chicken and meatballs and other convenience products to have on hand for the craziest of nights.

- Frozen fruits and veggies make it easy to have them on hand without going bad (like fresh produce does) or to use when the fresh options aren't in season.

- Shop often for fresh fruits and veggies to have available for meals and snacks. Bagged salads, refrigerated potatoes and precut veggies make it a hop, skip and jump to having dinner on the table.

- Dairy products like eggs, cheeses and sour cream in your fridge are great starts for simple dinners. Loaded omelets, quesadillas or grilled cheese make delicious, fast dinners.

USE UP WHAT YOU'VE GOT

Your fridge and freezer might look bare . . . but take another look. Dinner might be just a few combinations of ingredients away.

- **Combine ingredients.** If you don't have enough of one ingredient, look for things you can combine. Pastas can be combined and cooked together. Start cooking the types that take the longest to cook, then add the shorter-cooking ones later so they all get done at the same time. Not enough chicken for a meal? Add some shrimp from the freezer or a can of black beans from the pantry.

- **Get creative.** Look for ingredients that could be used to make any of these standbys: stuffed baked potatoes, stir-fries, quesadillas, rice bowls, pasta dishes, pizzas or omelets. Keep in mind that not everyone's dinner has to be the same. Customize them to each person's tastes and what you have on hand.

- **Do a fridge sweep.** Before you go to the store again, do a sweep of what you already have and make soup. (Did you know that that is how restaurants get their "soup of the day"?) See Chicken "Fridge Sweep" Chowder, page 196, for inspiration.

GO-TO DINNERS

On those nights when you just can't come up with what to put on the table, look to these last-minute ideas to solve the dinner dilemma.

Everyone's Eating at Different Times

Have the food ready to reheat as needed.

Steakhouse Sloppy Joes, page 70
 Creamy coleslaw
 Chips

Colorful Ham Salad Sandwiches, page 97
 Clusters of grapes
 Carrot sticks

Make-Ahead Meals

Make it ahead so dinner is ready when you are!

BBQ Beef Biscuit Stacks, page 82
 Green beans

Oven-Roasted Pulled Pork, page 86
 Tortillas
 Sliced bell peppers
 Rice

No Time to Cook

Have super-quick meals ready in 20 minutes.

Asian Beef Noodle Bowls, page 78
 Apple or pear slices

Chicken with Pan-Roasted Cauliflower and Orzo, page 42
 Green salad

QUICK, THROW-TOGETHER MEALS

There's work, school and a host of activities, with no chance to catch your breath. All of a sudden it's dinnertime—what do you do? On those nights when there's no plan and magician-like skills are needed, don't head for the drive-thru! Pick one of these ideas and customize it by repurposing whatever foods and ingredients you have on hand. You'll have dinner on the table in minutes (and you'll wish you could high-five yourself for the creative effort).

Anything goes! Don't feel like you need to start with plain leftover meat or chicken or cooked veggies. Sauced and seasoned foods will add a new twist of flavor to these incredibly easy dinners. If it's in a lot of sauce, simply use a slotted spoon (to remove the food from the majority of the sauce) when you are ready to use it, and discard or repurpose any remaining sauce.

RICE BOWLS

Grain bowls might seem fancy and time-consuming, but when you've got leftovers, they're a snap to put together.

1. **Create a base.** Choose any kind of rice, quinoa or couscous. Reheat leftovers or cook up some fresh from your pantry in minutes.

2. **Layer up.** Spoon some protein over the rice or grain. Thoroughly reheat whatever leftover meat, poultry or cooked beans you have on hand. Or heat a can of rinsed and drained beans in a microwavable bowl.

3. **Sprinkle with shredded cheese.** Adding cheese to your bowl on top of the warm protein will help the cheese to melt and cling to ingredients you put on top.

4. **Top with veggies.** This is the place to use up those leftover cooked veggies (reheated and drained if necessary) or raid your kitchen for green onions, tomatoes, cucumbers, canned corn (heat before using), olives, etc.

MYO PASTA

Feel "chefy" when you make your own customized pasta dish—from what seems like nothing!

1. **Cook up pasta.** Reheat leftover cooked pasta by plunging it in boiling water for a minute; drain. Or cook a batch from your pantry. While it cooks, prepare the rest of the dish. Drain the pasta—but be sure to save some of the cooking liquid—and return the pasta to the pan.

2. **Cook up veggies.** What do you have on hand? Use any leftover cooked veggies—or cook up broccoli, carrots or cauliflower—and add onion to round out the flavor and bulk up the dish. Undercook them a minute or two. See the Fresh Veggie Cooking Chart on page 10 for details.

3. **Toss it all together.** Add the veggie mixture to the pasta, along with bite-size pieces of cooked meat or poultry or a can of drained beans. Toss gently over low heat, long enough to heat through. Add some of the reserved cooking liquid to moisten all the ingredients.

4. **Go for the greens.** Now's the time to bulk up the dish even more, if you like. Throw in fresh arugula or baby spinach or kale leaves and toss just until wilted.

5. **Finish with more flavor.** Add grated Parmesan, Romano or Asiago cheese or toasted bread crumbs to tie all the ingredients together into a yummy dish.

BEEFED-UP GRILLED CHEESE

You might think of grilled cheese as a lunch sandwich. These simple steps turn grilled cheese into a delicious dinner twist.

1. **Butter it up.** Butter one side of each slice of bread with about 2 teaspoons softened butter. (The butter will help the sandwich get golden-brown and toasty.) Place one slice buttered-side down to build the sandwich. It's a lot easier to do it now, rather than after the sandwich is built.
2. **Start with cheese.** Sprinkle with shredded cheese or add a layer of thinly sliced cheese on top of the piece of bread.
3. **Top with cooked meat.** Use a little finely chopped or sliced cooked (reheated) beef, pork or chicken.
4. **Sprinkle on flavor.** Add sliced olives, pickles, sliced green onions or other tasty ingredients.
5. **More cheese, please.** Add a little more shredded or thinly sliced cheese on top of the meat.
6. **Top it.** Finish with the second slice of bread, buttered side up; press sandwich lightly together.
7. **Cook it.** Cook sandwich uncovered in hot skillet or griddle over low heat until golden brown on both sides and cheese is melted.

"TACO" SALAD

Whatever you have on-hand will take this salad on a tasty new adventure. Your creation may not even be Mexican-flavored at all!

1. **Build a base.** Use tortilla, nacho or corn chips. Or coarsely crush tortilla shells with your hands onto individual microwavable plates.
2. **Add meat or beans.** Reheat leftover cooked beef, pork or chicken, or use drained canned beans; spoon over the chips.
3. **Sprinkle with cheese.** Use your favorite shredded cheese. Microwave uncovered 30 seconds to 1 minute on High or until the cheese is melted.
4. **Top with your favorite ingredients.** Shredded or bite-size pieces of salad greens and reheated leftover cooked and drained veggies, chopped tomatoes, olive tapenade, black bean relish or pickle slices are all great choices.
5. **Sauce it up.** Dollop or drizzle with a sauce or two for added moisture and flavor. Ranch dressing, artichoke dip, barbecue sauce, salsa and sour cream are all yummy options.

FRESH VEGGIE COOKING CHART

Here's a handy chart to use with the preferred cooking methods for most popular veggies. Use this to help get dinner on the table in a jiffy, with veggies cooked to perfection!

- **To Steam:** In saucepan or skillet, place steamer basket in ½ inch water (water should not touch bottom of basket). Place veggies in steamer basket. Cover tightly and heat to boiling; reduce heat to low. Steam for amount of time in chart.

- **To Roast:** Heat oven to 425°F. Toss cut (unless stated otherwise) veggies with about 1 tablespoon olive oil and season as desired. Place vegetables in baking pan. Roast for amount of time in chart.

- **To Microwave:** Use microwavable dish with cover or use plastic wrap to cover. When using paper towels or plastic wrap in the microwave, use products that are microwave safe. Add 2 tablespoons water, unless stated otherwise, to dish with vegetables. Microwave on High, unless stated otherwise, for amount of time in chart; drain. Stir or rearrange vegetables once or twice during cooking. Let vegetables stand covered 1 to 2 minutes to finish cooking.

VEGETABLE	PREPARATION	CONVENTIONAL DIRECTIONS	MICROWAVE DIRECTIONS
Artichokes, Globe (4 medium)	Remove discolored leaves; trim stem even with base. Cut 1 inch off top. Snip tips off leaves. To retain color, dip in cold water mixed with lemon juice.	Steaming or roasting not recommended.	Place 1 or 2 artichokes in dish; add ¼ cup water. Microwave 5 to 7 minutes or until leaves pull out easily and bottom is tender when pierced with a knife.
Artichokes, Jerusalem (1 lb)	Leave whole, or cut as desired. To retain color, toss with cold water mixed with lemon juice.	Steam: 15 to 20 minutes or until crisp-tender.	5 to 7 minutes or until crisp-tender.
Asparagus (1½ lb)	Break off ends of spears. Leave whole, or cut into 1-inch pieces.	Steam: 6 to 8 minutes or until crisp-tender. Roast (whole): 10 to 12 minutes.	4 to 6 minutes or until crisp-tender.
Beans, Green, Purple Wax and Yellow Wax (1 lb)	Remove ends. Leave beans whole, or cut into 1-inch pieces.	Steam: 10 to 12 minutes or until crisp-tender. Roast (whole): 6 to 8 minutes.	8 to 10 minutes or until crisp-tender.
Beets (5 medium)	Cut off all but 2 inches of tops. Leave whole with root ends attached. Peel after cooking.	Steam: 45 to 50 minutes or until tender. Roast: 35 to 40 minutes.	12 to 16 minutes or until tender.
Broccoli (1½ lb)	Trim off large leaves; remove tough ends of stems. Cut as desired.	Steam: 10 to 11 minutes or until crisp-tender.	5 to 6 minutes or until crisp-tender.
Brussels Sprouts (1 lb)	Remove discolored leaves; cut off ends of stems. Cut large sprouts in half.	Steam: 8 to 12 minutes or until tender. Roast: 12 to 15 minutes.	5 to 6 minutes or until tender.
Carrots (6 or 7 medium)	Peel; cut off ends. Leave ready-to-eat baby carrots whole, or cut as desired.	Steam: 8 to 10 minutes or until crisp-tender. Roast: 25 to 30 minutes.	5 to 9 minutes or until crisp-tender.
Cauliflower (1 medium head)	Remove outer leaves and stem; cut off any discoloration. Leave whole, or separate into florets.	Steam: 8 to 12 minutes or until tender. Roast: 15 to 20 minutes.	8 to 10 minutes or until tender.

VEGETABLE	PREPARATION	CONVENTIONAL DIRECTIONS	MICROWAVE DIRECTIONS
Corn (4 ears)	Husk ears and remove silk just before cooking.	Steam: 5 to 7 minutes or until crisp-tender.	Wrap ears in waxed paper or place in dish. 1 ear: Microwave 2 to 3 minutes. 2 ears: Microwave 3 to 4 minutes.
Greens: Beet, Chicory, Collard, Escarole, Kale, Mustard, Spinach, Swiss Chard, Turnip (1 lb)	Remove root ends and imperfect leaves.	Steam: 5 to 8 minutes or until tender.	Beet, chicory or escarole: 8 to 10 minutes or until tender. Collards, kale, mustard, spinach, Swiss chard or turnips: 4 to 6 minutes or until tender.
Mushrooms (1 lb)	Wipe each mushroom with damp paper towel to remove dirt. Trim off stem. Leave whole, or cut as desired.	Sauté: 4 to 6 minutes with 1 tablespoon butter or until tender. Roast: 5 to 10 minutes.	Place mushrooms in dish; add 1 tablespoon butter. Microwave 3 to 4 minutes or until tender.
Parsnips (6 to 8 medium)	Peel; cut off ends. Leave whole, or cut as desired.	Steam: 9 to 15 minutes or until tender. Roast: 25 to 30 minutes.	5 to 6 minutes or until tender.
Peas, Sugar Snap (1 lb)	Snip off stem ends and remove strings.	Steam: 6 to 7 minutes or until crisp-tender.	6 to 7 minutes or until crisp-tender.
Peas, Sweet (2 lb)	Shell just before cooking.	Steam: 8 to 10 minutes or until tender.	4 to 6 minutes or until tender.
Peppers, Bell (2 medium)	Remove stems, seeds and membranes. Leave whole to stuff and bake, or cut as desired.	Steam: 4 to 6 minutes or until crisp-tender. Sauté: 3 to 5 minutes, with 1 tablespoon butter. Roast: 15 to 20 minutes.	3 to 4 minutes or until crisp-tender.
Potatoes, Fingerling (10 to 12) Small, Red and White (10 to 12)	Leave whole, or cut as desired.	Steam: 18 to 22 minutes or until tender. Roast: 25 to 30 minutes.	Place in dish; add ¼ cup water. Microwave 9 to 11 minutes or until tender.
Potatoes, Red or White (6 medium), Russet (4 medium), Yukon Gold (6 medium)	Leave whole, or peel and cut as desired.	Steam: 15 to 20 minutes or until tender. Roast: 40 to 45 minutes.	Pierce whole potatoes for steam to escape; place on paper towel. 1 or 2 potatoes: Microwave 4 to 6 minutes or until tender. Cover; let stand 5 minutes. 3 or 4 potatoes: Microwave 8 to 12 minutes or until tender. Cover; let stand 5 minutes.
Potatoes, Sweet (4 medium)	Leave whole, or peel and cut as desired.	Steam: 15 to 20 minutes or until tender. Roast: 40 to 45 minutes.	Pierce whole potatoes to allow steam to escape; place on paper towel. Microwave 9 to 11 minutes or until tender.
Squash, Summer: Chayote, Crookneck, Zucchini, Pattypan, Straightneck (1½ lb)	Remove stem and blossom ends but do not peel. Cut as desired.	Steam: 5 to 7 minutes or until tender. Sauté: 5 to 10 minutes, with 1 tablespoon olive oil or until tender.	Place in dish. Microwave 4 to 6 minutes or until almost tender.
Squash, Winter: Acorn, Buttercup, Butternut, Pumpkin, Spaghetti (2 lb)	Halve or cut into pieces; remove seeds.	Steam: 10 to 15 minutes or until tender.	Whole squash except spaghetti: Pierce with knife in several places to allow steam to escape. Place on paper towel. Microwave uncovered 5 minutes or until squash feels warm to the touch. Cut in half; remove seeds. Arrange halves in dish. Microwave 5 to 8 minutes or until tender. Whole spaghetti squash: Pierce with knife in several places to allow steam to escape. Microwave uncovered 18 to 23 minutes or until tender. Cut in half; remove seeds and fibers. Place on paper towel.

Chapter One

CHICKEN

AND

TURKEY

GRILLED SRIRACHA CHICKEN WITH GARLIC-CILANTRO RICE

4 servings | Prep Time: 20 Minutes | Start to Finish: 55 Minutes

CHICKEN

- 8 (8-inch) bamboo skewers
- 1 teaspoon vegetable oil
- 1 tablespoon Sriracha sauce
- 1 tablespoon reduced-sodium soy sauce
- 1 teaspoon grated gingerroot
- 1 lb boneless skinless chicken breasts, cut into 32 pieces (about 1½ inches each)
  Grilling spray

RICE

- 1 cup uncooked long-grain rice
- 2 cups water
- 4 cloves garlic, finely chopped
- ¼ teaspoon salt
- ½ cup chopped fresh cilantro

GARNISH

Lime wedges, if desired

1 Soak skewers in water 15 minutes.

2 In medium bowl, mix oil, Sriracha sauce, soy sauce and gingerroot. Add chicken pieces; toss to coat. On each skewer, thread 4 pieces of chicken; refrigerate until ready to grill.

3 In 2-quart saucepan, heat rice, water, garlic and salt to boiling over high heat. Stir; reduce heat to low. Cover; cook 15 minutes. Remove from heat; let stand 5 minutes. Fluff with fork; stir in cilantro. Cover to keep warm.

4 Meanwhile, spray grill with grilling spray. Heat gas or charcoal grill. Place chicken skewers on grill over medium heat. Cover grill; cook 8 to 10 minutes, turning occasionally to cook on all sides, until chicken is no longer pink in center.

5 Serve skewers over rice with lime wedges.

1 Serving: Calories 340; Total Fat 5g (Saturated Fat 1.5g, Trans Fat 0g); Cholesterol 70mg; Sodium 470mg; Total Carbohydrate 42g (Dietary Fiber 0g); Protein 30g **Exchanges:** 1½ Starch, 1½ Other Carbohydrate, 3½ Very Lean Meat, ½ Fat **Carbohydrate Choices:** 3

IN A SNAP If the weather doesn't cooperate with your grilling plans, cook these skewers indoors on a grill pan. Heat the pan over medium heat. You may need to add a couple of minutes to the cook time.

USE IT UP If you have any leftover takeout packets of soy sauce—here's the perfect recipe to use one! If it's not reduced-sodium soy sauce, you can expect this dish to taste saltier, however.

TEN-MINUTE BOAT TACOS

6 servings | Prep Time: 10 Minutes | Start to Finish: 10 Minutes

1   tablespoon vegetable oil

1¼ lb boneless skinless chicken breasts, cut into very small thin strips

1   package (1 oz) taco seasoning mix

12 mini boat-shaped soft flour tortillas (from two 6.7-oz packages)

½   cup guacamole

½   cup crumbled queso fresco cheese (2 oz)

Chopped tomatoes, sliced jalapeño chiles and fresh cilantro leaves, if desired

1 In 10-inch nonstick skillet, heat oil over medium heat. Cook chicken in oil, stirring occasionally, until browned. Sprinkle with taco seasoning mix. Cook, stirring occasionally, just until chicken is no longer pink in center.

2 Meanwhile, heat tortillas as directed on package.

3 Divide chicken mixture among warmed tortillas. Top with guacamole, cheese, tomatoes, chiles and cilantro.

1 Serving (**2 Tacos**): Calories 270; Total Fat 12g (Saturated Fat 3.5g, Trans Fat 0g); Cholesterol 60mg; Sodium 730mg; Total Carbohydrate 17g (Dietary Fiber 1g); Protein 23g **Exchanges:** ½ Starch, ½ Other Carbohydrate, 2 Very Lean Meat, 1 Medium-Fat Meat, 1 Fat **Carbohydrate Choices:** 1

USE IT UP
If all you are missing to make this family favorite is queso fresco . . . don't let that stop you! Get creative and substitute whatever type of shredded cheese you have in the fridge. Mexican cheese blend, Colby-Monterey Jack or Cheddar are all great choices.

Mix tomatoes with leftover chopped red onion and cilantro leaves as we did in the photo, for more flavor and eye-catching interest.

IN A SNAP
If you have regular flour tortillas at home, don't make a special trip to the store. Place the toppings on one side of the tortilla, fold over and enjoy! Crispy tostada shells would also be perfect for serving open-face.

If you have the ingredients to make your own guacamole, try this easy version: In medium bowl with a potato masher or fork, mash 3 pitted, peeled ripe avocados with 1 seeded, chopped jalapeño, ¼ cup chopped fresh cilantro, ½ teaspoon salt and the juice of 1 lime.

If you have some guac leftover after dinner, dip with tortilla chips when the late-night hungries hit . . . or use as a sandwich spread the next day.

EASY MEDITERRANEAN CHICKEN

4 servings | Prep Time: 25 Minutes | Start to Finish: 25 Minutes

4   boneless skinless chicken breasts (5 oz each)

¼   teaspoon salt

6   tablespoons chopped fresh basil leaves

1   tablespoon olive oil

1½   cups cherry tomatoes (about 10 oz), halved

¼   cup olive tapenade

1   Place chicken on sheet of waxed paper. Sprinkle evenly with ⅛ teaspoon of the salt and 2 tablespoons of the basil; press lightly. Turn chicken over. Sprinkle with remaining ⅛ teaspoon salt and another 2 tablespoons basil. Cover with a second sheet of waxed paper. Pound chicken with rolling pin or meat mallet to ½-inch thickness.

2   In 12-inch skillet, heat oil over medium-high heat. Cook chicken in oil 10 to 12 minutes, turning once, until golden brown on outside and no longer pink in center. Remove chicken to plate; cover to keep warm.

3   Add tomatoes and tapenade to skillet. Cook over medium-high heat 2 to 3 minutes, stirring constantly, until tomatoes just begin to soften and mixture is hot. Serve tomato mixture over chicken; sprinkle with remaining 2 tablespoons basil.

1 Serving: Calories 220; Total Fat 8g (Saturated Fat 2g, Trans Fat 0g); Cholesterol 90mg; Sodium 240mg; Total Carbohydrate 3g (Dietary Fiber 1g); Protein 32g **Exchanges:** ½ Vegetable, 4½ Very Lean Meat, 1 Fat **Carbohydrate Choices:** 0

MAKE A MEAL
A salad of fresh greens, sliced cucumber and red onion, drizzled with a Greek vinaigrette, would complement this entree nicely.

USE IT UP
Tapenade makes a great topper for crackers for a late-night snack. Or toss a little into a green salad for an extra burst of flavor.

Olive tapenade can be made with green or black olives, or a mixture. A small amount contributes a lot of flavor. Look for olive tapenade near the olives, roasted peppers and other condiments in your supermarket.

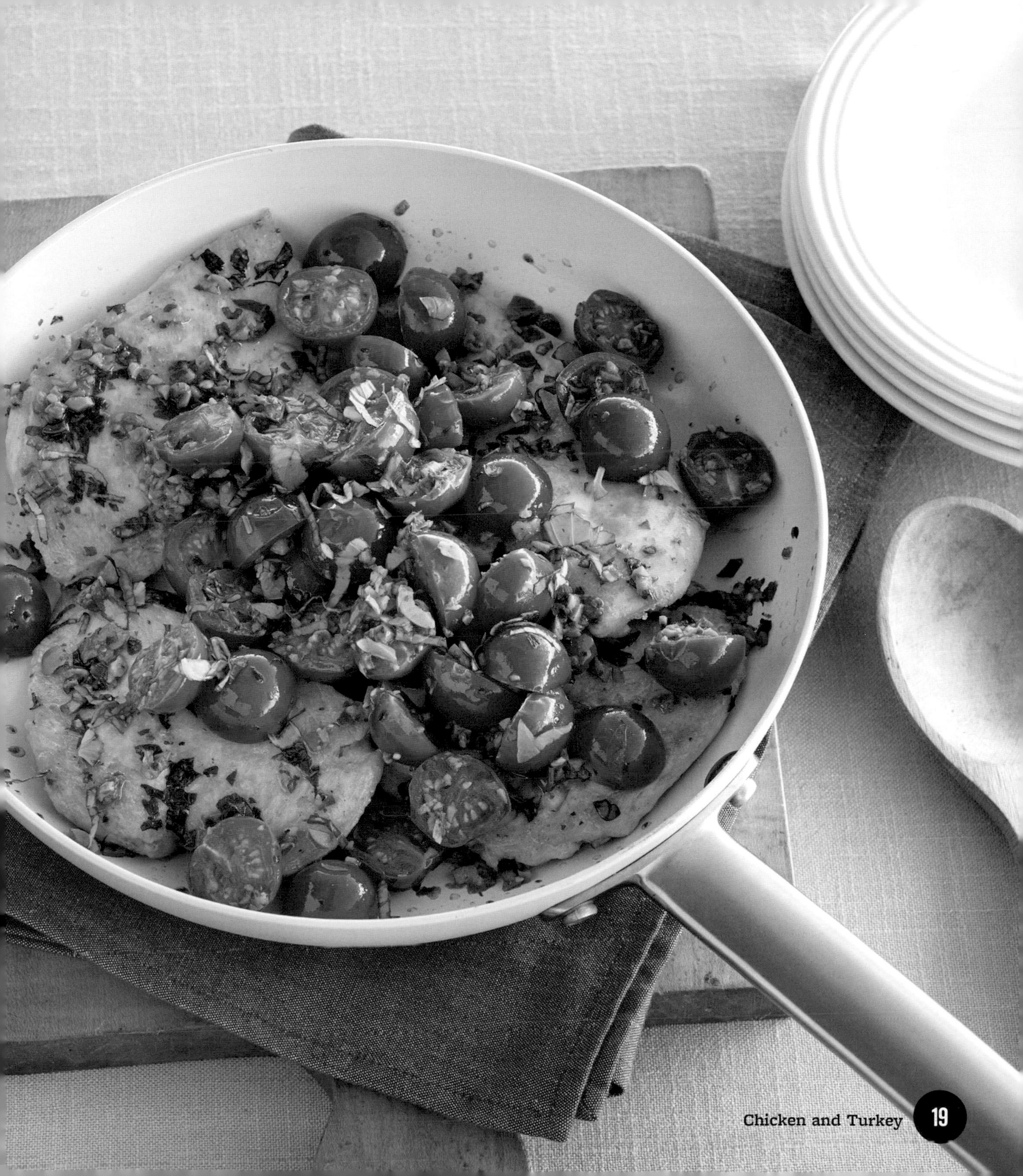

SINGAPORE NOODLES WITH CHICKEN

4 servings | Prep Time: 30 Minutes | Start to Finish: 30 Minutes

NOODLES

- 8 cups water
- 4 oz uncooked rice stick noodles

CHICKEN

- 2 tablespoons soy sauce
- 1 tablespoon sugar
- ½ teaspoon curry powder
- 1 teaspoon chili garlic sauce or sriracha sauce
- ½ cup water
- 2 tablespoons vegetable oil
- ½ lb boneless skinless chicken breasts, cut into ¾-inch pieces
- ¼ teaspoon salt
- 1 medium red bell pepper, cut into thin strips
- 4 oz fresh sugar snap peas, cut diagonally in half
- 6 medium green onions, thinly sliced, white and green parts separated

1 In large microwavable bowl, microwave 8 cups water uncovered on High 4 to 5 minutes or until boiling. Soak noodles in hot water until softened, about 8 minutes; drain. Using kitchen scissors, cut noodles into 4-inch pieces; set aside.

2 In small bowl, mix soy sauce, sugar, curry powder and chili garlic sauce. Stir in ½ cup water.

3 In 12-inch nonstick skillet or wok, heat oil over medium-high heat. Sprinkle chicken with salt; cook chicken in oil 4 to 5 minutes, turning once, until browned on both sides. Add bell pepper, peas and white parts of onions. Cook 3 to 4 minutes, stirring frequently, until vegetables soften and begin to brown on edges and chicken is no longer pink in center.

4 Add soy sauce mixture and drained noodles to skillet; stir to combine. Reduce heat to medium. Cook 1 to 2 minutes, stirring constantly, until sauce is absorbed. Stir in green parts of onions.

1 Serving: Calories 300; Total Fat 10g (Saturated Fat 2g, Trans Fat 0g); Cholesterol 35mg; Sodium 640mg; Total Carbohydrate 34g (Dietary Fiber 3g); Protein 19g **Exchanges:** 1 Starch, 1 Other Carbohydrate, ½ Vegetable, 2 Very Lean Meat, 1½ Fat **Carbohydrate Choices:** 2

IN A SNAP
Have all ingredients measured and cut before heating your pan to make stir-frying a breeze.

USE IT UP
If you have boneless chicken thighs on hand, you can use them in place of the chicken breasts.

EASY CHICKEN ALFREDO WITH BISCUITS

6 servings | Prep Time: 20 Minutes | Start to Finish: 35 Minutes

1 tablespoon olive oil

1¼ lb boneless skinless chicken breasts, cut into 1-inch cubes

3 cups sliced zucchini (about 4 medium or 1 lb)

2 cups Original Bisquick® mix

½ cup shredded Parmesan cheese (2 oz)

3 tablespoons chopped fresh basil leaves

⅔ cup milk

¾ cup Alfredo pasta sauce

1 cup chopped tomatoes

1 Heat oven to 400°F. In 12-inch ovenproof skillet, heat oil over medium-high heat. Cook chicken and zucchini in oil 5 to 7 minutes, stirring occasionally, until chicken is no longer pink.

2 Meanwhile, in medium bowl, stir together Bisquick mix, cheese, 2 tablespoons of the basil and the milk until soft dough forms.

3 Stir Alfredo sauce into chicken mixture. Move mixture toward center of skillet. Drop 12 heaping tablespoonfuls of dough around edge of skillet.

4 Bake 12 to 14 minutes or until biscuits are golden brown. Spoon tomatoes over chicken mixture. Sprinkle with remaining 1 tablespoon basil.

1 Serving: Calories 470; Total Fat 24g (Saturated Fat 10g, Trans Fat 1.5g); Cholesterol 95mg; Sodium 840mg; Total Carbohydrate 33g (Dietary Fiber 2g); Protein 31g **Exchanges:** 1 Starch, 1 Other Carbohydrate, 1 Vegetable, 3½ Lean Meat, 2½ Fat **Carbohydrate Choices:** 2

USE IT UP This is a great go-to recipe when you find yourself with a bumper crop of zucchini, basil and tomatoes.

Change up the vegetables with fresh broccoli and red bell pepper, or try half yellow summer squash and half zucchini.

TACO SHELLS OR TORTILLAS

TACO SHELLS

- **Crunch Them** Crumble over your favorite casserole before baking.

- **Toss Them** Add to a salad instead of croutons.

- **Coat Nuggets** For crispy chicken or fish nuggets, cut 1 pound of boneless chicken or fish into 1-inch pieces. Mix ¼ cup flour and ½ teaspoon seasoned salt in a gallon storage bag; add pieces and shake to cover evenly. Dip pieces into ¼ cup melted butter. Place 1 cup of crushed taco shells in another bag; add pieces and shake until evenly coated. Bake at 400°F for 15 to 20 minutes or until chicken is no longer pink inside or fish flakes easily with a fork.

TORTILLAS

- **Make Pizza** Place tortillas on a cookie sheet; top with your favorite toppings and bake at 350°F for about 15 minutes. For a crisper crust, bake a minute or two before topping.

- **Roll Up a Sandwich** Spread peanut butter and jelly, or tuna or egg salad over tortilla; roll up.

- **Make Quesadillas** Heat skillet sprayed with cooking spray over medium-low heat. Add a tortilla and top with fillings, such as finely chopped meat and veggies and shredded cheese. Top with another tortilla. Cook until bottom is deep golden brown (press quesadilla lightly together as the cheese melts). Turn; cook until bottom is golden brown. Cut into wedges with a pizza cutter and serve with your favorite dipping sauce.

MEXICAN STUFFED CHICKEN BREASTS

4 servings | Prep Time: 20 Minutes | Start to Finish: 55 Minutes

4 boneless skinless chicken breasts (6 to 8 oz each)

1 cup shredded pepper Jack cheese (4 oz)

4 oz (half of 8-oz package) cream cheese, softened

1 can (4.5 oz) chopped green chiles

1 package (1 oz) taco seasoning mix

2 tablespoons olive oil

¾ cup shredded mozzarella cheese (3 oz)

¼ cup sliced green onions (4 medium)

¼ cup fresh cilantro leaves

1 Heat oven to 400°F. Line 15x10-inch pan with foil. Place wire cooling rack or roasting pan rack in pan; spray rack with cooking spray.

2 In thick side of each chicken breast, cut 3-inch-long pocket to within ¼ inch of opposite side.

3 In medium bowl, mix pepper Jack cheese, cream cheese, chiles and 1 tablespoon of the taco seasoning mix. Spoon about ⅓ cup cheese mixture into pocket in each chicken breast; secure with toothpicks. (Try to secure bottom of chicken up and over stuffing so it doesn't spill out while baking.) Place chicken on rack in pan.

4 In small bowl, mix remaining taco seasoning mix and the oil. Brush mixture over chicken.

5 Bake 25 to 30 minutes or until meat thermometer inserted into center of stuffing reads 160°F. Sprinkle mozzarella cheese over chicken; bake 3 to 5 minutes longer or until cheese is melted. Top with onions and cilantro.

1 Serving: Calories 560; Total Fat 35g (Saturated Fat 16g, Trans Fat 1g); Cholesterol 175mg; Sodium 1190mg; Total Carbohydrate 10g (Dietary Fiber 1g); Protein 50g **Exchanges:** ½ Other Carbohydrate, 5 Very Lean Meat, 2 High-Fat Meat, 3½ Fat **Carbohydrate Choices:** ½

USE IT UP

Save money by purchasing shredded cheese in larger quantities, and keep it fresh by storing in the freezer for up to 6 months. Take out what you need—no need to thaw it first. You may need to add a minute or two to the bake time.

Use the remaining cream cheese to spread on bagels or to stir into hot mashed potatoes, for extra creaminess.

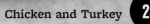

SOY–BROWN SUGAR–GLAZED CHICKEN THIGHS

4 servings | Prep Time: 15 Minutes | Start to Finish: 40 Minutes

¼ cup packed brown sugar
¼ cup soy sauce
1 tablespoon rice vinegar
½ teaspoon ground ginger
1 clove garlic,
finely chopped
1½ lb skin-on bone-in
chicken thighs
1 tablespoon vegetable oil

1 Heat oven to 375°F. In small bowl, beat brown sugar, soy sauce, vinegar, ginger and garlic with whisk until well combined. Set aside.

2 Heat 10-inch ovenproof skillet or roasting pan over medium-high heat. Rub chicken with oil; place, skin side down, in skillet. Sear chicken, without moving, 3 to 5 minutes or until skin is browned and chicken releases easily from skillet.

3 Transfer chicken to plate. Pour off drippings from skillet. Return chicken, skin side up, to skillet. Pour soy–brown sugar mixture over chicken.

4 Bake uncovered 15 to 25 minutes or until juice of chicken is clear when thickest part is cut to bone (at least 165°F). Serve chicken with sauce from pan.

1 Serving: Calories 330; Total Fat 17g (Saturated Fat 4g, Trans Fat 0g); Cholesterol 90mg; Sodium 1000mg; Total Carbohydrate 15g (Dietary Fiber 0g); Protein 30g **Exchanges:** 1 Other Carbohydrate, 4 Lean Meat, 1 Fat **Carbohydrate Choices:** 1

IN A SNAP To avoid the cutting board entirely, use chopped garlic from a jar or substitute ½ teaspoon garlic powder.

GLUTEN-FREE CHICKEN TETRAZZINI

6 servings | Prep Time: 25 Minutes | Start to Finish: 40 Minutes

2 tablespoons vegetable oil

1 package (8 oz) sliced fresh mushrooms (about 3 cups)

3 cups gluten-free chicken broth

8 oz uncooked gluten-free spaghetti, broken into pieces

1 can (18.5 oz) ready-to-eat creamy mushroom soup

2 cups chopped gluten-free cooked chicken breast

4 oz (half of 8-oz package) gluten-free cream cheese, cut into cubes

1 teaspoon garlic salt

⅛ teaspoon pepper

1 cup frozen sweet peas, thawed

1 cup gluten-free shredded Italian cheese blend (4 oz)

1 cup gluten-free oven-toasted corn cereal, coarsely crushed

1 Heat oven to 375°F. In 4-quart ovenproof Dutch oven, heat oil over medium-high heat. Cook mushrooms in oil 4 to 5 minutes, stirring occasionally, until tender. Remove mushrooms to plate; set aside.

2 In same Dutch oven, heat broth to boiling over high heat. Add spaghetti; cook 4 minutes, stirring occasionally. Reduce heat to medium. Stir in soup, chicken, cream cheese, garlic salt and pepper; cook about 2 minutes or until warm. Add mushrooms, peas and cheese blend; stir well. Top with crushed cereal.

3 Bake uncovered about 15 minutes or until bubbly.

1 Serving: Calories 510; Total Fat 22g (Saturated Fat 9g, Trans Fat 0g); Cholesterol 75mg; Sodium 1220mg; Total Carbohydrate 47g (Dietary Fiber 3g); Protein 30g **Exchanges:** 3 Starch, 2 Very Lean Meat, 1 Medium-Fat Meat, 3 Fat **Carbohydrate Choices:** 3

IN A SNAP Skip the fresh mushrooms and stir in 2 (4.5-ounce) jars of mushrooms (drained) along with the peas and cheese.

USE IT UP The cereal adds a great crunch, but you could also rummage through your pantry and use what you have on hand. Try gluten-free pretzels, chips or cubed bread for a delicious new twist.

COOKING GLUTEN FREE? Always read labels to make sure *each* recipe ingredient is gluten free. Products and ingredient sources can change.

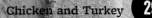

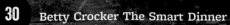

PARMESAN-CHICKEN ZITI WITH ARTICHOKES AND SPINACH

8 servings | Prep Time: 35 Minutes | Start to Finish: 35 Minutes

4   cups water

2   cans (12 oz each) evaporated milk

1   teaspoon salt

2   cloves garlic, finely chopped

1   package (16 oz) ziti pasta

2   teaspoons cornstarch

2   cups shredded deli rotisserie chicken (from 2-lb chicken)

1   can (14 oz) artichoke hearts, drained, coarsely chopped

6   oz shredded Parmesan cheese (1½ cups)

    Juice of 2 medium lemons (about ⅔ cup)

2   tablespoons butter

4   cups fresh baby spinach (5-oz bag)

½   teaspoon pepper, if desired

1 In 5-quart Dutch oven or stockpot, heat water, 1 can of the evaporated milk, the salt, garlic and pasta to simmering over medium heat. Cook 12 to 14 minutes, stirring frequently, until pasta is tender.

2 In medium bowl, beat remaining can of evaporated milk and the cornstarch; stir in chicken and artichoke hearts. Add to pasta mixture; return to simmering. Cook 1 to 3 minutes or until sauce is thickened and coats back of spoon.

3 Remove from heat; stir in half of the cheese and all the lemon juice. Stir until cheese melts, then add remaining cheese (reserving ¼ cup for serving, if desired) and butter; stir again.

4 Add spinach; stir until wilted. Serve with pepper and reserved cheese.

1 Serving (1½ Cups): Calories 540; Total Fat 16g (Saturated Fat 8g, Trans Fat 0g); Cholesterol 65mg; Sodium 1040mg; Total Carbohydrate 65g (Dietary Fiber 6g); Protein 34g **Exchanges:** 4 Starch, ½ Vegetable, 1 Very Lean Meat, 2 Lean Meat, 1½ Fat **Carbohydrate Choices:** 4

IN A SNAP
Pull off this recipe without the need for a rotisserie chicken. Bake, broil or grill chicken for dinner a day or two before you plan to make this recipe, cooking a few more pieces than you need—2 to 3 chicken breast halves will equal about 2 cups of shredded or chopped chicken. Just cover and refrigerate the extra pieces to use in this dish.

USE IT UP
What's in your fridge? Baby kale or chard make great stand-ins for spinach in this recipe.

FETTUCCINE WITH CHICKEN AND VEGETABLES

4 servings | Prep Time: 20 Minutes | Start to Finish: 20 Minutes

1 package (9 oz) refrigerated fresh fettuccine

2 cups fresh small broccoli florets

½ cup Italian dressing

1 lb uncooked chicken breast strips for stir-fry

1 medium red onion, cut into thin wedges

¼ teaspoon garlic-pepper blend

½ cup sliced drained roasted red bell peppers (from a jar)

Shredded Parmesan cheese, if desired

1 Cook fettuccine and broccoli together as directed on fettuccine package. Drain and return to saucepan. Toss with 2 tablespoons of the dressing. Cover to keep warm.

2 Meanwhile, in 12-inch nonstick skillet, heat 2 tablespoons dressing over medium-high heat. Cook chicken, onion and garlic-pepper blend in dressing 4 to 6 minutes, stirring occasionally, until chicken is no longer pink in center.

3 Stir roasted peppers and remaining ¼ cup dressing into chicken mixture. Cook 2 to 3 minutes, stirring occasionally, until warm. Serve chicken mixture over fettuccine and broccoli. Serve with cheese.

1 Serving: Calories 320; Total Fat 11g (Saturated Fat 2g, Trans Fat 0g); Cholesterol 90mg; Sodium 570mg; Total Carbohydrate 25g (Dietary Fiber 2g); Protein 30g **Exchanges:** 1½ Starch, ½ Vegetable, 3½ Very Lean Meat, 1½ Fat **Carbohydrate Choices:** 1½

USE IT UP
Boneless skinless chicken breasts, cut crosswise into ¼-inch slices, can be substituted for the stir-fry strips.

If you don't have garlic-pepper blend on hand, substitute ⅛ teaspoon each garlic powder and coarse ground black pepper.

CHEESE

- **Swap It** Experiment using whatever cheese you've got on hand rather than buying another kind for a recipe.

- **Top Chili** Sprinkle shredded cheese on top of steaming bowls of chili. Don't have enough of one kind for everyone? Use different types on different bowls and then let everyone pick which one they want, or mix a variety together before sprinkling it on the chili.

- **Broil It** Make cheesy toast to serve with soup. Place 1-inch-thick slices of French bread on cookie sheet; brush lightly with butter and sprinkle with grated cheese (pick ones that melt well, such as mozzarella, 4-cheese or Monterey Jack). Broil 5 to 6 inches from heat about 3 minutes or until melted.

- **Grate It** Stuck with little bits of block cheese? Grate them with a box grater in minutes. You can combine types and use the mix to make great chips and cheese, grilled cheese sandwiches or quesadillas.

- **Sauce It** Make an easy cheese sauce for veggies or eggs. Melt 2 tablespoons butter in a saucepan over low heat and stir in 2 tablespoons flour until it's smooth and bubbly. Gradually stir in 1 cup milk. Cook and stir over medium heat until boiling; boil and stir 1 minute. Stir in about ½ cup shredded cheese a little at a time, until melted.

- **Store It** Keep a bag of the grated bits to add to casseroles, mashed potatoes and creamy soups. You can freeze cheese in resealable food-storage plastic bags up to 2 months.

THAI PEANUT CHICKEN PASTA

6 servings | Prep Time: 40 Minutes | Start to Finish: 40 Minutes

1 carton (32 oz) chicken broth (4 cups)

1½ cups water

⅔ cup creamy peanut butter

3 tablespoons soy sauce

2 tablespoons honey

2 tablespoons Sriracha sauce

1 tablespoon toasted sesame oil or olive oil

1 teaspoon ground ginger

1 box (16 oz) linguine, broken in half

1 medium red bell pepper, cut into ½-inch strips

1 medium orange or yellow bell pepper, cut into ½-inch strips

2 cups shredded deli rotisserie chicken (from 2-lb chicken)

2 tablespoons lime juice

3 tablespoons chopped fresh cilantro

3 tablespoons chopped dry-roasted peanuts

3 tablespoons thinly sliced green onions

1 In 4-quart Dutch oven or stockpot, heat broth and water to boiling over medium-high heat. Add peanut butter, soy sauce, honey, Sriracha sauce, oil and ginger; stir until well blended.

2 Add linguine and bell peppers. Reduce heat to medium-low; cook 13 to 15 minutes, stirring occasionally, until linguine and vegetables are tender and sauce is reduced and thickened. Stir in chicken; cook until hot.

3 Stir in lime juice. Top individual servings with cilantro, peanuts and onions.

1 Serving: Calories 700; Total Fat 25g (Saturated Fat 5g, Trans Fat 0g); Cholesterol 45mg; Sodium 1470mg; Total Carbohydrate 85g (Dietary Fiber 6g); Protein 35g **Exchanges:** 3 Starch, 2½ Other Carbohydrate, 2½ Very Lean Meat, 1 High-Fat Meat, 3 Fat **Carbohydrate Choices:** 5½

IN A SNAP
This recipe makes great leftovers! If necessary, add a little extra chicken broth or water to the mixture before reheating.

USE IT UP
You can use cooked cubed chicken if you don't have rotisserie chicken. A green bell pepper would also work along with red, orange or yellow bell pepper.

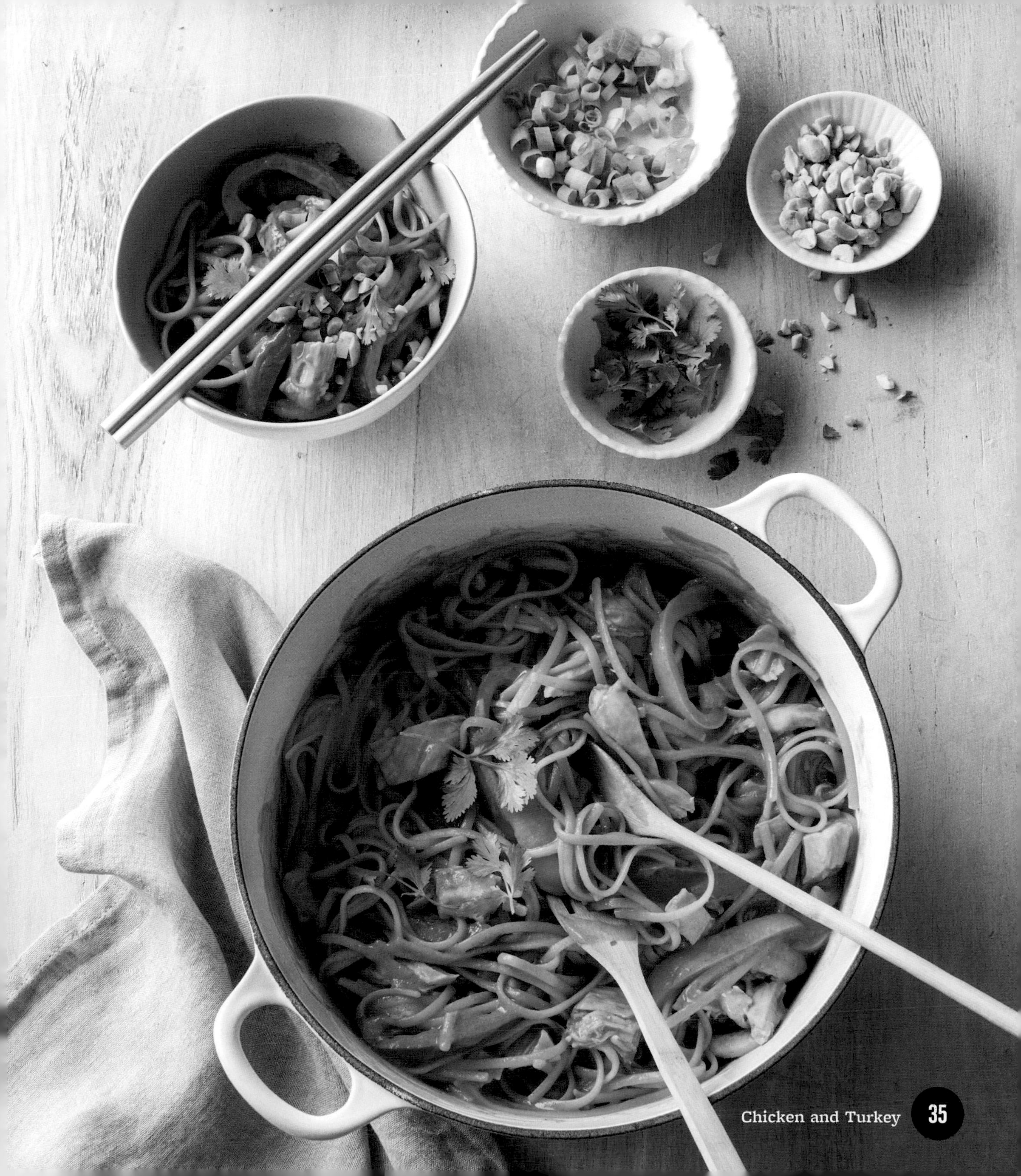

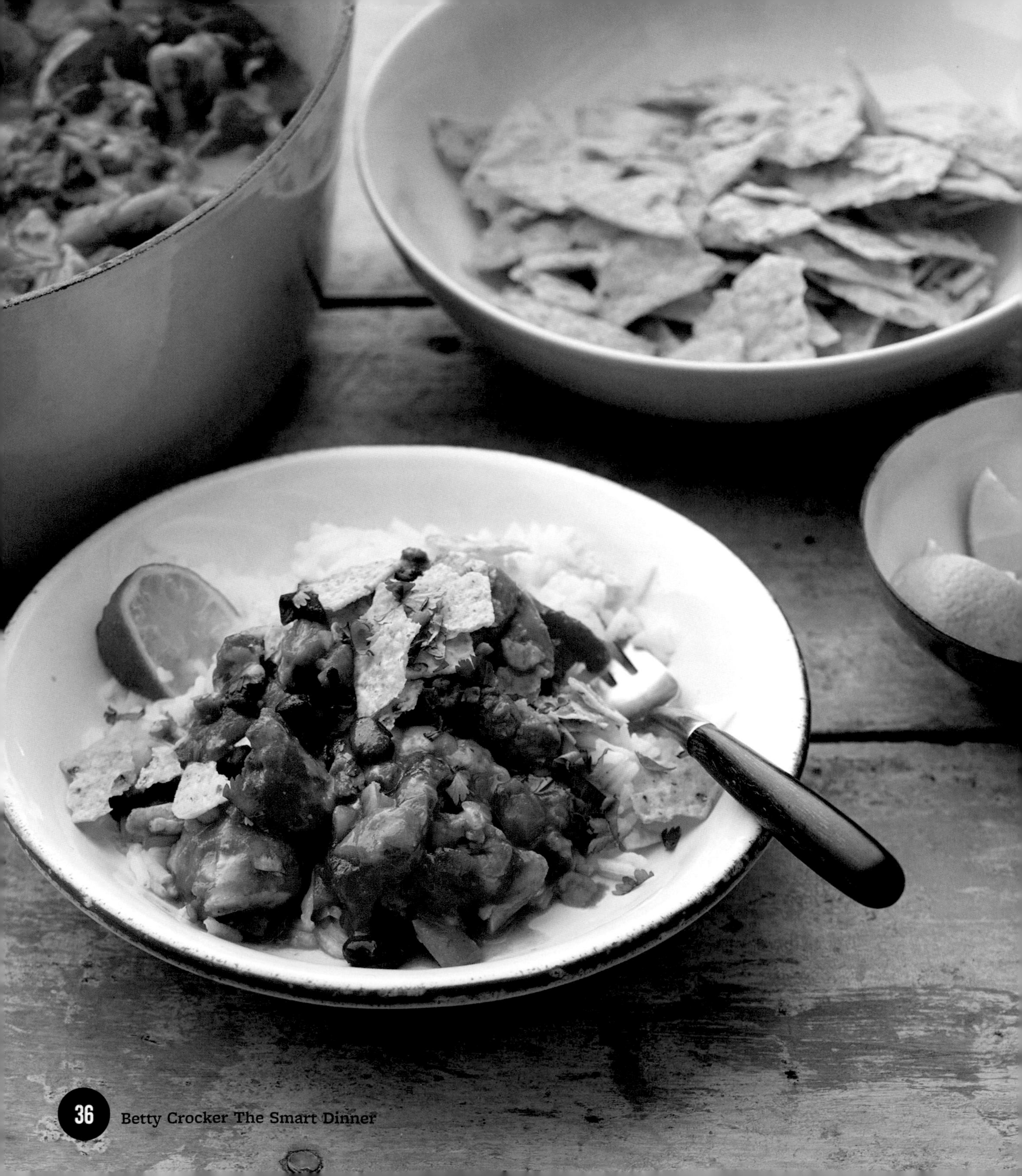

CHEESY CHICKEN AND SAUSAGE

6 servings | Prep Time: 40 Minutes | Start to Finish: 40 Minutes

2 tablespoons olive oil

½ lb fresh chorizo or bulk pork sausage

1¼ lb boneless skinless chicken thighs, cut into 1-inch pieces

1 large onion, chopped (1 cup)

½ teaspoon salt

1 tablespoon taco seasoning mix (from 1-oz package)

1 can (4.5 oz) chopped green chiles

1 can (28 oz) whole tomatoes, undrained

1 can (15 oz) black beans, drained, rinsed

2 cups shredded Monterey Jack or pepper Jack cheese (8 oz)

4½ cups hot cooked rice; or 6 flour tortillas (6 inch), heated as directed on package, if desired

2 cups coarsely crushed tortilla chips

¼ cup chopped fresh cilantro

6 lime wedges

1 In 4-quart Dutch oven or stockpot, heat 1 tablespoon of the oil over medium heat. Cook sausage in oil 6 to 10 minutes, stirring occasionally, until no longer pink. Drain. Transfer sausage to plate; set aside.

2 Add chicken to Dutch oven; cook 6 to 10 minutes, stirring occasionally, until no longer pink in center. Transfer to plate with sausage.

3 Add remaining 1 tablespoon oil to Dutch oven. Add onion and salt. Cook 4 to 5 minutes or until onion is softened. Stir in taco seasoning mix and chiles; cook 1 minute longer. Add tomatoes. Heat to simmering. Stir in sausage and chicken and the beans. Return to simmering; cook 5 minutes for flavors to combine. Stir in cheese.

4 Serve over rice or in tortillas. Top with chips and cilantro. Serve with lime wedges.

1 Serving (1⅓ **Cups**)**:** Calories 730; Total Fat 42g (Saturated Fat 16g, Trans Fat 0g); Cholesterol 130mg; Sodium 1460mg; Total Carbohydrate 42g (Dietary Fiber 8g); Protein 46g **Exchanges:** 1½ Starch, 1 Other Carbohydrate, 1 Vegetable, 3 Lean Meat, 2½ High-Fat Meat, 2½ Fat **Carbohydrate Choices:** 3

USE IT UP
Wondering what to do with leftover taco seasoning? Stir into softened butter, then brush on corn on the cob before grilling . . . stir into sour cream for a zippy dip . . . or mix into an oil-and-vinegar dressing for a south-of-the-border twist.

CHEESY CHICKEN ENCHILADA PASTA

6 servings | Prep Time: 30 Minutes | Start to Finish: 30 Minutes

3 cups uncooked medium pasta shells (8 oz)

1 can (14.5 oz) fire roasted diced tomatoes, undrained

1 can (10 oz) mild enchilada sauce

2 cups water

1 bunch green onions, thinly sliced, white and green parts separated

2 teaspoons chili powder

1 can (15 oz) black beans, drained, rinsed

1 can (11 oz) whole kernel corn, drained

2 cups finely chopped deli rotisserie chicken (from 2-lb chicken)

2 cups shredded sharp Cheddar cheese (8 oz)

Lime wedges and sour cream, if desired

1 In large colander, rinse and drain uncooked pasta. In 4-quart saucepan, mix pasta, tomatoes, enchilada sauce, water, white parts of onions and chili powder. Heat to boiling over high heat; reduce heat. Simmer uncovered 14 to 16 minutes, stirring frequently, until pasta is tender; do not drain.

2 Stir in beans, corn and chicken; return to simmering. Cook 2 minutes longer for flavors to combine. Remove from heat; stir in cheese.

3 Top with green parts of onions. Serve with lime wedges and sour cream.

1 Serving (1½ Cups): Calories 550; Total Fat 19g (Saturated Fat 8g, Trans Fat 0.5g); Cholesterol 80mg; Sodium 1000mg; Total Carbohydrate 61g (Dietary Fiber 9g); Protein 34g **Exchanges:** 2 Starch, 2 Other Carbohydrate, ½ Vegetable, 3 Very Lean Meat, 1 High-Fat Meat, 1½ Fat **Carbohydrate Choices:** 4

IN A SNAP Rinsing the dry pasta removes extra starch from the shells, so it can be used in this one-pot dish without causing it to become too thick.

USE IT UP If you have medium-spicy enchilada sauce or pepper Jack cheese, you can use them instead of the mild sauce and Cheddar cheese for a spicier dish.

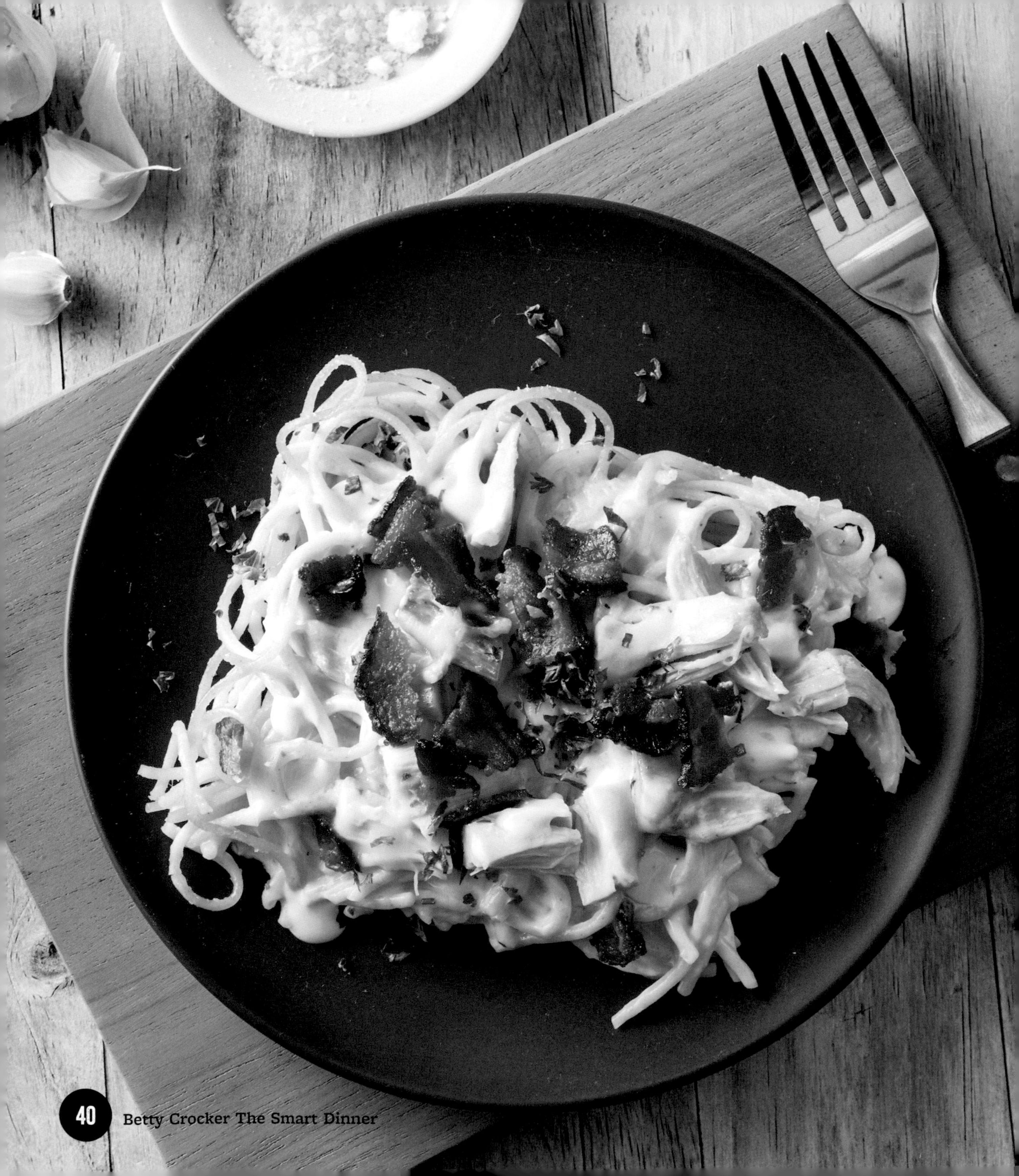

WHITE SPAGHETTI-PIZZA BAKE

8 servings | Prep Time: 20 Minutes | Start to Finish: 50 Minutes

1   lb uncooked spaghetti

⅔   cup milk

2   eggs

2   cloves garlic,
     finely chopped

3   cups shredded
     mozzarella cheese
     (12 oz)

½   cup shredded
     Parmesan cheese

1   jar (15 oz) Alfredo
     pasta sauce

2   cups diced
     cooked chicken

6   slices bacon, chopped,
     cooked

1   tablespoon chopped
     fresh parsley

1 Heat oven to 400°F. Spray 15x10x1-inch pan with cooking spray.

2 In 5-quart Dutch oven or stockpot, cook and drain spaghetti as directed on package. Rinse spaghetti; return to Dutch oven.

3 In small bowl, beat milk and eggs with fork or whisk. Stir in garlic.

4 Add egg mixture, 1 cup of the mozzarella cheese and the Parmesan cheese to spaghetti; stir until well blended. Pour spaghetti mixture evenly into pan. Cover with nonstick foil.

5 Bake 15 minutes. Reduce oven temperature to 350°F. Remove foil. Evenly spread Alfredo sauce over spaghetti crust. Top with chicken, remaining 2 cups of the mozzarella cheese and bacon. Bake 10 to 15 minutes longer or until cheese is melted. Sprinkle with parsley.

1 Serving: Calories 750; Total Fat 37g (Saturated Fat 20g, Trans Fat 1g); Cholesterol 180mg; Sodium 860mg; Total Carbohydrate 59g (Dietary Fiber 3g); Protein 43g **Exchanges:** 3½ Starch, ½ Other Carbohydrate, 3 Very Lean Meat, 1½ High-Fat Meat, 4½ Fat **Carbohydrate Choices:** 4

USE IT UP Have fun with toppings! Try ripe olives, bell peppers, mushrooms or your favorite pizza toppings.

MAKE A MEAL Serve with a fresh garden salad.

CHICKEN WITH PAN-ROASTED CAULIFLOWER AND ORZO

4 servings | Prep Time: 20 Minutes | Start to Finish: 20 Minutes

1 tablespoon olive oil

2 cups bite-size fresh cauliflower florets

1½ cups chicken broth

1¼ lb boneless skinless chicken thighs, cut into bite-size pieces

1 cup uncooked orzo or rosamarina pasta (6 oz)

¼ cup thinly sliced green onions (4 medium)

1 can (14.5 oz) diced tomatoes with basil, garlic and oregano, drained

2 cups packed arugula

½ cup shredded Parmesan cheese (2 oz)

1 In 12-inch nonstick skillet, heat oil over medium heat. Cook cauliflower in oil about 5 minutes, stirring occasionally, until lightly browned.

2 Add broth, chicken, orzo, onions and tomatoes. Heat to boiling; reduce heat. Cover; simmer 8 to 10 minutes, stirring occasionally, until chicken is no longer pink in center and orzo is tender. Remove from heat.

3 Stir in arugula. Cover; let stand about 1 minute or until arugula is partially wilted. Sprinkle with cheese.

1 Serving (1½ Cups): Calories 380; Total Fat 14g (Saturated Fat 5g, Trans Fat 0g); Cholesterol 55mg; Sodium 780mg; Total Carbohydrate 35g (Dietary Fiber 3g); Protein 28g **Exchanges:** 1½ Starch, 2 Vegetable, ½ Lean Meat, 2½ Medium-Fat Meat **Carbohydrate Choices:** 2

USE IT UP You can substitute chicken breasts for the thighs. Have fresh baby spinach on hand? Go ahead and substitute it for the arugula.

BUFFALO CHICKEN BITES WITH BLUE CHEESE DIPPING SAUCE

6 servings | Prep Time: 25 Minutes | Start to Finish: 55 Minutes

CHICKEN BITES

- 1 egg white
- ⅓ cup hot Buffalo wing sauce
- 1 lb boneless skinless chicken breasts, cut into 40 (1-inch) pieces
- ¾ cup Original Bisquick mix
- 3 tablespoons cornmeal
- 1 teaspoon salt
- ½ teaspoon pepper
  Vegetable oil for frying

DIPPING SAUCE

- ¾ cup crumbled blue cheese (3 oz)
- 6 tablespoons sour cream
- 6 tablespoons light mayonnaise
- 3 tablespoons milk

1 In medium bowl, mix egg white and Buffalo wing sauce. Stir in chicken. Cover; refrigerate 30 minutes.

2 Line cookie sheet with waxed paper. In large resealable food-storage plastic bag, shake Bisquick mix, cornmeal, salt and pepper. With slotted spoon, remove one-fourth of the chicken pieces from bowl; place in bag of Bisquick mixture. Seal bag; shake to coat. Shake excess Bisquick mixture from chicken; place on cookie sheet. Repeat with remaining chicken.

3 In small bowl, mix sauce ingredients until blended. Cover; refrigerate until serving time.

4 In 10-inch nonstick skillet, heat ¼ inch oil to medium-high heat (375°F). Working in batches, cook chicken bites in oil 3 to 4 minutes, turning once, until golden brown. Drain on paper towels. Serve chicken with sauce.

1 Serving: Calories 360; Total Fat 23g (Saturated Fat 8g, Trans Fat 0g); Cholesterol 70mg; Sodium 1100mg; Total Carbohydrate 16g (Dietary Fiber 0g); Protein 23g **Exchanges:** ½ Starch, ½ Low-Fat Milk, 2½ Very Lean Meat, 4 Fat **Carbohydrate Choices:** 1

MAKE A MEAL
These yummy bites are the start to a great salad. Serve them over chopped lettuce and tomatoes with the dipping sauce as the dressing. Add blue cheese crumbles and croutons, if you like.

CHICKEN WITH TOMATOES AND ARTICHOKES

4 servings | Prep Time: 15 Minutes | Start to Finish: 4 Hours 45 Minutes

- 4 **bone-in chicken breasts (2½ lb)**
- 3 **tablespoons fat-free balsamic vinaigrette or Italian dressing**
- 1 **teaspoon Italian seasoning**
- ½ **teaspoon salt**
- ¼ **teaspoon pepper**
- 1 **cup thinly sliced onion**
- ¼ **cup sliced green olives**
- 4 **cloves garlic, finely chopped**
- 1 **can (14.5 oz) diced tomatoes, drained**
- 1 **can (14 oz) artichoke hearts, drained, cut into quarters**
- 2 **to 3 tablespoons chopped fresh parsley**

1 Spray 3- to 4-quart slow cooker with cooking spray. Remove skin and any fat from chicken. Brush chicken with dressing; place in slow cooker. Sprinkle with Italian seasoning, salt and pepper. Top with onion, olives, garlic, tomatoes and artichoke hearts.

2 Cover; cook on Low heat setting 4 hours 30 minutes to 5 hours 30 minutes.

3 Skim off any fat from top of chicken mixture. Serve in shallow bowls; sprinkle with parsley.

1 Serving: Calories 340; Total Fat 9g (Saturated Fat 2g, Trans Fat 0g); Cholesterol 125mg; Sodium 950mg; Total Carbohydrate 17g (Dietary Fiber 9g); Protein 49g **Exchanges:** ½ Other Carbohydrate, 2 Vegetable, 6½ Very Lean Meat, 1 Fat **Carbohydrate Choices:** 1

IN A SNAP If you're serving on plates rather than in shallow bowls, use a slotted spoon to remove the chicken mixture from the slow cooker.

MAKE A MEAL Serve the chicken with your favorite instant rice pilaf blend for an easy side.

BBQ CHIPOTLE CHICKEN–CHEDDAR SLIDERS

12 sandwiches | Prep Time: 15 Minutes | Start to Finish: 15 Minutes

1 cup barbecue sauce

2 tablespoons chopped fresh cilantro

1 chipotle chile in adobo sauce (from 7-oz can), finely chopped

3 cups chopped cooked chicken

3 cups mixed baby greens (from 5-oz package)

3 slices (¾ oz each) sharp Cheddar cheese, cut into quarters

36 dill pickle flavor or kettle-cooked jalapeño potato chips

1 package (15 oz) slider buns (12 buns)

1 In 2-quart saucepan, heat barbecue sauce, cilantro and chile to boiling over medium heat, stirring frequently. Stir in chicken. Heat to boiling; reduce heat. Cover; simmer about 5 minutes, stirring occasionally, until thoroughly heated.

2 For each sandwich, place about ¼ cup greens, ¼ cup chicken mixture, 1 piece cheese and 3 potato chips on bun bottom; cover with bun tops.

1 Sandwich: Calories 240; Total Fat 7g (Saturated Fat 2g, Trans Fat 0g); Cholesterol 35mg; Sodium 500mg; Total Carbohydrate 30g (Dietary Fiber 1g); Protein 15g **Exchanges:** 2 Starch, 1½ Very Lean Meat, 1 Fat **Carbohydrate Choices:** 2

USE IT UP Chips add a fun and salty crunch to these simple sandwiches. Instead of dill pickle potato chips, check out your cupboard to see what other chips you have on hand. Nacho-flavored tortilla chips, corn chips or regular potato chips would all be good options.

Chop remaining chiles from the adobo sauce and then stir back into the sauce. Spoon the mixture onto a strip of plastic wrap, 4 to 5 inches long. Wrap the plastic wrap around the chiles, forming a log-like shape; freeze. Whenever you need a chopped chile in sauce, slice about 1 inch off. Or stir it into scrambled eggs, when cooking rice or cooked ground beef for tacos.

EASY GENERAL TSO'S CHICKEN

4 servings | Prep Time: 35 Minutes | Start to Finish: 35 Minutes

2   tablespoons chili garlic sauce

2   tablespoons sugar

1   tablespoon rice vinegar

¼   cup all-purpose flour

2   tablespoons cornstarch

1   egg white

1   tablespoon soy sauce

10   oz boneless skinless chicken thighs, cut into bite-size pieces (about 3 chicken thighs)

2   tablespoons vegetable oil

1   bunch broccoli florets, cut into bite-size pieces (about 3 cups)

6   medium green onions, thinly sliced diagonally (⅔ cup)

2   cups cooked white rice

    Sesame seed, if desired

1 In small bowl, mix chili garlic sauce, sugar and vinegar; set aside. In large bowl, mix flour and cornstarch with whisk; set aside.

2 In medium bowl, beat egg white and soy sauce. Add chicken; toss to coat. Transfer chicken a few pieces at a time to bowl with flour mixture; toss to coat, then transfer to plate. Discard any remaining egg mixture and flour mixture.

3 In 12-inch nonstick skillet, heat oil over medium heat. Add chicken to skillet, separating the pieces; cook 6 to 7 minutes, turning once, until chicken is crispy and browned on outside. If pieces of chicken stick together, break apart with spatula.

4 Add broccoli to skillet; cook 3 to 4 minutes, stirring frequently, until broccoli is softened and browned on edges, and chicken is no longer pink in center. Add chili garlic sauce mixture to pan; cook 1 to 2 minutes longer, stirring until mixture is thoroughly coated. Stir in green onions.

5 Divide rice among 4 bowls. Divide chicken mixture over rice. Sprinkle with sesame seed.

1 Serving: Calories 370; Total Fat 11g (Saturated Fat 2g, Trans Fat 0g); Cholesterol 70mg; Sodium 670mg; Total Carbohydrate 48g (Dietary Fiber 2g); Protein 21g **Exchanges:** 1½ Starch, 1½ Other Carbohydrate, 1 Vegetable, 2 Lean Meat, 1 Fat **Carbohydrate Choices:** 3

USE IT UP Don't have chicken thighs? Breasts work just as well in this recipe.

HONEY-SRIRACHA CHICKEN PACKETS

4 servings | Prep Time: 15 Minutes | Start to Finish: 50 Minutes

½ cup uncooked instant brown rice

½ cup water

1 box (7 oz) frozen sliced carrots, sugar snap peas, black beans and edamame with butter sauce, thawed

4 boneless skinless chicken breasts (1¼ lb)

2 tablespoons honey

2 tablespoons lime juice

1 tablespoon Sriracha sauce

1 tablespoon chopped fresh cilantro

IN A SNAP Is your family eating at different times? Bake enough packets as directed for those who are eating now. Refrigerate remaining packets for later, baking them as needed.

1 Heat oven to 350°F. In small bowl, mix rice and water. Soak 5 minutes; drain. Stir in thawed vegetables.

2 Cut 4 (10x12-inch) sheets of heavy-duty foil. Spray center of one side of each sheet with cooking spray. Spoon one-fourth of the rice mixture onto center of each sheet. Top each with 1 chicken breast.

3 In small bowl, mix honey, lime juice and Sriracha sauce. Spoon evenly over chicken.

4 Bring up 2 sides of foil over chicken so edges meet. Seal edges, making tight ½-inch fold; fold again, allowing space for heat circulation and expansion. Fold other sides to seal. Place packets on ungreased cookie sheet.

5 Bake about 30 minutes or until juice of chicken is clear when center of thickest part is cut (at least 165°F). Let stand 5 minutes. To serve, cut large X across top of each packet; carefully fold back foil to allow heat to escape. Sprinkle with cilantro.

To Grill Packets: Place packets on grill over medium-low heat. Cover grill; cook 20 to 30 minutes, rotating packets one-half turn after 10 minutes, until juice of chicken is clear when center of thickest part is cut (at least 165°F).

1 Serving: Calories 310; Total Fat 6g (Saturated Fat 1.5g, Trans Fat 0g); Cholesterol 75mg; Sodium 280mg; Total Carbohydrate 34g (Dietary Fiber 5g); Protein 31g **Exchanges:** 2 Starch, ½ Vegetable, 3½ Very Lean Meat, ½ Fat **Carbohydrate Choices:** 2

HOMEMADE TAKEOUT BURRITOS

8 burritos | Prep Time: 20 Minutes | Start to Finish: 30 Minutes

1½ cups cooked white rice

Juice of 1 medium lime

⅓ cup chopped fresh cilantro

2 cups shredded deli rotisserie chicken (from 2-lb chicken)

1 cup seasoned black beans (from 15-oz can)

8 flour tortillas (8 inch)

1 cup pico de gallo salsa

1 cup shredded romaine lettuce, if desired

½ cup sour cream

1 Place rice in medium microwavable bowl; cover with microwavable plastic wrap. Microwave on High about 1 minute or until hot. Stir in lime juice, cilantro and chicken, fluffing with fork.

2 Place beans in small microwavable bowl; cover with microwavable plastic wrap. Microwave on High about 45 seconds or until hot.

3 Wrap tortillas between two microwavable paper towels. Microwave on High 30 seconds. Place 1 tortilla on work surface. Spoon ¼ cup chicken mixture onto middle of tortilla. Top with beans, salsa, lettuce and sour cream.

4 Roll up, folding sides in. Repeat to make 8 burritos. Wrap in foil if desired. Cut in half before serving.

1 Burrito: Calories 310; Total Fat 10g (Saturated Fat 3.5g, Trans Fat 1.5g); Cholesterol 40mg; Sodium 810mg; Total Carbohydrate 39g (Dietary Fiber 2g); Protein 16g
Exchanges: 2 Starch, ½ Other Carbohydrate, 1 Very Lean Meat, ½ Lean Meat, 1½ Fat
Carbohydrate Choices: 2½

USE IT UP
Here's a great way to use up leftover takeout rice or any cooked rice.

When using cilantro in a dish, feel free to chop as much of the stems as you wish with the leaves.

CHEESY CHICKEN AND BACON NO-BOIL PASTA BAKE

4 servings | Prep Time: 30 Minutes | Start to Finish: 1 Hour 10 Minutes

- 8 oz uncooked spaghetti, broken in half
- ½ lb boneless skinless chicken breasts, cut into bite-size pieces
- ½ teaspoon salt
- 2 cups chicken broth
- 1 package (8 oz) cream cheese, cut into 1-inch pieces, softened
- 6 slices bacon, crisply cooked, crumbled
- ½ cup shredded Parmesan cheese (2 oz)
- ½ cup Italian style panko crispy bread crumbs
- 2 tablespoons butter, melted

1 Heat oven to 400°F. Spray 8-inch square (2-quart) glass baking dish with cooking spray. Spread spaghetti evenly in dish; set aside.

2 Sprinkle chicken with salt. In 12-inch nonstick skillet, cook chicken over medium-high heat 4 to 5 minutes, turning once, until browned. Reduce heat to medium. Add broth and cream cheese; heat to simmering. Cook 1 to 2 minutes, stirring to break up cream cheese pieces, until combined. (Mixture may appear grainy but will become smooth during baking.)

3 Pour chicken mixture over spaghetti in baking dish; stir. Cover tightly with foil. Bake 28 to 30 minutes or until spaghetti is soft and chicken is no longer pink in center.

4 In medium bowl, mix bacon, Parmesan cheese, bread crumbs and melted butter. Stir spaghetti mixture; sprinkle with topping. Bake uncovered 8 to 10 minutes or until crumbs are golden brown and cheese is melted. Serve immediately.

1 Serving: Calories 750; Total Fat 37g (Saturated Fat 19g, Trans Fat 1g); Cholesterol 135mg; Sodium 1410mg; Total Carbohydrate 63g (Dietary Fiber 3g); Protein 39g **Exchanges:** 3 Starch, 1 Other Carbohydrate, 4 Very Lean Meat, ½ Lean Meat, 6½ Fat **Carbohydrate Choices:** 4

USE IT UP Try using other types of cheese besides Parmesan on the top—shredded Gruyère and mozzarella are both tasty options.

IN A SNAP Short on time? Use packaged precooked bacon.

No breadcrumbs on hand? Pulse a piece of day-old sandwich bread in the food processor into fine crumbs; toss with ¼ teaspoon Italian seasoning. If your bread is fresh, partially toast it in the toaster before placing in the food processor.

PINEAPPLE-CHICKEN PIZZA POCKETS

8 servings | Prep Time: 35 Minutes | Start to Finish: 55 Minutes

3 cups Original Bisquick mix, plus more for dusting

⅔ cup very warm water (120°F to 130°F)

2 tablespoons olive oil

½ cup tomato pasta or marinara sauce

1 cup shredded cooked chicken

⅓ cup chopped green bell pepper

½ cup canned pineapple tidbits (from 8-oz can), drained

¾ cup shredded Monterey Jack cheese (3 oz)

1 Heat oven to 450°F. Line cookie sheet with foil; spray foil with cooking spray.

2 In medium bowl, stir together Bisquick mix, water and oil until moistened. Let stand 15 minutes.

3 Knead dough slightly to form ball. Divide dough into 8 equal pieces. On surface lightly dusted with additional Bisquick mix, roll each dough piece with rolling pin to 6-inch round about ⅛ inch thick.

4 In small bowl, stir together pasta sauce, chicken and bell pepper. Spoon 1 heaping tablespoon chicken mixture onto each dough round. Top each with 1 tablespoon pineapple and 1 tablespoon cheese. Fold dough over; seal edge with fork. Place on cookie sheet.

5 Bake 12 to 18 minutes or until golden brown. Sprinkle pizza pockets evenly with remaining ¼ cup cheese. Bake 1 to 2 minutes longer or until cheese is melted.

1 Serving: Calories 300; Total Fat 15g (Saturated Fat 6g, Trans Fat 0g); Cholesterol 25mg; Sodium 680mg; Total Carbohydrate 31g (Dietary Fiber 0g); Protein 11g
Exchanges: 1½ Starch, ½ Other Carbohydrate, ½ Very Lean Meat, ½ High-Fat Meat, 2 Fat
Carbohydrate Choices: 2

MAKE AHEAD These pizza pockets can be frozen for a fast meal on another day. Bake as directed, then cool completely, wrap in plastic wrap and freeze for up to 3 months. To reheat, remove from plastic wrap and wrap in microwavable paper towel. Microwave on High 30 to 45 seconds or until hot in center (filling will be hot). Microwaves vary; sandwiches may take more or less time to become hot in center.

USE IT UP If you have canned chicken in your pantry, you can substitute it for the cooked chicken.

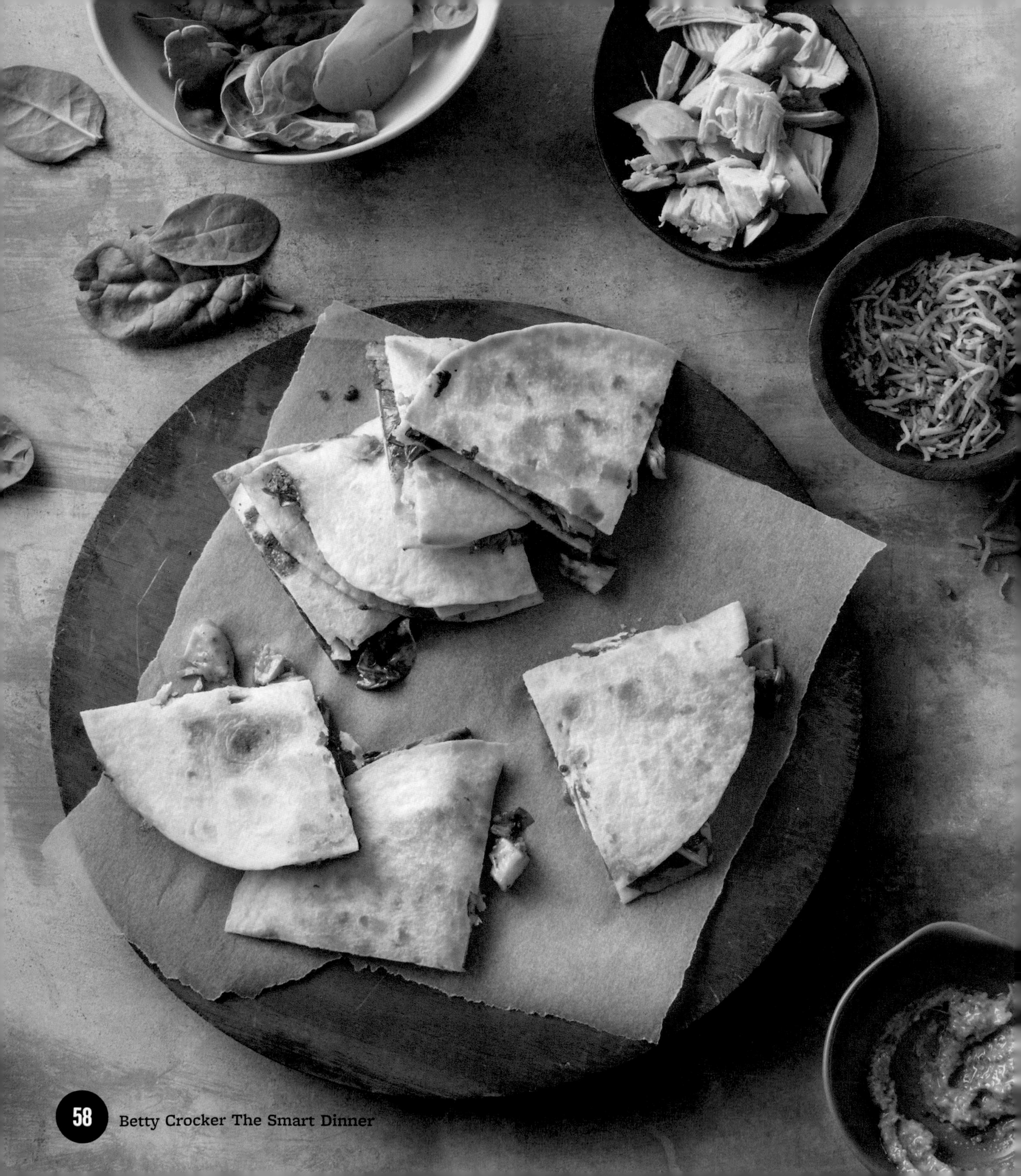

CHICKEN-PESTO QUESADILLAS

4 servings | Prep Time: 15 Minutes | Start to Finish: 15 Minutes

8   flour tortillas (6 inch)

3   tablespoons basil pesto

1   cup shredded
    cooked chicken

1   cup packed fresh baby
    spinach leaves

1   cup shredded Mexican
    cheese blend (4 oz)

2   tablespoons butter

1 On one side of each of 4 tortillas, spread about 2 teaspoons pesto. Top each with ¼ cup chicken, ¼ cup spinach and ¼ cup cheese. Cover with remaining tortillas.

2 In 12-inch skillet, heat 1 tablespoon of the butter over medium-low heat. Place 2 quesadillas in skillet. Cook about 2 minutes or until bottoms are lightly browned. Carefully turn; cook 2 minutes longer or until second sides are lightly browned and cheese is melted. Repeat with remaining 1 tablespoon butter and remaining 2 quesadillas.

3 To serve, cut each quesadilla into 4 wedges.

1 Serving: Calories 440; Total Fat 26g (Saturated Fat 12g, Trans Fat 1g); Cholesterol 75mg; Sodium 660mg; Total Carbohydrate 29g (Dietary Fiber 2g); Protein 22g **Exchanges:** 2 Starch, ½ Very Lean Meat, ½ Lean Meat, 1 High-Fat Meat, 3 Fat **Carbohydrate Choices:** 2

IN A SNAP Make this even quicker by using a griddle to cook all 4 quesadillas at once.

USE IT UP Have some deli turkey in the fridge? Use it in place of the shredded chicken.

TASTIEST TURKEY MEAT LOAF

6 servings | Prep Time: 20 Minutes | Start to Finish: 1 Hour 35 Minutes

MEAT LOAF

1¼	lb ground turkey breast
1	container (6 oz) fat-free Greek plain yogurt
¼	cup ketchup
¾	cup seasoned bread crumbs
1	tablespoon Worcestershire sauce
¾	teaspoon salt
¼	teaspoon ground sage
¼	teaspoon pepper
2	cloves garlic, finely chopped, or ¼ teaspoon garlic powder
1	small onion, chopped (⅓ cup)
1	egg, slightly beaten

TOPPING

½	cup ketchup
½	teaspoon ground mustard
1	tablespoon packed brown sugar

1 Heat oven to 375°F. In large bowl, mix meat loaf ingredients. Spread mixture in ungreased 8x4- or 9x5-inch loaf pan, or shape into 9x5-inch loaf in ungreased 13x9-inch pan.

2 In small bowl, mix topping ingredients; spread over loaf.

3 Bake uncovered 1 hour to 1 hour 10 minutes or until meat thermometer inserted in center of loaf reads 165°F. Let stand 5 minutes; drain.

1 Serving: Calories 240; Total Fat 3.5g (Saturated Fat 1g, Trans Fat 0g); Cholesterol 80mg; Sodium 760mg; Total Carbohydrate 23g (Dietary Fiber 1g); Protein 28g **Exchanges:** ½ Starch, 1 Other Carbohydrate, 3½ Very Lean Meat, ½ Fat **Carbohydrate Choices:** 1½

USE IT UP
If you have barbecue sauce, you can use it in place of the topping to save a few minutes and add a different flavor to the meat loaf.

Leftover meat loaf is perfect for sandwiches. Serve cold slices on your favorite bread, with mayonnaise or ketchup if desired, for a delicious lunch at work or an on-the-go meal.

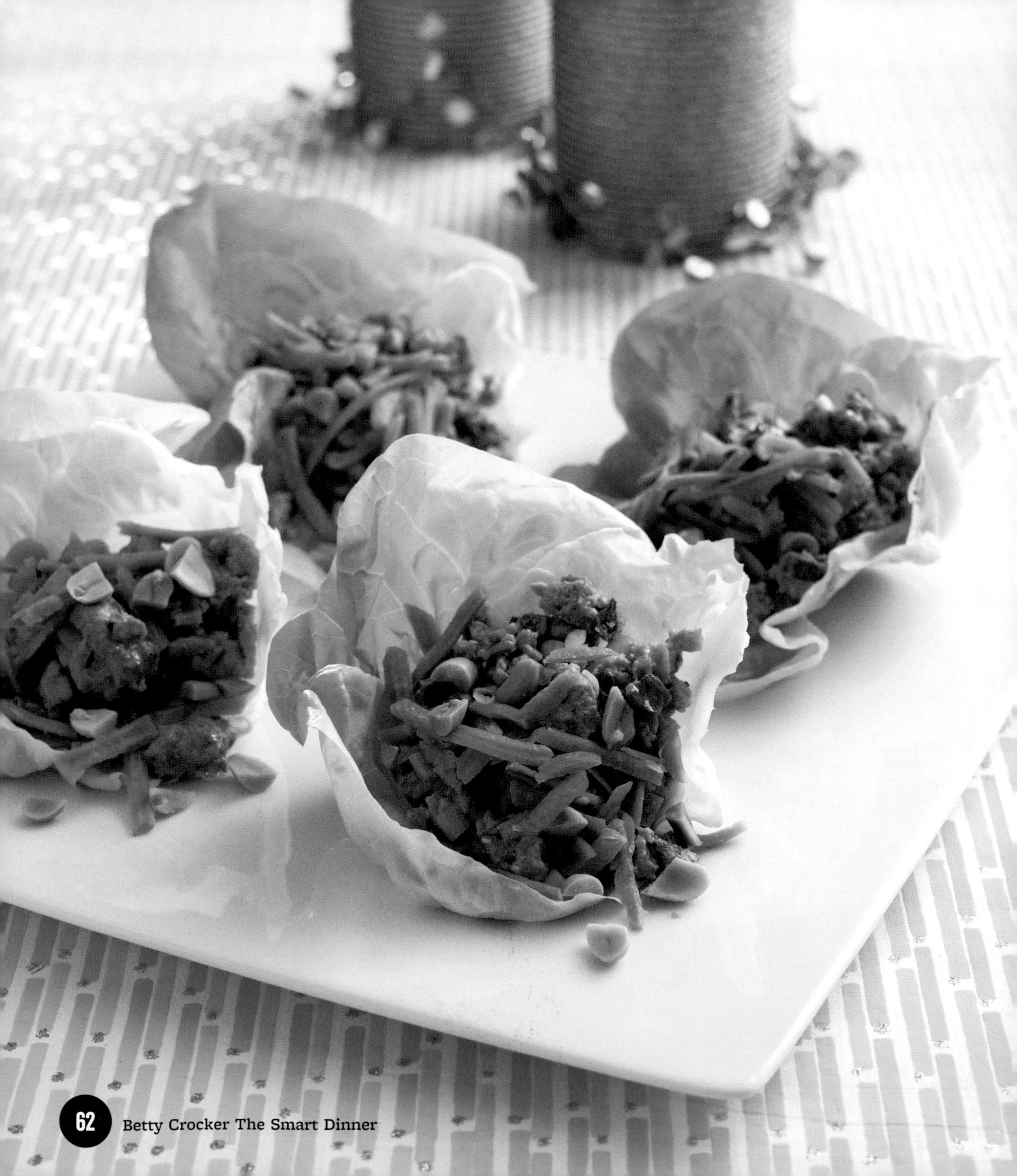

THAI TURKEY LETTUCE WRAPS

12 lettuce wraps | Prep Time: 30 Minutes | Start to Finish: 30 Minutes

1¼ lb ground turkey

¼ cup chopped green onions (4 medium)

3 tablespoons chopped fresh cilantro

1 tablespoon chopped fresh mint

2 tablespoons fresh lime juice

2 tablespoons fish sauce

3 tablespoons creamy peanut butter

2 teaspoons chili garlic paste or sauce

1 teaspoon sugar

½ teaspoon crushed red pepper flakes

1 cup shredded carrots

⅓ cup chopped salted peanuts

12 medium Bibb lettuce leaves*

1 In 10-inch nonstick skillet, cook turkey over medium-high heat, stirring frequently, until thoroughly cooked; drain. Stir in onions, cilantro, mint, lime juice, fish sauce, peanut butter, chili paste, sugar and pepper flakes. Cook 3 to 4 minutes, stirring frequently, until hot.

2 To serve, spoon 2 heaping tablespoons turkey mixture, about 2 tablespoons carrots and about 1 teaspoon peanuts onto each lettuce leaf; wrap around filling. Serve warm.

1 Lettuce Wrap: Calories 140; Total Fat 8g (Saturated Fat 1.5g, Trans Fat 0g); Cholesterol 35mg; Sodium 330mg; Total Carbohydrate 4g (Dietary Fiber 1g); Protein 11g **Exchanges:** ½ Other Carbohydrate, 1½ Very Lean Meat, 1½ Fat **Carbohydrate Choices:** 0

*We recommend Bibb lettuce for this recipe because of its sturdiness.

IN A SNAP If you like to dip your wraps in sauce, pull your store-bought spicy peanut sauce out of the fridge.

USE IT UP A pound of ground chicken or beef could be used instead of the turkey. Feel free to use what you have. You'll have slightly less filling, but you won't even notice once the wraps are rolled.

Here's a great time to use up those red pepper flakes that came with a delivery pizza.

Chapter Two

BEEF

....

AND

....

PORK

BEEF AND KASHA MEXICANA

6 servings | Prep Time: 30 Minutes | Start to Finish: 30 Minutes

1 lb extra-lean (at least 90%) ground beef

1 small onion, chopped (⅓ cup)

1 cup uncooked buckwheat kernels or groats (kasha)

1 can (14.5 oz) diced tomatoes, undrained

1 can (4.5 oz) chopped green chiles, undrained

1 package (1 oz) 40% less-sodium taco seasoning mix

2 cups frozen corn, thawed

1½ cups water

1 cup shredded reduced-fat Cheddar cheese (4 oz)

2 tablespoons chopped fresh cilantro, if desired

2 tablespoons sliced pitted ripe olives, if desired

1 In 12-inch skillet, cook beef and onion over medium-high heat 5 to 7 minutes, stirring occasionally, until beef is thoroughly cooked; drain. Add kasha; stir until kernels are moistened.

2 Stir in tomatoes, chiles, taco seasoning mix, corn and water. Heat to boiling; reduce heat to low. Cover; simmer 5 to 7 minutes, stirring occasionally, until kasha is tender.

3 Sprinkle cheese over beef mixture. Cover; cook 2 to 3 minutes or until cheese is melted. Sprinkle with cilantro and olives.

1 Serving (1⅓ Cups): Calories 360; Total Fat 11g (Saturated Fat 5g, Trans Fat 0g); Cholesterol 60mg; Sodium 570mg; Total Carbohydrate 39g (Dietary Fiber 5g); Protein 25g **Exchanges:** 2½ Starch, ½ Vegetable, 2 Lean Meat, ½ High-Fat Meat **Carbohydrate Choices:** 2½

USE IT UP
If you have soft corn or flour tortillas on hand, spoon the mixture onto the tortillas and roll up to make a delicious handheld dinner.

BREAD AND BUNS

- **Whip Up French Toast** For 8 slices of leftover bread; beat 3 eggs, ¾ cup milk, ¼ teaspoon ground cinnamon, ¼ teaspoon vanilla and ⅛ teaspoon salt. Dunk bread slices in egg mixture and cook on hot griddle over medium-high heat until golden brown on both sides.

- **Toss Together a Panzanella** See our fresh take on this lovely bread salad on page 245.

- **Toast Up Croutons** Cut firm slices of bread or rolls into cubes. Toss 4 cups cubes with ¼ cup melted butter. (If you like, add 3 cloves chopped garlic to the butter, or use olive oil and stir in 2 teaspoons Italian seasoning and ½ teaspoon salt.) Bake at 300°F for about 30 minutes, stirring occasionally, until golden brown. Cool completely before using.

- **Whirl It** Process bread in your food processor and use the crumbs to add bulk to meatballs, meat loaf or our cod cakes, page 115. Or toss crumbs with a little melted butter for a delicious oven casserole topping (sprinkle on during the last 20 minutes of bake time).

- **Make Garlic Bread** Mix 2 to 3 tablespoons softened butter with about ⅛ teaspoon garlic powder; brush on cut sides of leftover buns or bread; place butter-side up on cookie sheet. Broil on high about 4 inches from heat 2 to 3 minutes or until toasted.

- **Save It** If the bread isn't totally stale or moldy, throw it in an airtight freezer storage bag and freeze for up to 3 months, then use in any of the ideas above.

PASTA BOLOGNESE

6 servings | Prep Time: 25 Minutes | Start to Finish: 40 Minutes

2 tablespoons olive oil

3 cups diced onions

1 cup diced carrots

1 teaspoon salt

1 lb lean (at least 80%) ground beef

¼ cup tomato paste (from 6-oz can)

1 can (28 oz) fire roasted diced tomatoes, undrained

1 carton (32 oz) beef broth (4 cups)

½ teaspoon crushed red pepper flakes

2 teaspoons Italian seasoning

1 package (16 oz) spaghetti

½ cup shredded Parmesan cheese (2 oz)

¼ cup thinly sliced fresh basil leaves

1 In 4-quart Dutch oven or stockpot, heat oil over medium-high heat. Cook onions, carrots and salt in oil 5 to 8 minutes, stirring occasionally, until softened. Add beef; cook 5 to 8 minutes longer, stirring frequently, until browned.

2 Stir in tomato paste and tomatoes. Stir in broth, pepper flakes and Italian seasoning; heat to simmering. Break spaghetti in half; rinse under cold water. Tuck spaghetti into simmering liquid, covering completely. Reduce heat to medium-low; cook 13 to 15 minutes or until spaghetti is soft and sauce is reduced slightly.

3 Top individual servings with cheese and basil.

1 Serving (1⅔ Cups): Calories 630; Total Fat 18g (Saturated Fat 6g, Trans Fat 0.5g); Cholesterol 55mg; Sodium 1520mg; Total Carbohydrate 86g (Dietary Fiber 7g); Protein 32g **Exchanges:** 2 Starch, 3 Other Carbohydrate, 2 Vegetable, 3 Lean Meat, 2 Fat **Carbohydrate Choices:** 6

IN A SNAP Spoon remaining tomato paste by tablespoonfuls onto a waxed paper–lined cookie sheet. Freeze until firm; transfer to a freezer-proof resealable storage bag. Pull out as many tablespoons at a time as you need!

USE IT UP You can use whatever type of pasta you have. If it's a thicker pasta, such as penne or fusilli, you may need to cook it a few extra minutes.

If there's some fresh spinach or baby kale looking lonely in your fridge, put it to use by stirring up to 2 cups of the leaves into the pasta mixture just before serving.

STEAKHOUSE SLOPPY JOES

8 sandwiches | Prep Time: 30 Minutes | Start to Finish: 30 Minutes

1 lb ground beef

1 cup chicken or beef broth

2 tablespoons steak sauce

1 tablespoon Dijon mustard

2 tablespoons butter

1 package (8 oz) sliced fresh mushrooms (about 3 cups)

1 large onion, chopped (1 cup)

1 teaspoon Montreal steak grill seasoning

2 tablespoons all-purpose flour

8 burger buns, toasted if desired

½ cup shredded sharp Cheddar cheese (2 oz)

1 In 12-inch skillet, cook beef over medium-high heat 5 to 7 minutes, stirring occasionally, until thoroughly cooked; drain. Set beef aside. In medium bowl, mix broth, steak sauce and mustard; set aside.

2 Add butter to skillet. Cook mushrooms, onion and steak seasoning in butter 7 to 8 minutes, stirring occasionally, until onion is translucent and mushrooms are browned.

3 Sprinkle flour over vegetables. Cook 1 to 2 minutes, stirring constantly, until flour begins to brown. Return beef to skillet; stir in broth mixture. Return to simmering; cook 3 to 4 minutes or until thickened.

4 For each sandwich, spoon about ⅓ cup beef mixture on a bun bottom, top with 1 tablespoon cheese and cover with bun top.

1 Sandwich: Calories 190; Total Fat 12g (Saturated Fat 6g, Trans Fat 0.5g); Cholesterol 50mg; Sodium 350mg; Total Carbohydrate 6g (Dietary Fiber 0g); Protein 14g **Exchanges:** ½ Other Carbohydrate, ½ Vegetable, 2 Lean Meat, 1 Fat **Carbohydrate Choices:** ½

USE IT UP
Wondering what else Montreal steak grill seasoning can be used on? Think of foods that cozy up to bold seasoning: steaks, other roasted or grilled beef or pork, potato dishes or eggs.

For a bold flavor twist, use crumbled blue cheese or Gorgonzola instead of Cheddar.

IN A SNAP
If you don't have Montreal seasoning, you could make up a simplified mix by combining 1½ teaspoons each dried minced onion, dried minced garlic and paprika with ½ teaspoon each coarse ground black pepper and crushed red pepper flakes. Add ¼ teaspoon each ground coriander and salt if desired. Use 1 teaspoon of the seasoning for this recipe, and save the remaining mixture for another use.

GREEK BURGERS WITH TZATZIKI SAUCE

8 burgers | Prep Time: 30 Minutes | Start to Finish: 30 Minutes

SAUCE

- ½ medium cucumber, peeled, seeded and shredded
- 1 cup plain fat-free yogurt
- 4 medium green onions, chopped (¼ cup)
- 1 clove garlic, finely chopped
- 1 tablespoon olive oil
- 1 teaspoon lemon juice
- ¼ teaspoon salt

BURGERS

- 1 lb extra-lean (at least 90%) ground beef
- ½ cup frozen (thawed) chopped spinach, squeezed to drain
- ¼ cup crumbled feta cheese (1 oz)
- ¼ cup finely chopped red onion
- 2 cloves garlic, finely chopped
- ½ teaspoon salt
- ¼ teaspoon pepper
- 8 whole wheat burger buns, split
- 2 medium plum (Roma) tomatoes, sliced
- 4 leaves romaine lettuce, torn in half

1 Place shredded cucumber in clean dish towel; squeeze to remove any excess liquid. In small bowl, mix cucumber and remaining sauce ingredients. Cover; refrigerate until serving time.

2 Heat gas or charcoal grill. In large bowl, mix beef, spinach, cheese, red onion, 2 cloves garlic, ½ teaspoon salt and the pepper. Shape into 8 patties, ¼ inch thick.

3 Place patties on grill over medium heat. Cover grill; cook 5 to 8 minutes, turning once, until meat thermometer inserted in center of patties reads 160°F.

4 Spoon 2 tablespoons sauce on each bun bottom. Top with burger, tomato and lettuce. Cover with bun tops.

1 Burger: Calories 210; Total Fat 6g (Saturated Fat 1.5g, Trans Fat 1.5g); Cholesterol 0mg; Sodium 540mg; Total Carbohydrate 27g (Dietary Fiber 2g); Protein 12g **Exchanges:** 1½ Starch, 1 Vegetable, 1 Medium-Fat Meat **Carbohydrate Choices:** 2

IN A SNAP The tzatziki sauce can be made ahead and kept covered in the refrigerator for up to 1 day, making it easier to get dinner on the table and allowing the flavors of the sauce to blend at the same time.

USE IT UP Got plain Greek yogurt in the fridge? Feel free to use it instead of the regular yogurt. It will make the tzatziki sauce thicker and creamier.

Fresh spinach can be substituted for the frozen; just chop baby or regular spinach leaves to measure ¾ cup and stir into the beef with the other ingredients.

GRILLED CHEDDAR BURGER AND VEGGIE PACKETS

4 servings | Prep Time: 40 Minutes | Start to Finish: 40 Minutes

6 medium green onions

1 lb lean (at least 80%) ground beef

1 cup shredded Cheddar cheese (4 oz)

1 tablespoon Worcestershire sauce

1½ teaspoons peppered seasoned salt

2 medium Yukon Gold potatoes, thinly sliced

1½ cups ready-to-eat baby-cut carrots

12 cherry tomatoes, cut in half if desired

1 Heat gas or charcoal grill. Cut 4 (18x12-inch) sheets of heavy-duty foil; spray one side of each sheet with cooking spray.

2 Slice 4 of the onions; set aside. Chop remaining 2 onions. In large bowl, mix chopped onions, beef, cheese, Worcestershire sauce and 1 teaspoon of the peppered seasoned salt. Shape mixture into 4 patties, about 1 inch thick.

3 Divide potatoes among foil sheets. Top each with beef patty, carrots, tomatoes and sliced onions; sprinkle with remaining ½ teaspoon peppered seasoned salt. Bring up 2 sides of foil over patties and vegetables so edges meet. Seal edges, making tight ½-inch fold; fold again, allowing space for heat circulation and expansion. Fold other sides to seal.

4 Place packets on grill over medium heat. Cover grill; cook 17 to 20 minutes, rotating packets one-half turn after 10 minutes, or until potatoes are tender. To serve, cut large X across top of each packet; carefully fold back foil to allow heat to escape.

1 Serving: Calories 420; Total Fat 23g (Saturated Fat 10g, Trans Fat 1g); Cholesterol 100mg; Sodium 830mg; Total Carbohydrate 26g (Dietary Fiber 4g); Protein 29g **Exchanges:** 1 Starch, 1½ Vegetable, 2 Medium-Fat Meat, 1 High-Fat Meat, 1 Fat **Carbohydrate Choices:** 2

USE IT UP
If you don't have peppered seasoned salt, use 1 teaspoon seasoned salt or ½ teaspoon salt and ¼ teaspoon pepper for each teaspoon of peppered seasoned salt.

MAKE A MEAL
These colorful packets are almost a meal in themselves. Add slices of garlic bread and a cluster of grapes for hearty appetites.

IN A SNAP
If you'd rather bake these packets, place them on a large cookie sheet. Bake at 450°F for 35 to 40 minutes.

FRENCH BREAD TACO PIZZA

4 servings | Prep Time: 15 Minutes | Start to Finish: 30 Minutes

1   loaf (1 lb) French bread

½   lb ground beef

2   tablespoons taco seasoning mix (from 1-oz package)

⅓   cup water

1   can (16 oz) refried beans

1   medium yellow bell pepper, cut into ¾-inch pieces

½   cup thinly sliced red onion

1½   cups shredded Mexican cheese blend (6 oz)

1   cup shredded lettuce

1   medium tomato, chopped (¾ cup)

1 Heat oven to 425°F. Line large cookie sheet with foil. Cut bread in half lengthwise, then in half crosswise. Place bread, cut sides up, on cookie sheet. Bake about 5 minutes just until lightly toasted.

2 Meanwhile, in 6- to 8-inch skillet, cook beef over medium-high heat 5 to 7 minutes, stirring occasionally, until thoroughly cooked; drain. Add taco seasoning mix and water; cook until thickened.

3 Spread refried beans over toasted bread. Top with beef mixture, bell pepper, onion and cheese. Bake 10 to 12 minutes or until cheese is melted. Top with lettuce and tomato.

1 Serving: Calories 710; Total Fat 24g (Saturated Fat 12g, Trans Fat 1g); Cholesterol 75mg; Sodium 1540mg; Total Carbohydrate 86g (Dietary Fiber 8g); Protein 38g **Exchanges:** 2 Starch, 3½ Other Carbohydrate, ½ Vegetable, 1 Very Lean Meat, 2 Medium-Fat Meat, 1½ High-Fat Meat **Carbohydrate Choices:** 6

IN A SNAP For a quick and easy meal, cook the ground beef mixture ahead and refrigerate. Then all you have to do at dinnertime is reheat the beef, top the French bread and bake.

ASIAN BEEF NOODLE BOWLS

4 servings | Prep Time: 20 Minutes | Start to Finish: 20 Minutes

4 oz uncooked angel hair pasta (capellini), broken in half

8 oz fresh sugar snap peas

5 teaspoons vegetable oil

1 lb boneless beef sirloin steak, cut into ¼-inch strips

1 medium carrot, thinly sliced (½ cup)

½ cup teriyaki baste and glaze* (from 12-oz bottle)

4 medium green onions with tops, sliced (¼ cup)

½ cup honey-roasted peanuts, chopped

1 Cook pasta as directed on package. Meanwhile, cut off stem ends of sugar snap peas and remove strings if desired. Drain pasta; cover to keep warm.

2 In 12-inch nonstick skillet or wok, heat 3 teaspoons of the oil over medium-high heat. Stir-fry beef in oil 2 to 3 minutes or until no longer pink. Remove from skillet; keep warm.

3 In same skillet, heat remaining 2 teaspoons oil over medium-high heat. Stir-fry peas and carrot in oil 3 to 4 minutes or until crisp-tender. Stir in pasta, beef and teriyaki glaze; toss until well blended.

4 Serve in bowls; sprinkle with onions and peanuts.

*Teriyaki baste and glaze has a thick, syrup-like consistency and shouldn't be confused with teriyaki marinade or sauce.

1 Serving (1¼ Cups): Calories 490; Total Fat 18g (Saturated Fat 3.5g, Trans Fat 0g); Cholesterol 65mg; Sodium 1040mg; Total Carbohydrate 47g (Dietary Fiber 5g); Protein 36g **Exchanges:** 1 Starch, 1½ Other Carbohydrate, 1½ Vegetable, 4 Very Lean Meat, 3 Fat **Carbohydrate Choices:** 3

IN A SNAP
Beef is easier to cut into thin strips if partially frozen first for 30 to 60 minutes.

USE IT UP
The honey-roasted peanuts add a nice contrasting crunch to this dish. But use whatever you have on hand—slivered almonds, pepitas (roasted pumpkin seeds) or hulled sunflower seeds.

AMAZING BACON-CHEESEBURGER TACOS

6 servings | Prep Time: 25 Minutes | Start to Finish: 25 Minutes

1 lb lean (at least 80%) ground beef

1 medium onion, chopped (½ cup)

1 package (1 oz) 40% less sodium taco seasoning mix

⅔ cup water

½ cup cheese 'n salsa dip (from 15-oz jar)

1 box (7.4 oz) hard and soft taco shells (6 hard corn shells and 6 soft flour tortillas)

1½ cups shredded lettuce

1 large tomato, seeded, chopped (1 cup)

6 slices bacon, crisply cooked, crumbled

1 In 10-inch nonstick skillet, cook beef and onion over medium-high heat 5 to 7 minutes, stirring occasionally, until beef is thoroughly cooked; drain.

2 Stir in taco seasoning mix and water. Reduce heat to medium; cook 3 to 4 minutes, stirring frequently, until thickened. Stir in dip until well mixed. Meanwhile, heat taco shells and tortillas as directed on box.

3 Fill heated taco shells and tortillas with beef mixture, lettuce, tomato and bacon.

1 Serving (2 Tacos): Calories 350; Total Fat 18g (Saturated Fat 6g, Trans Fat 1g); Cholesterol 55mg; Sodium 950mg; Total Carbohydrate 27g (Dietary Fiber 1g); Protein 19g **Exchanges:** 1½ Starch, ½ Vegetable, 2 Medium-Fat Meat, 1½ Fat **Carbohydrate Choices:** 2

USE IT UP
If your store doesn't carry the dip, substitute 4 ounces Mexican prepared cheese product, cubed, or another soft cheese that melts easily. If you prefer less spice, use regular prepared cheese product.

Have leftover cheese dip? Heat it and drizzle over tortilla chips for an easy appetizer or late-night snack.

BBQ BEEF BISCUIT STACKS

16 sandwiches | Prep Time: 25 Minutes | Start to Finish: 8 Hours 45 Minutes

BEEF

- 1 boneless beef rump roast (4 lb)
- 2 cups barbecue sauce
- 1 bottle (12 oz) dark beer

CREAMY COLESLAW

- 1 container (6 oz) fat-free Greek plain yogurt
- ¼ cup mayonnaise
- 1 tablespoon sugar
- 3 tablespoons cider vinegar
- ¼ teaspoon salt
- 4 cups thinly sliced cabbage
- 2 tablespoons chopped green onions (2 medium)

CHEESE BISCUITS

- 4 cups Original Bisquick mix
- 1½ cups milk
- 1 cup shredded Cheddar cheese (4 oz)
- ½ cup butter, melted

1 Spray 4- to 5-quart slow cooker with cooking spray. Place beef in slow cooker. In small bowl, mix barbecue sauce and beer; pour over beef. Cover; cook on Low heat setting 8 to 10 hours or until beef is tender.

2 Meanwhile, in large bowl, mix yogurt, mayonnaise, sugar, vinegar and salt until smooth. Stir in cabbage and onions. Cover; refrigerate until serving time.

3 About 30 minutes before serving, remove beef from slow cooker to cutting board or plate. Shred beef, using 2 forks; return to slow cooker to keep warm.

4 Heat oven to 425°F. In medium bowl, stir biscuit ingredients until soft dough forms. Drop dough by 16 spoonfuls onto ungreased large cookie sheet. Bake 16 to 18 minutes or until golden brown.

5 Split biscuits in half. For each sandwich, spoon about ½ cup beef mixture and 3 tablespoons coleslaw onto biscuit bottom; cover with biscuit top.

1 Sandwich: Calories 340; Total Fat 11g (Saturated Fat 3.5g, Trans Fat 2g); Cholesterol 65mg; Sodium 690mg; Total Carbohydrate 32g (Dietary Fiber 0g); Protein 27g **Exchanges:** 1½ Starch, ½ Other Carbohydrate, ½ Vegetable, 2 Lean Meat, 1 Medium-Fat Meat **Carbohydrate Choices:** 2

IN A SNAP
Make this full recipe when you have a crowd to feed, or save half of the beef, coleslaw and biscuits (all stored separately) for a second meal or lunches.

STEAK BIBIMBAP

4 servings | Prep Time: 30 Minutes | Start to Finish: 30 Minutes

KOREAN BARBECUE SAUCE

- 2 tablespoons ketchup
- 2 tablespoons barbecue sauce
- 2 teaspoons Sriracha sauce
- 2 teaspoons soy sauce
- ½ teaspoon toasted sesame oil
- 1½ teaspoons miso paste (any variety)

STEAK AND VEGETABLES

- 3 large carrots with tops
- 2 tablespoons vegetable oil
- 1 medium onion, finely chopped (½ cup)
- 2 teaspoons finely chopped garlic
- 1½ cups thinly sliced cooked steak
- ⅛ teaspoon salt
- ⅛ teaspoon pepper
- 1 large red bell pepper, cut into thin strips
- 1 teaspoon seasoned rice vinegar
- 1 package (5 oz) fresh baby spinach leaves (6 cups)
- 1 tablespoon water
- 1 teaspoon soy sauce
- 2 cups hot cooked brown rice, quinoa, couscous or other grain

1 In small bowl, stir together sauce ingredients. Set aside.

2 Cut off carrot tops; chop leafy tops to measure 2 tablespoons. Shred carrots. Set aside.

3 In 10-inch nonstick skillet or wok, heat 1 tablespoon of the oil over medium heat. Cook onion and garlic in oil 3 to 4 minutes, stirring frequently, until softened. Stir in steak and 2 tablespoons of the barbecue sauce. Reduce heat to low; cook 1 to 2 minutes, stirring constantly, until hot. Remove from skillet to bowl; cover to keep warm.

4 Wipe skillet with paper towel. Heat 2 teaspoons oil over medium heat. Cook carrots 2 to 3 minutes, stirring frequently, until crisp-tender. Stir in salt and pepper. Remove from skillet; keep warm.

5 Add remaining 1 teaspoon oil to skillet. Cook bell pepper 3 to 4 minutes, stirring frequently, until crisp-tender. Season with vinegar. Remove from skillet; keep warm. Add spinach and water to skillet; toss over high heat until spinach is wilted. Stir in soy sauce.

6 Divide rice among 4 individual bowls; arrange beef, carrots, bell pepper and spinach around rice. Sprinkle with reserved carrot tops. Serve with remaining barbecue sauce.

1 Serving: Calories 350; Total Fat 11g (Saturated Fat 2.5g, Trans Fat 0g); Cholesterol 40mg; Sodium 690mg; Total Carbohydrate 41g (Dietary Fiber 6g); Protein 20g
Exchanges: 1 Starch, 1 Other Carbohydrate, 1½ Vegetable, 2 Lean Meat, 1 Fat
Carbohydrate Choices: 3

USE IT UP This is a great recipe to make with leftover steak.

OVEN-ROASTED PULLED PORK

10 cups | Prep Time: 15 Minutes | Start to Finish: 7 Hours 15 Minutes

Use this recipe as a base to have on hand for Creamy Pulled-Pork Pasta, page 89, and Fajita Pulled-Pork Wraps with Avocado-Onion Slaw, page 90.

1   boneless pork shoulder roast (5 lb)
20   cloves garlic, peeled
¼   cup olive oil
2   teaspoons salt
2   teaspoons pepper

IN A SNAP We recommend freezing the pork in 2-cup portions, but make it work for you by creating whatever size portions you need to feed your family for one meal. It's a great start to homemade meals in minutes.

USE IT UP This delicious shredded pork can be used to make quick barbecue pork sandwiches. Stir in barbecue sauce with the pork and heat until hot. Spoon onto buns.

1 Heat oven to 325°F. In 13x9-inch (3-quart) glass baking dish, place pork, fat side up. With sharp knife, cut (20) 1-inch slits in fat; tuck 1 clove garlic into each slit. Rub pork with oil. Sprinkle with salt and pepper; rub into meat.

2 Cover tightly with foil. Roast 5 hours 30 minutes to 6 hours 30 minutes or until meat thermometer inserted in center of roast reads 190°F. Let stand until cool enough to handle, about 30 minutes.

3 Shred meat with 2 forks; discard garlic. Toss shredded pork in some of the pan juices (if any) to coat. Divide pork into 2-cup portions; place in freezer containers or resealable freezer plastic bags. Seal tightly; refrigerate until completely cooled, at least 1 hour. Freeze up to 3 months.

½ **Cup:** Calories 160; Total Fat 12g (Saturated Fat 4g, Trans Fat 0g); Cholesterol 45mg; Sodium 270mg; Total Carbohydrate 0g (Dietary Fiber 0g); Protein 12g **Exchanges:** 1½ Medium-Fat Meat, 1 Fat **Carbohydrate Choices:** 0

CANNED BEANS (DRAINED)

- **Top a Salad** The protein and fiber in beans will help fill you up and keep you full.

- **Bulk Up Soup** Toss beans into soup while preparing it, or at the end just to heat them through. A great addition to prepared soup, too!

- **Stuff a Taco** Heat beans in the microwave and then spoon into a tortilla or taco shell. Sprinkle with your favorite Mexican fillings, such as shredded cheese, chopped tomato, sour cream and guacamole.

- **Stir Up Succotash** Make a simple succotash by mixing canned beans, cooked and cooled corn and cherry tomato halves. Toss with a little melted butter or whipping cream, and season with salt and pepper and your favorite herbs.

- **Perk Up Pizza** Sprinkle beans on your pizza instead of sausage or pepperoni. Add the beans either right after or right before the shredded cheese so the cheese can hold the beans in place.

- **Toss with Rice** Toss beans in during the last few minutes of cooking rice so they have a chance to get warm. Use about ½ cup of beans for every 1 cup uncooked rice. Or add beans to leftover rice before reheating (about ½ cup for 2 cups of rice). If you like, dress the rice up with chopped fresh tomatoes or bell pepper and chopped jalapeño or herbs.

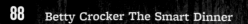

CREAMY PULLED-PORK PASTA

8 servings | Prep Time: 35 Minutes | Start to Finish: 35 Minutes

Make the Oven-Roasted Pulled Pork, page 86, to have on hand for making this dish in a jiffy.

1 box (16 oz) campanelle pasta

2 tablespoons butter

1 large onion, sliced (1 cup)

½ teaspoon salt

1 package (8 oz) sliced fresh mushrooms (about 3 cups)

¼ cup sherry vinegar*

2 cups frozen Oven-Roasted Pulled Pork (page 86), thawed

1 cup whipping cream

1 package (5 oz) baby arugula

½ cup shredded Parmesan cheese (2 oz)

Additional sherry vinegar, if desired

1 In 4- to 5-quart Dutch oven or stockpot, cook pasta as directed on package. Drain, reserving ¼ cup cooking water. Return pasta to Dutch oven; cover to keep warm.

2 Meanwhile, in 10-inch skillet, melt butter over medium heat. Add onion and salt; cook 5 to 7 minutes, stirring frequently, until edges of onion slices are browned and soft. Add mushrooms; cook 5 to 7 minutes until mushrooms release juices, liquid evaporates and mushrooms are browned.

3 Add vinegar; scrape up any bits from bottom of pan and stir until liquid is almost completely evaporated. Stir in pork. Add whipping cream and reserved pasta cooking water; cook 2 to 3 minutes or until thickened. Add pork mixture to pasta in Dutch oven; toss to coat. Fold in arugula; stir until arugula wilts.

4 Divide pasta mixture among 8 bowls. Top each with cheese. Drizzle with a few drops vinegar.

*Cider vinegar or white balsamic vinegar can be substituted for the sherry vinegar. Avoid regular balsamic vinegar, which will give the pasta a brownish cast.

1 Serving (1¼ Cups): Calories 500; Total Fat 24g (Saturated Fat 12g, Trans Fat 0.5g); Cholesterol 75mg; Sodium 660mg; Total Carbohydrate 52g (Dietary Fiber 3g); Protein 19g **Exchanges:** 2½ Starch, 1 Other Carbohydrate, 1½ Lean Meat, 3½ Fat **Carbohydrate Choices:** 3½

USE IT UP Don't have campanelle pasta? Try bow-tie (farfalle), penne or ziti. Any sturdy pasta shape in your pantry will work well with this hearty sauce.

FAJITA PULLED-PORK WRAPS
WITH AVOCADO-ONION SLAW

6 servings | Prep Time: 15 Minutes | Start to Finish: 15 Minutes

Make the Oven-Roasted Pulled Pork, page 86, to have on hand for making this dish in a snap.

2 cups frozen Oven-Roasted Pulled Pork (page 86), thawed

¾ cup chunky-style salsa

¼ cup water

1 teaspoon chili powder

¾ teaspoon ground cumin

3 tablespoons mayonnaise or salad dressing

1 tablespoon white vinegar

¼ teaspoon salt

1 medium avocado, pitted, peeled and cubed

1 medium onion, halved, thinly sliced

12 flour tortillas (6 inch), heated as directed on package

¼ cup chopped fresh cilantro

1 In 3-quart saucepan, stir together pork, salsa, water, chili powder and cumin. Heat to boiling; reduce heat. Cover; simmer 5 minutes, stirring occasionally, to blend flavors.

2 In medium bowl, mix mayonnaise, vinegar and salt. Gently stir in avocado and onion.

3 Spoon pork mixture onto warmed tortillas; top with avocado-onion slaw and cilantro.

1 Serving (**2 Wraps**): Calories 430; Total Fat 23g (Saturated Fat 5g, Trans Fat 0.5g); Cholesterol 50mg; Sodium 960mg; Total Carbohydrate 35g (Dietary Fiber 4g); Protein 21g **Exchanges:** 2 Starch, ½ Vegetable, 2 Very Lean Meat, 4 Fat **Carbohydrate Choices:** 2

USE IT UP The avocado-onion slaw adds creaminess as well as crunch, but for those who aren't avocado fans, try substituting diced tomato and/or shredded lettuce.

If you don't have chili powder or cumin, substitute 1¾ teaspoons taco seasoning mix (from 1-oz package).

ROASTED PORK LOIN SHEET PAN DINNER

6 servings | Prep Time: 20 Minutes | Start to Finish: 1 Hour

2 tablespoons olive oil

4 cloves garlic, finely chopped

1 teaspoon dried thyme leaves

1 teaspoon salt

½ teaspoon pepper

1 pork tenderloin (1½ lb)

1 small red onion, cut into ½-inch wedges

1 lb Brussels sprouts, halved

1 lb small red potatoes, quartered

4 slices thick-sliced bacon, cut into 1-inch pieces

1 Heat oven to 425°F. Spray large rimmed sheet pan with cooking spray. In small bowl, stir oil, garlic, thyme, salt and pepper until well mixed.

2 Place pork in center of pan; rub with 1 tablespoon of the oil mixture.

3 In large bowl, toss onion, Brussels sprouts, potatoes and remaining 1 tablespoon oil mixture until well coated. Spoon vegetables around pork. Sprinkle with bacon.

4 Roast uncovered 30 to 35 minutes or until thermometer inserted in thickest part of pork reads 145°F and vegetables are browned and tender. Let stand 5 minutes.

5 Cut pork into ½-inch-thick slices. Serve with vegetables.

1 Serving: Calories 310; Total Fat 12g (Saturated Fat 3g, Trans Fat 0g); Cholesterol 75mg; Sodium 570mg; Total Carbohydrate 21g (Dietary Fiber 4g); Protein 31g **Exchanges:** 1 Starch, 1 Vegetable, 3½ Very Lean Meat, 2 Fat **Carbohydrate Choices:** 1½

MAKE A MEAL Serve this one-pan meal with slices of crusty baguette.

USE IT UP If you like butternut squash, feel free to substitute it for the Brussels sprouts. Already cubed squash can often be found in your supermarket's refrigerated produce section and is a great help when you need to get dinner on the table quickly.

CITRUSY PORK CHOP SKILLET

4 servings | Prep Time: 45 Minutes | Start to Finish: 45 Minutes

1 tablespoon Dijon mustard

1 teaspoon salt

½ teaspoon pepper

4 bone-in pork loin chops, ½ to ¾ inch thick

2 teaspoons chopped fresh or 1 teaspoon dried thyme leaves

3 tablespoons olive oil

1 medium onion, chopped (½ cup)

2 cloves garlic, finely chopped

½ lb small Brussels sprouts, cut in half (if large, cut into quarters)

¼ head red cabbage, cut into ½-inch slices (about 2 cups)

Grated peel and juice of 1 large orange (about ½ cup juice)

Grated peel and juice of 1 large lemon (about ¼ cup juice)

2 tablespoons packed brown sugar

2 teaspoons cornstarch

1 In small bowl, stir together mustard, ½ teaspoon of the salt and ¼ teaspoon of the pepper. Brush mixture over pork chops; sprinkle evenly with thyme.

2 In 12-inch skillet, heat 1 tablespoon of the oil over medium-high heat. Cook pork chops in oil 6 to 8 minutes, turning once, until browned. Remove from skillet; cover to keep warm.

3 In same skillet, heat remaining 2 tablespoons oil over medium-high heat. Cook onion, garlic and Brussels sprouts in oil 3 to 5 minutes, stirring frequently, until lightly browned. Add cabbage; cook 3 minutes.

4 In small bowl, stir together orange and lemon peel and juice, brown sugar, cornstarch and remaining ½ teaspoon salt and ¼ teaspoon pepper. Pour over vegetables in skillet. Heat to boiling; reduce heat. Place pork chops on top of vegetables.

5 Cover; cook 5 minutes or until pork is no longer pink when cut near bone and meat thermometer reads 145°F.

1 Serving: Calories 370; Total Fat 19g (Saturated Fat 4.5g, Trans Fat 0g); Cholesterol 65mg; Sodium 750mg; Total Carbohydrate 24g (Dietary Fiber 4g); Protein 25g **Exchanges:** 1 Other Carbohydrate, 2 Vegetable, 3 Very Lean Meat, 3½ Fat **Carbohydrate Choices:** 1½

IN A SNAP The method of this recipe is much like stir-frying and happens quickly, so make sure to measure out all ingredients and have everything handy and ready to go before heating the skillet.

MAKE A MEAL You'll want to sop up all the terrific flavor this dish offers by serving the sauce, veggies and pork over cooked brown rice or mashed potatoes.

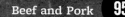

COLORFUL HAM SALAD SANDWICHES

6 sandwiches | Prep Time: 15 Minutes | Start to Finish: 15 Minutes

½ cup mayonnaise

1 teaspoon curry powder

2 cups finely chopped cooked ham

1 cup finely chopped fresh broccoli

½ cup finely shredded carrot

¼ cup raisins

¼ cup cashew pieces

Lettuce leaves or other greens

1 small apple, thinly sliced

6 burger buns, split

1 In medium bowl, mix mayonnaise and curry powder. Stir in ham, broccoli, carrot, raisins and cashews.

2 For each sandwich, place lettuce and apple slices on bun bottom; top with about ½ cup ham salad. Cover with bun tops.

1 Sandwich: Calories 400; Total Fat 22g (Saturated Fat 4.5g, Trans Fat 0g); Cholesterol 35mg; Sodium 1020mg; Total Carbohydrate 34g (Dietary Fiber 3g); Protein 16g **Exchanges:** 2 Starch, ½ Vegetable, 1½ Lean Meat, 3½ Fat **Carbohydrate Choices:** 2

MAKE A MEAL
For heartier appetites, use 4 larger buns, like Kaiser or brioche buns, and fill with ¾ cup ham salad. Serve with chips and a green salad.

CUBAN FRIED RICE

4 servings | Prep Time: 40 Minutes | Start to Finish: 40 Minutes

2 tablespoons vegetable oil

1 medium onion, chopped (½ cup)

1 medium red bell pepper, chopped (1 cup)

3 cups cold cooked regular long-grain white or brown rice

1½ cups cubed cooked ham

1 cup black beans (from 15-oz can), drained, rinsed

½ cup frozen sweet peas

1 small jalapeño chile, seeded, chopped

2 cloves garlic, finely chopped

3 eggs, slightly beaten

3 tablespoons soy sauce

½ cup chopped green onions (8 medium)

1 In 12-inch skillet or wok, heat 1 tablespoon of the oil over medium-high heat. Cook onion and bell pepper in oil 3 to 4 minutes, stirring frequently, until crisp-tender.

2 Reduce heat to medium. Add rice, ham, beans, peas, chile and garlic; cook about 5 minutes, stirring and breaking up rice, until mixture is hot.

3 Move rice mixture to side of skillet. Add remaining 1 tablespoon oil to other side of skillet. Cook eggs in oil, stirring constantly, until eggs are thickened throughout but still moist. Stir eggs into rice mixture. Stir in soy sauce. Sprinkle with green onions.

1 Serving: Calories 460; Total Fat 16g (Saturated Fat 4g, Trans Fat 0g); Cholesterol 170mg; Sodium 2090mg; Total Carbohydrate 54g (Dietary Fiber 7g); Protein 25g **Exchanges:** 2 Starch, 1½ Other Carbohydrate, 1 Vegetable, 1 Very Lean Meat, ½ Lean Meat, 1 Medium-Fat Meat, 1½ Fat **Carbohydrate Choices:** 3½

IN A SNAP Using leftover rice makes this meal even quicker! So next time you're making rice, make extra and keep it in the fridge for fried rice. If you don't have leftover rice, to make 3 cups long-grain white rice, heat 1 cup rice and 2 cups water to boiling in 4-quart saucepan. Reduce heat to low. Cover and simmer 15 minutes or until liquid is absorbed and rice is tender.

USE IT UP If you don't have a jalapeño, you can add a little heat with ¼ to ½ teaspoon crushed red pepper flakes.

SPINACH, RICOTTA AND SAUSAGE CALZONES

8 calzones | Prep Time: 25 Minutes | Start to Finish: 1 Hour

1 box (9 oz) frozen
chopped spinach

½ lb bulk Italian sausage,
browned, drained

1 cup whole milk
ricotta cheese

1 cup shredded mozzarella
cheese (4 oz)

4 tablespoons grated
Parmesan cheese

1 teaspoon
Italian seasoning

1 lb frozen pizza dough
(from 3-lb bag), thawed

1 egg, slightly beaten

Pizza sauce or marinara
sauce, if desired

1 Heat oven to 375°F. Spray cookie sheet with cooking spray.

2 Cook spinach as directed on box. When cool enough to handle, squeeze between paper towels to remove excess moisture. Place spinach in large bowl. Add cooked sausage, ricotta, mozzarella, 3 tablespoons of the Parmesan and the Italian seasoning; stir until well combined.

3 Divide pizza dough into 8 balls. Roll and press each ball into 5- to 6-inch round. Spoon meat mixture onto half of each round, leaving ½-inch border around edge. Fold dough over filling; pinch and roll edges to seal in filling.

4 Place calzones on cookie sheet. Brush tops with egg. Prick tops with fork to allow steam to escape.

5 Bake 20 to 22 minutes or until golden brown, topping with remaining 1 tablespoon Parmesan during last 3 minutes of baking. Cool 10 minutes. Serve warm with pizza sauce.

Freezer Directions: Make as directed in Steps 2 and 3. Place calzones on cookie sheet; freeze 4 hours or until firm. Place calzones in resealable freezer plastic bag; freeze up to 3 months. When ready to bake, place frozen calzones on cookie sheet and brush with egg. Bake as directed, adding 5 to 8 minutes to the baking time.

IN A SNAP Get a head start on this meal by browning the sausage the night before while preparing dinner. Then cover and refrigerate until ready to assemble the calzones and bake.

Put frozen pizza dough in the fridge the night before to thaw. Or check with your local pizza place about purchasing dough . . . or look for prepared pizza dough at larger supermarkets.

1 Calzone: Calories 450; Total Fat 21g (Saturated Fat 10g, Trans Fat 0g); Cholesterol 80mg; Sodium 1050mg; Total Carbohydrate 41g (Dietary Fiber 1g); Protein 24g **Exchanges:** 2 Starch, ½ Other Carbohydrate, ½ Milk, 1 Medium-Fat Meat, 1 High-Fat Meat, ½ Fat **Carbohydrate Choices:** 3

SAUSAGE-PIZZA QUINOA

8 servings | Prep Time: 40 Minutes | Start to Finish: 1 Hour 5 Minutes

1   lb bulk spicy Italian pork sausage

2   tablespoons olive oil

1   red onion, thinly sliced (about 2 cups)

1   medium green bell pepper, cut into thin strips (about 1 cup)

1   package (8 oz) sliced fresh mushrooms (about 3 cups)

1½ teaspoons salt

1   teaspoon Italian seasoning

1   package (12 oz) quinoa (2 cups), rinsed, well drained

4   cups milk

2   cups shredded mozzarella cheese (8 oz)

2   cups cherry tomatoes, cut into quarters

½ cup thinly sliced fresh basil leaves

    Grated or shredded Parmesan cheese, if desired

1 In 5-quart nonstick Dutch oven or stockpot, cook sausage over medium heat 8 to 10 minutes, stirring occasionally, until no longer pink. Drain; transfer to large bowl. Cover with foil; set aside.

2 Wipe out Dutch oven with paper towel. Add 1 tablespoon of the oil; heat over medium heat. Cook onion in oil 3 to 5 minutes, stirring occasionally, until softened. Add bell pepper; cook 3 to 5 minutes longer or until softened. Using slotted spoon, transfer onion and bell pepper to bowl with sausage; cover.

3 Add remaining 1 tablespoon oil to Dutch oven; heat over high heat. Cook mushrooms, salt and Italian seasoning in oil 5 to 7 minutes or until mushrooms are browned and liquid is evaporated. Transfer to bowl with sausage and vegetables; cover.

4 Wipe out Dutch oven. Add quinoa; cook over medium heat 1 to 2 minutes, stirring constantly, until fragrant. Slowly stir in milk. Heat to simmering over high heat, stirring occasionally; reduce heat to low. Cover; cook 20 to 25 minutes or until liquid is absorbed and quinoa is thoroughly cooked.

5 Add sausage-vegetable mixture to quinoa; stir to combine. Remove from heat; stir in mozzarella cheese. Top with tomatoes, basil and Parmesan cheese.

1 Serving (1½ Cups): Calories 450; Total Fat 22g (Saturated Fat 8g, Trans Fat 0g); Cholesterol 45mg; Sodium 890mg; Total Carbohydrate 39g (Dietary Fiber 4g); Protein 24g **Exchanges:** 2 Starch, 1 Vegetable, 1 Medium-Fat Meat, 1½ High-Fat Meat, 1 Fat **Carbohydrate Choices:** 2½

Betty Crocker The Smart Dinner

ISRAELI COUSCOUS RISOTTO WITH CARAMELIZED ONIONS AND SAUSAGE

4 servings | Prep Time: 35 Minutes | Start to Finish: 35 Minutes

1 teaspoon olive oil

1 large onion, diced (1 cup)

1 teaspoon sugar

3 links (4 oz each) lean sweet Italian turkey sausage, casings removed

1½ cups uncooked Israeli couscous

¼ cup white wine or chicken broth

2 cups unsalted chicken broth (from 32-oz carton)

1 cup water

¼ teaspoon crushed red pepper flakes

1 tablespoon freshly grated lemon peel

2 cups baby spinach leaves, coarsely chopped

⅓ cup shredded Parmesan cheese

1 Heat 4-quart Dutch oven or heavy-bottom saucepan over medium heat. Add oil and onion. Stir in sugar. Cook 5 to 10 minutes, stirring occasionally, until onion starts to brown. Add sausage. Cook, breaking up sausage with spoon, until browned.

2 Add couscous and stir, cooking 1 minute. Add wine; cook until wine has been absorbed by couscous. Add 1 cup of the broth; cook until broth is absorbed, stirring occasionally, about 5 minutes. Add remaining 1 cup broth, cooking until liquid is absorbed, stirring occasionally. Add water, cooking until liquid is absorbed, stirring occasionally.

3 Remove from heat. Stir in red pepper flakes, lemon peel, spinach leaves and cheese, stirring just until spinach wilts. Sprinkle with additional cheese, if desired. Serve immediately.

1 Serving: Calories 450; Total Fat 12g (Saturated Fat 3.5g, Trans Fat 0g); Cholesterol 60mg; Sodium 720mg; Total Carbohydrate 57g (Dietary Fiber 4g); Protein 27g **Exchanges:** 3½ Starch, ½ Vegetable, 2 Lean Meat, 1 Fat **Carbohydrate Choices:** 4

USE IT UP

Baby arugula leaves can easily be substituted for the spinach in this recipe; it adds a nice peppery flavor to round out the dish.

Add a little crunch to this dish by sprinkling pepitas, pine nuts or chopped walnuts over the risotto before serving.

BACON, TOMATO AND AVOCADO GRILLED CHEESE

4 sandwiches | Prep Time: 15 Minutes | Start to Finish: 15 Minutes

8 slices white or whole wheat bread

2 cups shredded Cheddar cheese (8 oz)

1 small onion, chopped (⅓ cup)

8 slices bacon, crisply cooked

1 medium tomato, thinly sliced

1 medium avocado, pitted, peeled and thinly sliced

⅓ cup butter, softened

1 On each of 4 bread slices, sprinkle ¼ cup cheese. Top evenly with onion, bacon, tomato and avocado. Top with remaining cheese and bread slices. Spread 2 teaspoons butter over each top slice of bread.

2 Heat griddle or skillet over medium-high heat (375°F). Place sandwiches, buttered side down, on griddle. Spread remaining butter over top slices of bread. Cook 6 to 8 minutes, turning once, until bread is golden brown and cheese is melted.

1 Sandwich: Calories 660; Total Fat 48g (Saturated Fat 25g, Trans Fat 1g); Cholesterol 120mg; Sodium 1110mg; Total Carbohydrate 31g (Dietary Fiber 4g); Protein 26g **Exchanges:** 2 Starch, ½ Medium-Fat Meat, 2½ High-Fat Meat, 5 Fat **Carbohydrate Choices:** 2

IN A SNAP Sometimes it can be hard to find ripe avocados. If possible, purchase them a few days before you need them. Speed up the ripening by placing them in a paper bag with an apple.

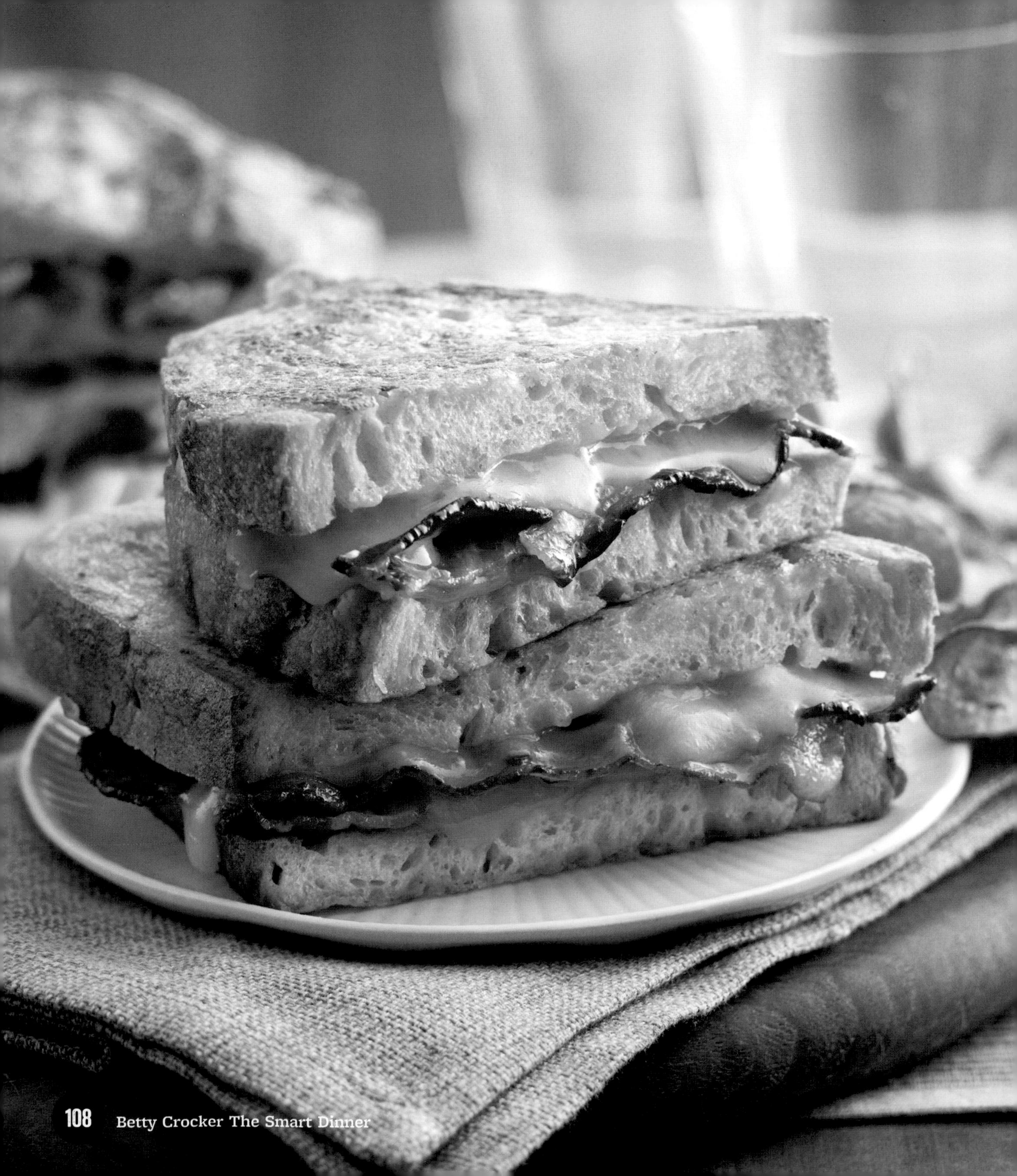

BEER-BATTERED GRILLED CHEESE SANDWICHES

2 sandwiches | Prep Time: 15 Minutes | Start to Finish: 15 Minutes

4   slices rustic white bread

2   slices (¾ oz each) provolone cheese

6   slices hickory-smoked bacon, crisply cooked

2   slices (¾ oz each) Cheddar cheese

1   egg

¾   cup pale ale beer

¼   cup all-purpose flour

¼   teaspoon chipotle chili pepper powder

1   tablespoon butter

1 On each of 2 bread slices, place 1 slice provolone cheese, 3 slices bacon and 1 slice Cheddar cheese. Top with remaining bread slices.

2 Heat griddle or skillet over medium-high heat (375°F). In shallow bowl, beat egg, beer, flour and chili powder with fork until smooth. Dip each sandwich into batter, giving it a few seconds on each side to absorb the batter; drain excess batter back into bowl.

3 Melt butter on griddle. Place sandwiches on griddle. Cook 6 to 8 minutes, turning once, until bread is golden brown and cheese is melted.

1 Sandwich: Calories 570; Total Fat 33g (Saturated Fat 16g, Trans Fat 1g); Cholesterol 170mg; Sodium 1220mg; Total Carbohydrate 40g (Dietary Fiber 2g); Protein 28g **Exchanges:** 2½ Starch, 3 High-Fat Meat, 1½ Fat **Carbohydrate Choices:** 2½

USE IT UP This recipe is very forgiving—use whatever kind of cheese, bacon, hearty bread and light-flavored beer you have. Any way you make it, it will be mouthwateringly delicious.

KANSAS CITY DOGS

8 sandwiches | Prep Time: 15 Minutes | Start to Finish: 15 Minutes

8   beef hot dogs

1   cup refrigerated original barbecue sauce with shredded pork (from 18-oz container)

8   hot dog buns, split

½   cup pickle slices

2   medium green onions, sliced (2 tablespoons)

    Mustard, if desired

1 Heat gas or charcoal grill. Place hot dogs on grill over medium heat. Cook uncovered 10 to 15 minutes, turning frequently, until hot.

2 Place sauce with pork in medium microwavable bowl; cover loosely. Microwave on high 45 to 60 seconds, stirring every 30 seconds, until hot.

3 Place hot dogs in buns. Spoon about 2 tablespoons sauce with pork onto each bun. Top with pickles, onions and mustard.

To Broil Hot Dogs: Set oven control to broil. Spray cookie sheet with cooking spray. Place hot dogs on cookie sheet. Broil with tops 4 to 6 inches from heat 4 to 5 minutes or until hot.

1 Sandwich: Calories 310; Total Fat 16g (Saturated Fat 6g, Trans Fat 1g); Cholesterol 30mg; Sodium 940mg; Total Carbohydrate 28g (Dietary Fiber 1g); Protein 12g **Exchanges:** 2 Starch, 1 Medium-Fat Meat, 2 Fat **Carbohydrate Choices:** 2

Chapter Three

FISH

AND

SHELLFISH

COD CAKES WITH RED PEPPER AIOLI

6 servings | Prep Time: 30 Minutes | Start to Finish: 30 Minutes

½ cup mayonnaise

½ cup roasted red peppers
   (from a jar)

2 cloves garlic, peeled

¾ lb cooked cod, walleye
   or tilapia

1 cup soft bread crumbs

½ cup sliced green onions
   (8 **medium**)

2 tablespoons chopped
   fresh parsley

2 cloves garlic,
   finely chopped

2 eggs, beaten

2 tablespoons olive oil

1 In blender or food processor, place mayonnaise, roasted peppers and 2 cloves garlic. Cover; process until smooth. Transfer aioli to small bowl. Cover; refrigerate until serving time.

2 In large bowl, stir together cod, bread crumbs, onions, parsley, chopped garlic and eggs, breaking up fish as necessary. Using about ½ cup mixture for each patty, shape into 6 (3-inch) patties (patties will be soft).

3 In 12-inch nonstick skillet, heat oil over medium heat. Cook patties in oil 6 to 8 minutes, turning once, until golden brown. Drain on paper towels. Serve cod cakes with aioli.

1 Serving: Calories 330; Total Fat 21g (Saturated Fat 3.5g, Trans Fat 0g); Cholesterol 100mg; Sodium 320mg; Total Carbohydrate 15g (Dietary Fiber 1g); Protein 18g **Exchanges:** 1 Starch, 2 Very Lean Meat, 4 Fat **Carbohydrate Choices:** 1

IN A SNAP
If you don't have leftover cooked fish, here's an easy way to cook it: Heat oven to 375°F. Place fish in a baking dish; drizzle with olive oil and sprinkle with salt and pepper. Bake uncovered 12 to 15 minutes or until fish flakes easily with fork. Cool to room temperature. Pat with paper towels to remove excess moisture and use as directed.

MAKE A MEAL
Serve cod cakes, topped with a spoonful of aioli, on burger buns (onion, plain or your favorite variety) lined with lettuce.

CRUNCHY PANKO FISH NUGGETS WITH LEMON-DILL SAUCE

4 servings | Prep Time: 15 Minutes | Start to Finish: 35 Minutes

LEMON-DILL SAUCE

- ¼ cup mayonnaise
- 2 tablespoons plain yogurt
- 1 teaspoon chopped fresh or ¼ teaspoon dried dill weed
- 1 teaspoon grated lemon peel
- 2 teaspoons fresh lemon juice

FISH NUGGETS

- 3 tablespoons all-purpose flour
- 1 teaspoon garlic salt
- 1 teaspoon paprika
- 1 egg
- 2 tablespoons water
- ½ teaspoon red pepper sauce
- 1¼ cups panko crispy bread crumbs
- 3 tablespoons butter, melted
- 1 lb cod fillets (½ inch thick), cut into about 1½-inch pieces

1 Heat oven to 425°F. Spray 15x10-inch pan with cooking spray.

2 In small bowl, stir together sauce ingredients. Cover; refrigerate until serving time.

3 In shallow dish, mix flour, garlic salt and paprika. In another shallow dish, beat egg, water and pepper sauce with whisk. In third shallow dish, mix bread crumbs and butter.

4 Coat fish with seasoned flour, dip into egg mixture, then coat with crumb mixture, pressing crumbs into fish if needed. Place in pan.

5 Bake 15 to 20 minutes or until fish flakes easily with fork. Serve with lemon-dill sauce.

1 Serving: Calories 430; Total Fat 23g (Saturated Fat 8g, Trans Fat 0g); Cholesterol 125mg; Sodium 570mg; Total Carbohydrate 31g (Dietary Fiber 0g); Protein 27g **Exchanges:** 2 Starch, 3 Very Lean Meat, 4 Fat **Carbohydrate Choices:** 2

IN A SNAP To make cleanup easier, line the cookie sheet with foil before baking. Use nonstick foil for the easiest removal.

BAKED LEMON-PEPPER FISH

4 servings | Prep Time: 10 Minutes | Start to Finish: 30 Minutes

⅔ cup Original Bisquick mix

1 teaspoon Italian seasoning

1 teaspoon lemon-pepper seasoning

1 egg

2 tablespoons water

1 lb cod, haddock or other medium-firm fish fillets (about ½ inch thick)

2 tablespoons butter, melted

Lemon wedges, if desired

1 Heat oven to 425°F. Spray 15x10-inch pan with cooking spray.

2 In shallow dish, stir together Bisquick mix, Italian seasoning and lemon-pepper seasoning. In another shallow dish, beat egg and water. Dip fish into egg mixture, then coat both sides with Bisquick mixture. Place in pan. Drizzle with melted butter.

3 Bake 10 minutes. Turn fillets; bake 5 to 10 minutes longer or until fish flakes easily with fork. Serve with lemon wedges.

1 Serving: Calories 200; Total Fat 9g (Saturated Fat 5g, Trans Fat 0g); Cholesterol 110mg; Sodium 310mg; Total Carbohydrate 6g (Dietary Fiber 0g); Protein 22g **Exchanges:** ½ Starch, 3 Very Lean Meat, 1½ Fat **Carbohydrate Choices:** ½

MAKE A MEAL

For an easy side, pair the fish with two-ingredient slaw: At the grocery store, just grab a bag of coleslaw mix and a jar of refrigerated coleslaw dressing.

CONDIMENTS

- **Magical Marinades** Use non-creamy salad dressings to marinate meat, poultry or mushrooms before cooking. Simply pour enough in a zip-top gallon-size bag to coat the food you are marinating. Close bag and shake. Marinate at least 30 minutes or up to 2 hours for mushrooms, or 24 hours for meat or poultry.

- **Quick Buffalo Sauce** Mix 2 parts sandwich spread with 1 part sriracha; add additional sriracha to taste. Brush the Buffalo sauce on chicken breasts while grilling, toss with chicken nuggets before baking or use as a sandwich spread. Or make a Buffalo pasta salad by tossing 8 ounces cooked small pasta (ziti, penne, shells) with ¼ cup of the Buffalo sauce and 2 to 3 tablespoons ranch dressing; add cut-up cooked chicken, bite-size pieces of raw veggies (such as bell pepper, broccoli or onion) and blue cheese crumbles.

- **Fruity BBQ Sauce** Mix 2 parts barbecue sauce and 1 part jelly or jam (raspberry, strawberry or apricot). Microwave about 30 seconds to partially melt jelly. During the last 10 to 15 minutes of cooking (to prevent burning), brush the fruity BBQ sauce on meat or poultry while grilling or baking.

- **Seasoned Sour Cream** Mix ½ cup sour cream, ¼ cup mayonnaise, 1 tablespoon chopped fresh parsley, 1 teaspoon seasoned salt and ⅛ teaspoon ground red pepper (cayenne). Serve with French fries or as a dip for veggies.

- **Tasty Tartar Sauce** Mix ½ cup mayonnaise or salad dressing with a tablespoon or two of finely chopped dill or sweet pickle. Add just enough pickle juice until desired consistency.

CAJUN CATFISH

8 servings | Prep Time: 40 Minutes | Start to Finish: 40 Minutes

2   cups vegetable oil

1   cup all-purpose flour

½   cup stone-ground cornmeal

2   tablespoons Cajun Creole seasoning

1   teaspoon onion powder

1   teaspoon garlic powder

½   teaspoon ground red pepper (cayenne)

1   egg

2   lb catfish nuggets, skin removed

Salt

¼   cup lemon juice

Tartar sauce, if desired

1 In heavy 3-quart saucepan, heat oil over medium-high heat to 375°F.

2 In shallow dish, stir together flour, cornmeal, Creole seasoning, onion powder, garlic powder and red pepper. In another shallow dish, beat egg with fork until foamy.

3 Sprinkle catfish nuggets with salt and lemon juice. Dip each nugget into beaten egg, then roll in flour mixture to coat. Drop 4 to 6 nuggets at a time into hot oil. Cook 2 minutes; turn and cook 1 minute longer or until deep golden brown. Remove from oil; drain on paper towels. Serve with tartar sauce.

1 Serving: Calories 360; Total Fat 22g (Saturated Fat 4g, Trans Fat 0g); Cholesterol 105mg; Sodium 450mg; Total Carbohydrate 15g (Dietary Fiber 1g); Protein 26g **Exchanges:** 1 Starch, 3 Lean Meat, 2½ Fat **Carbohydrate Choices:** 1

IN A SNAP If you can't find catfish nuggets at your supermarket, purchase 2 pounds of catfish fillets and cut them into about 2-inch pieces.

MAKE A MEAL A staple in Georgia and Mississippi, fried catfish morsels are dynamite dunked in tangy tartar sauce and served with coleslaw and baked beans.

ALMOND-CRUSTED COD WITH VEGGIES

4 servings | Prep Time: 45 Minutes | Start to Finish: 45 Minutes

¼ cup all-purpose flour

1 egg

½ cup sliced or slivered almonds, toasted*, finely ground

½ cup panko crispy bread crumbs

¼ cup shredded Parmesan cheese (1 oz)

1 teaspoon dried oregano leaves

¾ teaspoon coarse (kosher or sea) salt

¼ teaspoon pepper

6 tablespoons butter

1 large zucchini, sliced, quartered (about 2 cups)

1 large red bell pepper, cut into ¼-inch strips

4 cod fillets (4 oz each)

3 cups fresh baby spinach leaves

1 lemon, sliced

1 Place flour in shallow dish. In another shallow dish, beat egg. In third shallow dish, mix almonds, bread crumbs, cheese, oregano, ½ teaspoon of the salt and the pepper. Set aside.

2 In 12-inch nonstick skillet, melt 2 tablespoons of the butter over medium-high heat. Add zucchini, bell pepper and remaining ¼ teaspoon salt; cook 6 to 8 minutes, stirring occasionally, until vegetables are crisp-tender. Remove to bowl; cover to keep warm.

3 Dip fish fillets in flour, then in egg; coat both sides with bread crumb mixture.

4 In same skillet, melt remaining 4 tablespoons butter over medium heat. Cook fish in butter 6 to 12 minutes, turning once, until golden brown and fish flakes easily with fork.

5 To serve, place spinach on serving platter or individual plates. Top with fish and vegetables. Serve with lemon.

*To toast almonds, sprinkle in ungreased skillet. Cook over medium heat 5 to 7 minutes, stirring frequently until almonds begin to brown, then stirring constantly until nuts are light brown.

1 Serving: Calories 410; Total Fat 26g (Saturated Fat 12g, Trans Fat 0.5g); Cholesterol 140mg; Sodium 690mg; Total Carbohydrate 17g (Dietary Fiber 4g); Protein 27g **Exchanges:** ½ Starch, 1½ Vegetable, 3 Very Lean Meat, 5 Fat **Carbohydrate Choices:** 1

IN A SNAP
When you fry fish in a skillet, be sure the butter is hot enough, otherwise the fish will steam instead of fry. If possible, choose thin fillets so they will cook faster.

USE IT UP
Had a great catch? Walleye fillets can be substituted for the cod in this recipe.

SOFT AND CRUNCHY FISH TACOS

4 servings | Prep Time: 20 Minutes | Start to Finish: 20 Minutes

8   flour tortillas (6 inch)

8   taco shells

1   bag (12 oz) broccoli slaw mix (about 4 cups)

⅓   cup reduced-fat lime vinaigrette dressing or other vinaigrette dressing

¼   cup chopped fresh cilantro

1   package (1 oz) taco seasoning mix

4   tilapia or other mild-flavored, medium-firm fish fillets (about 1 lb)

1   tablespoon vegetable oil

1   cup guacamole

1   cup crumbled Cotija or feta cheese (4 oz), if desired

1 Heat tortillas and taco shells as directed on package. In medium bowl, toss broccoli slaw mix, dressing and cilantro; set aside.

2 In shallow dish, place taco seasoning mix. Coat both sides of fish with taco seasoning. In 12-inch nonstick skillet, heat oil over medium-high heat. Cook fish in oil 6 minutes, turning once, until fish flakes easily with fork. Divide fish into 8 pieces.

3 Spread 2 tablespoons guacamole over each flour tortilla. Place taco shell on center of tortilla. Using slotted spoon, spoon about ¼ cup slaw into each taco shell; top with 1 fish piece. Gently fold tortilla sides up to match taco shell sides. Top with 1 tablespoon cheese.

1 Serving (**2 Tacos**): Calories 680; Total Fat 30g (Saturated Fat 11g, Trans Fat 1g); Cholesterol 85mg; Sodium 2030mg; Total Carbohydrate 61g (Dietary Fiber 8g); Protein 40g **Exchanges:** 3½ Starch, 1 Vegetable, 3 Very Lean Meat, 1 Medium-Fat Meat, 4½ Fat **Carbohydrate Choices:** 4

USE IT UP
This is a great dish for chopping and using up cilantro stems with the leaves, if you like.

TILAPIA GYROS

4 servings | Prep Time: 25 Minutes | Start to Finish: 50 Minutes

TZATZIKI SAUCE

- ¼ cup fat-free Greek plain yogurt
- 2 tablespoons finely chopped cucumber
- 1 tablespoon finely chopped red onion
- 1 teaspoon chopped fresh dill weed or mint leaves

BAKED GREEK TILAPIA

- ⅔ cup panko crispy bread crumbs
- 1 teaspoon grated lemon peel
- ½ teaspoon dried oregano leaves
- ½ teaspoon salt
- ¼ teaspoon pepper
- 1 egg
- 4 tilapia or other mild-flavored, medium-firm fish fillets (about 1 lb)
- Cooking spray

PITA BREAD AND FILLING

- 4 whole wheat pita breads (6 inch)
- 4 leaves leaf lettuce, torn
- ½ cup thinly sliced cucumber
- 2 medium plum (Roma) tomatoes, seeded, coarsely chopped

1 Heat oven to 425°F. Spray cookie sheet with cooking spray. In small bowl, mix tzatziki sauce ingredients. Cover; refrigerate until serving time.

2 In small shallow dish, mix bread crumbs, lemon peel, oregano, salt and pepper. In another shallow dish, beat egg with fork. Dip 1 fish fillet into egg; shake off excess. Coat both sides with bread crumb mixture; shake off excess crumbs. Place on cookie sheet. Repeat with remaining fillets. Spray tops of breaded fish with cooking spray.

3 Bake 20 to 25 minutes or until fish flakes easily with fork. Wrap pita breads in foil; add to oven for last 10 minutes of bake time.

4 To serve, place lettuce on one side of each pita bread. Top with fish, sliced cucumber and tomato. Drizzle with tzatziki sauce; fold other half of pita bread over filling.

1 Serving: Calories 350; Total Fat 6g (Saturated Fat 1.5g, Trans Fat 0g); Cholesterol 85mg; Sodium 680mg; Total Carbohydrate 46g (Dietary Fiber 5g); Protein 27g **Exchanges:** 1½ Starch, 1½ Other Carbohydrate, ½ Vegetable, 3 Very Lean Meat, ½ Fat **Carbohydrate Choices:** 3

IN A SNAP Tzatziki sauce is a traditional Greek yogurt-based sauce with cucumber and mint. If you don't want to make it, look for it in the refrigerated section of the deli area at large supermarkets. Use leftovers as a salad dressing, dip for veggies or sandwich spread.

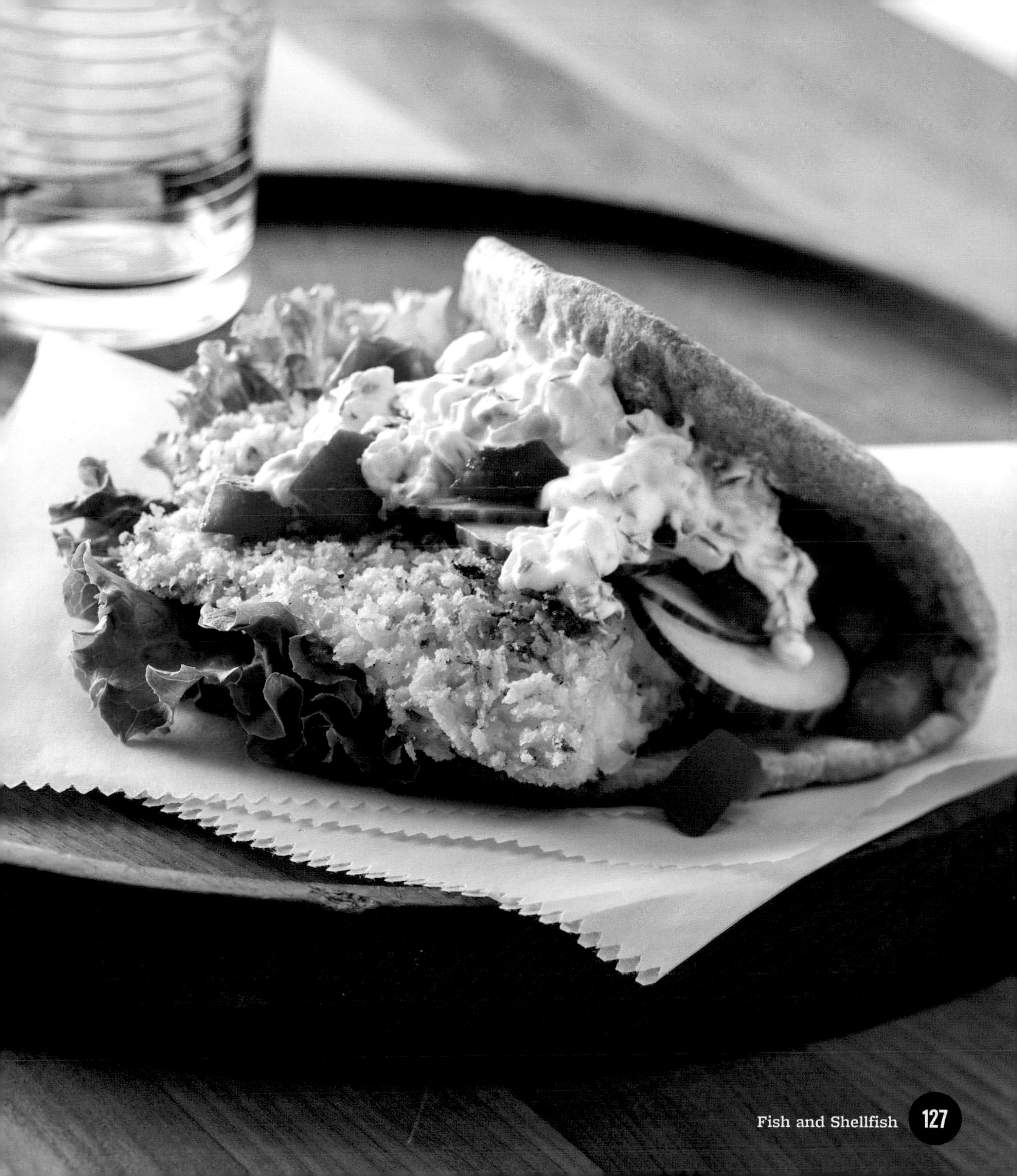

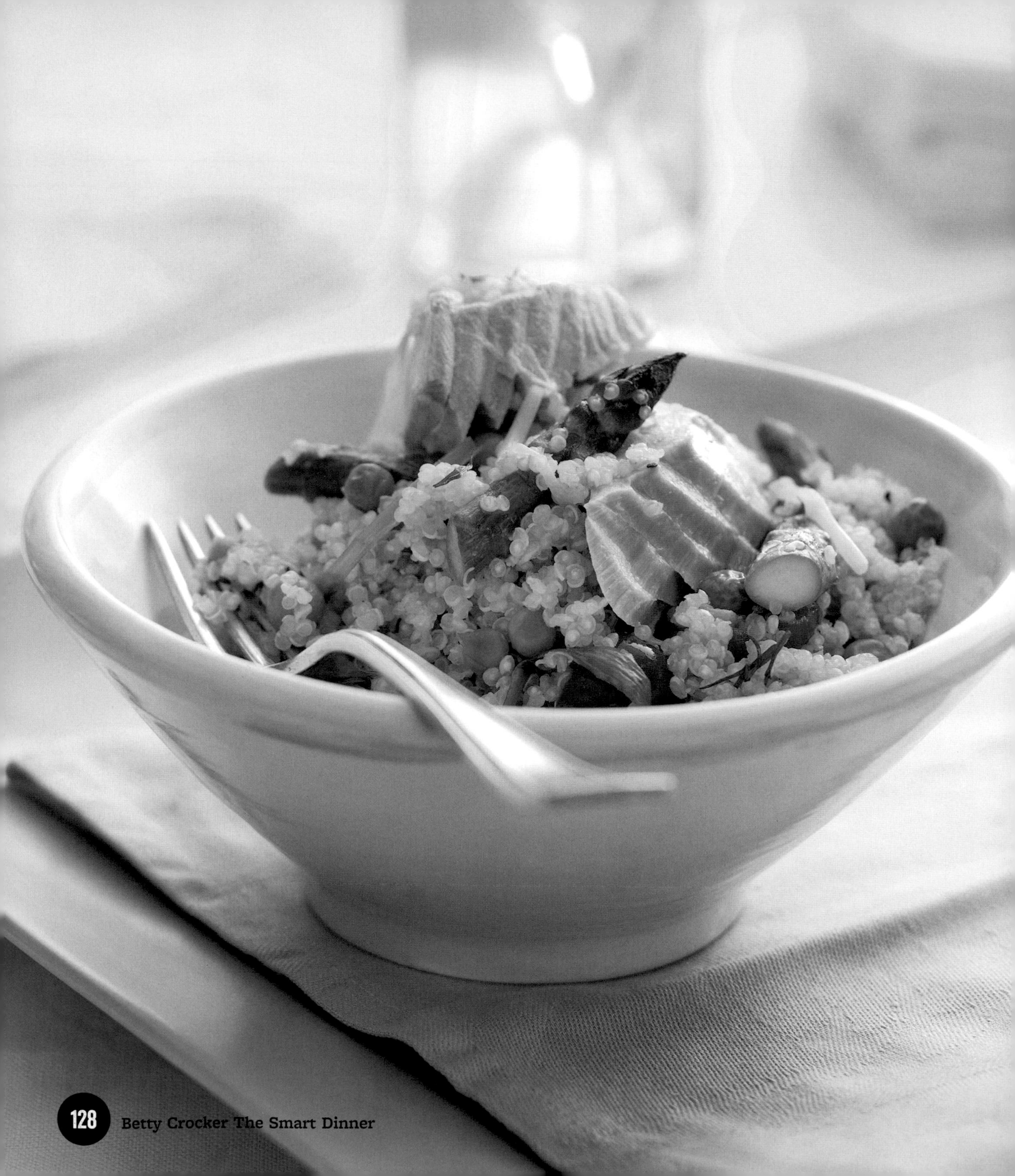

QUINOA PILAF WITH SALMON AND ASPARAGUS

4 servings | Prep Time: 35 Minutes | Start to Finish: 35 Minutes

6   cups water

1   cup uncooked quinoa, rinsed, well drained

1   vegetable bouillon cube

1   lb salmon fillets

2   teaspoons butter

20   medium stalks fresh asparagus, cut diagonally into 2-inch pieces (2 cups)

4   medium green onions, sliced (¼ cup)

1   cup frozen sweet peas, thawed

½   cup halved grape tomatoes

½   cup vegetable or chicken broth

1   teaspoon lemon-pepper seasoning

2   teaspoons chopped fresh or ½ teaspoon dried dill weed

1 In 2-quart saucepan, heat 2 cups of the water to boiling over high heat. Add quinoa; reduce heat to low. Cover; simmer 10 to 12 minutes or until water is absorbed.

2 Meanwhile, in 12-inch skillet, heat remaining 4 cups water and the bouillon cube to boiling over high heat. Add salmon, skin side up; reduce heat to low. Cover; simmer 10 to 12 minutes or until fish flakes easily with fork. Transfer with slotted spoon to plate; let cool. Discard water. Remove skin from salmon; break into large pieces.

3 Rinse and dry skillet. Melt butter in skillet over medium heat. Add asparagus; cook 5 minutes, stirring frequently. Add onions; cook 1 minute, stirring frequently. Stir in peas, tomatoes and broth; cook 1 minute.

4 Gently stir quinoa, salmon, lemon-pepper seasoning and dill into asparagus mixture. Cover; cook about 2 minutes or until hot.

1 Serving (1¾ Cups): Calories 380; Total Fat 12g (Saturated Fat 2.5g, Trans Fat 0g); Cholesterol 70mg; Sodium 600mg; Total Carbohydrate 37g (Dietary Fiber 6g); Protein 32g **Exchanges:** 2 Starch, 1½ Vegetable, 3½ Lean Meat **Carbohydrate Choices:** 2½

MAKE A MEAL
All this all-in-one meal needs is some fresh fruit on the side . . . and maybe a crusty roll, if you're ravenous.

SALMON TACOS WITH CHUNKY GUACAMOLE

10 servings | Prep Time: 30 Minutes | Start to Finish: 45 Minutes

GUACAMOLE

- 2 medium plum (Roma) tomatoes, chopped
- 2 medium avocados, peeled, chopped
- ¼ cup finely chopped onion
- 1 serrano chile, seeded, finely chopped
- ¼ cup chopped fresh cilantro
- 1 tablespoon lime juice
- ½ teaspoon salt

TACOS

- 3 tablespoons lime juice
- ½ teaspoon salt
- ½ teaspoon freshly ground pepper
- 1½ lb salmon fillets
- 2 tablespoons vegetable oil
- 10 soft corn or flour tortillas (6 inch), heated as directed on package if desired
- 2 cups finely shredded red cabbage

  Lime wedges

1 In medium bowl, mix guacamole ingredients. Cover; refrigerate until serving time.

2 In small bowl, mix lime juice, salt and pepper. Rub salmon fillets with lime juice mixture; let stand 15 minutes.

3 In 12-inch skillet, heat oil over medium heat. Cook salmon in oil 15 to 20 minutes, turning once, until fish flakes easily with fork. Remove and discard skin; cut salmon into serving-size pieces.

4 Fill tortillas with salmon and cabbage. Serve with guacamole and lime wedges.

To Grill Salmon: Heat gas or charcoal grill. Place salmon, skin side down, on grill over medium heat. Cover grill; cook 15 to 18 minutes or until fish flakes easily with fork (do not turn).

1 Serving (1 Taco and ¼ cup Guacamole): Calories 260; Total Fat 13g (Saturated Fat 2.5g, Trans Fat 0g); Cholesterol 45mg; Sodium 450mg; Total Carbohydrate 18g (Dietary Fiber 3g); Protein 17g **Exchanges:** 1 Starch, 2 Lean Meat, 1½ Fat **Carbohydrate Choices:** 1

IN A SNAP Use the grilling directions to skip dirtying a pan and you might just have the kitchen clean before sitting down to dinner!

HONEY-MUSTARD GLAZED SALMON

4 servings | Prep Time: 20 Minutes | Start to Finish: 35 Minutes

1 salmon fillet (1 lb)

1 tablespoon packed brown sugar

1 tablespoon butter, melted

1 tablespoon olive or vegetable oil

1 tablespoon honey

1 tablespoon soy sauce

1 tablespoon Dijon mustard

1 clove garlic, finely chopped

1 In shallow glass or plastic dish, place salmon, skin side down. In small bowl, mix remaining ingredients; pour over salmon. Cover; refrigerate at least 15 minutes but no longer than 1 hour.

2 Set oven control to broil. Remove salmon from marinade; reserve marinade. Place salmon, skin side down, on rack in broiler pan.

3 Broil with top 4 to 6 inches from heat 10 to 15 minutes, brushing 2 to 3 times with marinade, until fish flakes easily with fork. Discard any remaining marinade. Cut salmon into 4 serving pieces.

1 Serving: Calories 230; Total Fat 11g (Saturated Fat 3g, Trans Fat 0g); Cholesterol 0mg; Sodium 450mg; Total Carbohydrate 8g (Dietary Fiber 0g); Protein 24g **Exchanges:** ½ Other Carbohydrate, 3 Very Lean Meat, 1 Fat **Carbohydrate Choices:** ½

USE IT UP If you have a leftover soy sauce packet from takeout, you can use it here. One packet is about 1 tablespoon.

MAKE A MEAL Serve up some steamed fresh broccoli and your favorite rice dish for a simple supper that is restaurant-worthy.

ASIAN SALMON SHEET PAN DINNER

4 servings | Prep Time: 20 Minutes | Start to Finish: 55 Minutes

POTATOES

- 2 tablespoons toasted sesame oil
- 1 teaspoon chili garlic sauce
- 1 teaspoon soy sauce
- ¼ teaspoon salt
- 1 lb small red or white potatoes, cut into quarters

BROCCOLI AND SALMON

- 2 tablespoons packed brown sugar
- 2 tablespoons soy sauce
- 2 tablespoons butter, melted
- 1 tablespoon rice vinegar
- ¼ teaspoon salt
- 4 salmon fillets (4 oz each)
- 8 oz fresh broccoli florets (about 4 cups)
- 2 medium green onions, sliced diagonally

1 Heat oven to 425°F. Spray large rimmed sheet pan with cooking spray.

2 In large bowl, mix oil, chili garlic sauce, 1 teaspoon soy sauce and ¼ teaspoon salt. Add potatoes; toss to coat. Place potatoes in single layer in pan. Roast 20 minutes. Remove from oven. Stir potatoes; move to one side of pan.

3 In same large bowl, mix brown sugar, 2 tablespoons soy sauce, the butter, vinegar and ¼ teaspoon salt. Transfer 2 tablespoons of the mixture to medium bowl and add salmon; turn to coat. Add broccoli to large bowl; toss to coat. Place salmon, skin side down, in pan. Add broccoli to pan. Pour any remaining mixture from both bowls over salmon and broccoli.

4 Roast 12 to 15 minutes or until salmon flakes easily with fork and potatoes are tender. Top with onions.

1 Serving: Calories 410; Total Fat 22g (Saturated Fat 7g, Trans Fat 0g); Cholesterol 65mg; Sodium 950mg; Total Carbohydrate 31g (Dietary Fiber 4g); Protein 21g **Exchanges:** 1½ Starch, 1½ Vegetable, 2 Lean Meat, 3 Fat **Carbohydrate Choices:** 2

IN A SNAP
If some of your potatoes are larger, cut them into 6 or 8 pieces. Just make sure all of the pieces are about the same size so they'll cook evenly.

USE IT UP
If you find yourself left with a bunch of broccoli stalks when cutting the florets, place them all in a resealable freezer plastic bag. Add to it each time you have stalks, and when you have enough, use them to make broccoli soup.

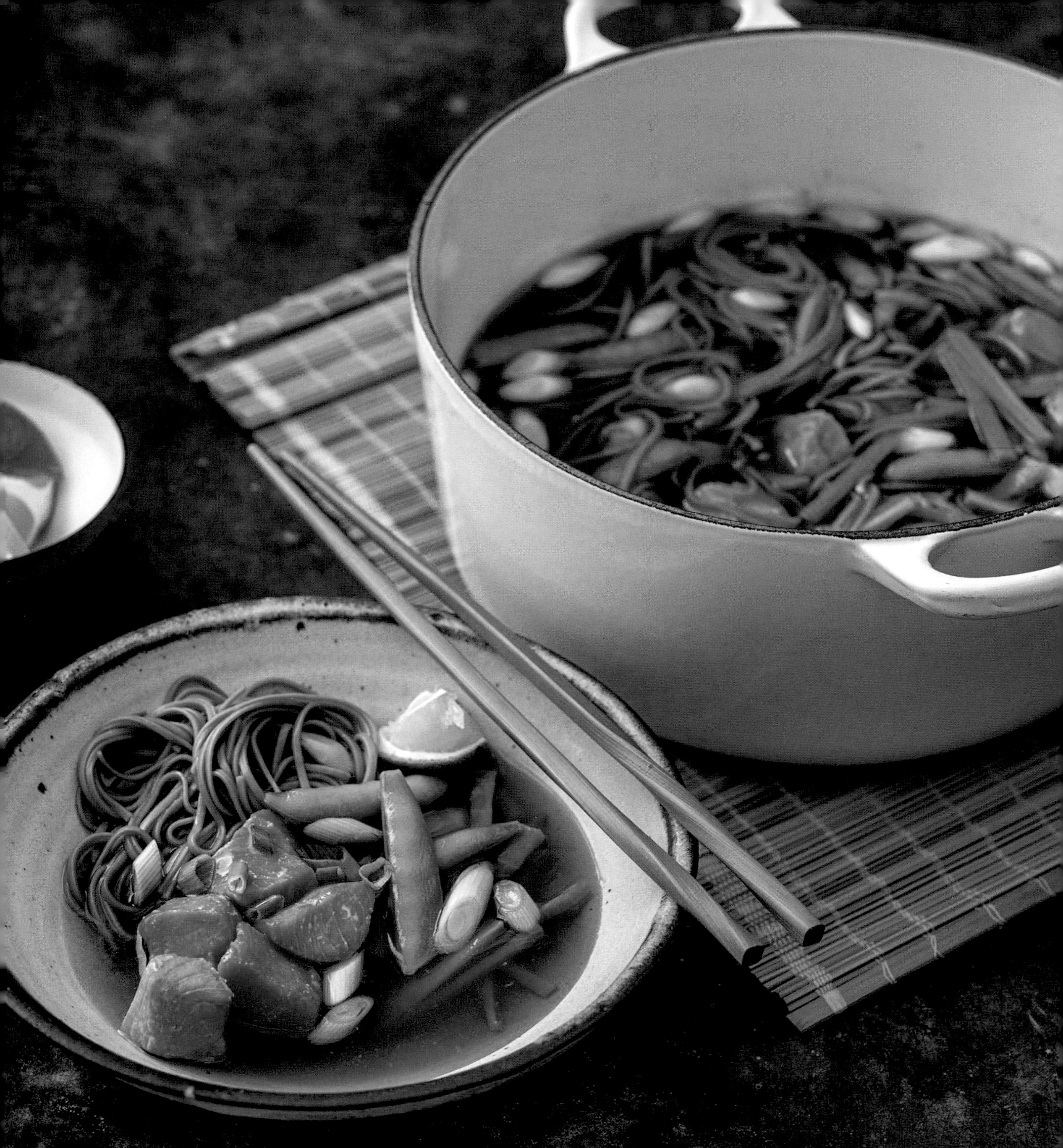

SOBA WITH SALMON

4 servings | Prep Time: 35 Minutes | Start to Finish: 35 Minutes

1 tablespoon sesame oil

1 tablespoon fincly chopped gingerroot

2 cloves garlic, finely chopped

¼ cup honey

4 cups water

½ cup reduced-sodium soy sauce

6 medium green onions, sliced diagonally, white and green parts separated

2 medium carrots, cut into matchstick pieces (about 1 cup)

1 lb salmon fillets, skin removed, cut into 1-inch cubes

6 oz uncooked soba (buckwheat) noodles

1 box (9 oz) frozen sugar snap peas

1 tablespoon lime juice

1 In 5-quart Dutch oven or stockpot, beat oil, gingerroot, garlic and honey with whisk. Beat in water and soy sauce. Heat to boiling over high heat.

2 Add white parts of onions, the carrots and salmon; return to boiling. Reduce heat to simmering; cook 2 minutes. Increase heat to high. Add noodles. Reduce heat to medium; cook 6 minutes longer.

3 Meanwhile, microwave frozen peas as directed on box; let stand 1 minute. Stir peas into noodle mixture. Cover; remove from heat. Let stand 1 minute. Stir in lime juice; top with green parts of onions.

1 **Serving** (2 Cups): Calories 510; Total Fat 16g (Saturated Fat 3g, Trans Fat 0g); Cholesterol 65mg; Sodium 1230mg; Total Carbohydrate 58g (Dietary Fiber 7g); Protein 33g **Exchanges:** 3 Starch, ½ Other Carbohydrate, 1 Vegetable, 3 Lean Meat, 1 Fat **Carbohydrate Choices:** 4

IN A SNAP
Peel and cut off about a 1-inch section of fresh gingerroot to chop for this recipe. Wrap remaining gingerroot in plastic wrap and store in a small resealable freezer plastic bag in the freezer for up to 2 months. Peel and chop a section each time you need fresh gingerroot.

USE IT UP
If you have angel hair pasta in your pantry, you can trade it for the soba noodles in a pinch.

This dish would be great with boneless skinless chicken thighs instead of salmon, if that's what is in your fridge.

TUNA MELTS

4 sandwiches | Prep Time: 15 Minutes | Start to Finish: 15 Minutes

4 slices whole-grain bread

2 cans (5 oz each) chunk albacore tuna in water, drained, flaked

1 can (8 oz) crushed pineapple in juice, well drained (½ cup)

¼ cup light or regular mayonnaise

2 tablespoons finely chopped red onion

1 tablespoon chopped fresh or ½ teaspoon dried tarragon leaves

8 thin slices plum (Roma) tomatoes (1 large or 2 small)

4 slices (¾ oz each) Swiss cheese

1 Set oven control to broil. Place bread slices on ungreased cookie sheet. Broil with tops about 5 inches from heat 2 to 4 minutes, turning once, until lightly toasted; set aside.

2 In medium bowl, stir together tuna, pineapple, mayonnaise, onion and tarragon until well blended. Spread evenly on toasted bread slices; top each with 2 tomato slices and 1 cheese slice.

3 Broil 3 to 5 minutes or until cheese is melted and sandwiches are hot.

1 Sandwich: Calories 300; Total Fat 13g (Saturated Fat 5g, Trans Fat 0g); Cholesterol 40mg; Sodium 460mg; Total Carbohydrate 23g (Dietary Fiber 3g); Protein 24g **Exchanges:** ½ Starch, 1 Other Carbohydrate, ½ Vegetable, 2½ Very Lean Meat, ½ High-Fat Meat, 1½ Fat **Carbohydrate Choices:** 1½

MAKE A MEAL Add some crunchy veggies, like pea pods or carrot sticks, and fresh fruit, and you've got a meal that is homemade and satisfying.

TUNA-NOODLE SKILLET SUPPER

6 servings | Prep Time: 10 Minutes | Start to Finish: 25 Minutes

1 tablespoon vegetable oil

1 large onion, coarsely chopped (1 cup)

4 cups water

4 cups uncooked medium egg noodles (8 oz)

1 package (8 oz) sliced fresh mushrooms (about 3 cups)

2 cans (5 oz each) solid white tuna in water, drained

1 jar (16 oz) Alfredo pasta sauce

1 cup seasoned croutons, coarsely crushed

1 In 12-inch nonstick skillet, heat oil over medium-high heat. Add onion; cook 2 to 3 minutes, stirring frequently, until softened.

2 Stir in water and noodles. Cover; heat to boiling. Boil 4 minutes.

3 Stir in mushrooms, tuna and pasta sauce (sauce will be thin). Reduce heat to medium; simmer uncovered 4 to 6 minutes, stirring occasionally, or until mushrooms are tender, sauce has thickened slightly and noodles are tender.

4 Remove from heat; let stand uncovered 5 minutes. Just before serving, top with croutons.

1 Serving: Calories 520; Total Fat 30g (Saturated Fat 16g, Trans Fat 1g); Cholesterol 120mg; Sodium 540mg; Total Carbohydrate 38g (Dietary Fiber 2g); Protein 24g **Exchanges:** 1½ Starch, 1 Fruit, 3 Lean Meat, 4 Fat **Carbohydrate Choices:** 2½

IN A SNAP
To save time, use frozen chopped onions. Look for them near the frozen breaded onion rings in the store.

USE IT UP
No croutons in your cupboard? Use whatever crunchy items you have on hand instead. Tasty ideas include coarsely crushed potato chips, crackers or corn chips. Pumpkin seeds or nuts such as slivered almonds would also be great.

CRACKERS AND CROUTONS

- **Top Casseroles and Crisps** Lightly break crackers up into bowls of steaming hot chili. Or give crackers or croutons a whirl in the food processor or crush them with a rolling pin in a resealable food-storage plastic bag, then use to top casseroles or fruit crisps.

- **Mix Them In** Add cracker crumbs to meat loaf, meatballs, crab cakes or other recipes calling for bread crumbs. Freeze the crumbs in a resealable freezer plastic bag up to 2 months.

- **Coat Nuggets** Use fine- or coarse-crushed crackers as a coating for chicken nuggets or whole breasts, pork chops or fish: Dip meat or fish in beaten egg, then roll in crushed crackers and bake. Use seasoned crackers for extra flavor, or toss crushed plain crackers with a sprinkling of dried herbs and pepper.

- **Create a Crust** Use crushed graham crackers or cinnamon grahams to make a pie crust: Mix 1½ cups crumbs with ⅓ cup melted butter and 3 tablespoons sugar; press into pan. Bake at 350°F for about 10 minutes or until light brown; cool before using. Experiment with other crackers for a sweet-salty ice cream pie crust. Buttery crackers, pretzel crackers or garlic-and-herb crackers could all work well with ice cream.

SPICY CHILI-GARLIC SHRIMP PASTA

3 servings | Prep Time: 25 Minutes | Start to Finish: 25 Minutes

1 tablespoon olive oil

¼ lb uncooked medium shrimp, peeled (tail shells removed), deveined and cut in half lengthwise

3 medium green onions, sliced diagonally, white and green parts separated

2 teaspoons chili garlic sauce

1 can (28 oz) fire roasted diced tomatoes, undrained

¾ cup water

4 oz uncooked spaghetti, broken in half

2 cups lightly packed fresh baby greens (such as spinach, kale or chard)

2 teaspoons lemon juice

1 In 12-inch nonstick skillet, heat oil over medium heat. Cook shrimp in oil 2 to 3 minutes, stirring frequently, until pink. Remove shrimp to small bowl; cover to keep warm.

2 Add white parts of onions and chili garlic sauce to skillet; cook 30 seconds. Add tomatoes and water; heat to boiling. Add spaghetti; return to boiling, stirring constantly to prevent noodles from sticking together.

3 Reduce heat to low. Cook 13 to 15 minutes, stirring frequently, until noodles are tender. Stir in shrimp and baby greens; cook about 30 seconds or until shrimp is hot and greens are slightly wilted.

4 Remove from heat; stir in lemon juice. Top with green parts of onions.

1 **Serving** (1⅓ **Cups**): Calories 320; Total Fat 6g (Saturated Fat 1g, Trans Fat 0g); Cholesterol 60mg; Sodium 730mg; Total Carbohydrate 50g (Dietary Fiber 5g); Protein 15g **Exchanges:** 2 Starch, 1 Other Carbohydrate, 1 Vegetable, 1 Very Lean Meat, 1 Fat **Carbohydrate Choices: 3**

IN A SNAP Cutting shrimp in half lengthwise may seem odd, but it reduces the cook time and also stretches the amount of shrimp to make each serving look a bit more robust.

GLUTEN-FREE CHILI-LIME SHRIMP BURRITO BOWLS

4 servings | Prep Time: 35 Minutes | Start to Finish: 35 Minutes

SHRIMP

- ¾ lb uncooked deveined, peeled small shrimp
- 1 tablespoon lime juice
- 1 tablespoon chili powder
- 1 teaspoon vegetable oil

VEGETABLES

- 1 teaspoon vegetable oil
- 1 large red bell pepper, cut into thin bite-size strips
- 1 large onion, coarsely chopped
- ⅛ teaspoon salt
- ⅛ teaspoon pepper

RICE AND BEANS

- 1 bag (10 oz) frozen brown rice
- 1 can (15 oz) black beans, drained, rinsed
- ¼ cup chopped fresh cilantro
- 1 tablespoon lime juice
- ¼ teaspoon salt

TOPPINGS

- ½ avocado, chopped
- ½ cup chopped tomato
- 4 tablespoons gluten-free sour cream
- Lime wedges, if desired

1 In medium bowl, mix shrimp, 1 tablespoon lime juice and the chili powder; set aside.

2 In 10-inch skillet, heat 1 teaspoon oil over medium-high heat. Add bell pepper and onion; sprinkle with ⅛ teaspoon salt and ⅛ teaspoon pepper. Cook 3 to 5 minutes, stirring frequently, until crisp-tender and beginning to brown. Remove from skillet to bowl; cover to keep warm.

3 Heat rice as directed on package. In medium microwavable bowl, microwave beans uncovered on High 1 to 2 minutes or until hot, stirring halfway through.

4 Meanwhile, return skillet to heat. Add shrimp mixture and 1 teaspoon oil. Cook 4 to 5 minutes, stirring occasionally, until shrimp turn pink and liquid is evaporated. Remove from heat; cover to keep warm.

5 Add rice, cilantro, 1 tablespoon lime juice and ¼ teaspoon salt to beans in bowl; mix well. Divide rice mixture, vegetables and shrimp evenly among 4 serving bowls. Top with avocado, tomato and sour cream; serve with lime wedges.

1 Serving: Calories 390; Total Fat 10g (Saturated Fat 2.5g, Trans Fat 0g); Cholesterol 135mg; Sodium 870mg; Total Carbohydrate 52g (Dietary Fiber 13g); Protein 25g **Exchanges:** ½ Starch, 2½ Other Carbohydrate, 1 Vegetable, 3 Very Lean Meat, 1½ Fat **Carbohydrate Choices:** 3½

COOKING GLUTEN FREE? Always read labels to make sure each recipe ingredient is gluten free. Products and ingredient sources can change.

CRISPY COCONUT SHRIMP

4 servings | Prep Time: 30 Minutes | Start to Finish: 30 Minutes

DIPPING SAUCE

- ⅓ cup orange marmalade
- ⅓ cup apricot preserves
- ¼ teaspoon crushed red pepper flakes
- 1 tablespoon water
- ½ teaspoon soy sauce

SHRIMP

- 2 eggs
- 1 cup Original Bisquick mix
- 1 cup shredded coconut
- ¼ teaspoon ground ginger
- ¼ teaspoon salt
- 1½ cups coconut oil
- 1 lb uncooked medium or large shrimp, peeled (with tail shells left on), deveined

1 In small microwavable bowl, mix dipping sauce ingredients. Microwave uncovered on High 30 to 50 seconds. Stir until blended; set aside.

2 In small bowl, beat eggs with whisk or fork. In medium bowl, stir together Bisquick mix, coconut, ginger and salt.

3 In 12-inch nonstick skillet, heat oil over medium heat. Dip each shrimp in eggs, then in Bisquick mixture. Dip shrimp again in eggs and Bisquick mixture. Cook shrimp in batches in hot oil 3 to 4 minutes, turning once, until coating is crisp and golden brown and shrimp are pink. Drain on paper towels.

4 Serve shrimp hot with dipping sauce.

1 Serving: Calories 770; Total Fat 44g (Saturated Fat 35g, Trans Fat 0g); Cholesterol 250mg; Sodium 750mg; Total Carbohydrate 66g (Dietary Fiber 1g); Protein 26g **Exchanges:** 1½ Starch, 3 Other Carbohydrate, 3 Very Lean Meat, 8½ Fat **Carbohydrate Choices:** 4½

IN A SNAP If you're in a hurry, skip the dipping sauce and serve the shrimp with purchased sweet-and-sour sauce, available in the Asian foods section of most grocery stores.

MAKE A MEAL These coconut shrimp pair beautifully with brown rice and a tropical fruit salad.

SPICY SHRIMP SHEET PAN DINNER

4 servings | Prep Time: 20 Minutes | Start to Finish: 20 Minutes

¼ cup olive oil

2 tablespoons chili garlic sauce

1 tablespoon honey

½ teaspoon salt

1 lb uncooked large shrimp, peeled (tail shells removed), deveined

2 cups halved cherry tomatoes

1 can (15 to 19 oz) chick peas or garbanzo beans, drained, rinsed

4 cups fresh baby spinach leaves

½ cup crumbled feta cheese (2 oz)

1 Set oven control to broil. Spray large rimmed sheet pan with cooking spray.

2 In large bowl, mix oil, chili garlic sauce, honey and salt. Add shrimp, tomatoes and chick peas; gently toss to coat. Spread in even layer in pan.

3 Broil with top 4 inches from heat 5 minutes; stir. Broil 2 to 3 minutes longer or until shrimp are pink.

4 Divide spinach among 4 plates. Top with shrimp mixture. Sprinkle with cheese.

1 Serving: Calories 420; Total Fat 20g (Saturated Fat 4.5g, Trans Fat 0g); Cholesterol 170mg; Sodium 800mg; Total Carbohydrate 30g (Dietary Fiber 7g); Protein 30g **Exchanges:** 1½ Starch, 2 Vegetable, 3 Very Lean Meat, 3½ Fat **Carbohydrate Choices:** 2

USE IT UP
Here's a great place to experiment with other cheeses in your fridge. Try chèvre (goat) cheese, Parmesan or fresh mozzarella instead of the feta.

The liquid in the can of chick peas is known as aquafaba and has been found to be a great egg replacer in baked goods. Rather than throw it out, try it in baked goods and whipped egg dishes like meringues.

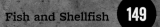

EASY SHRIMP PAELLA

6 servings | Prep Time: 30 Minutes | Start to Finish: 30 Minutes

2   tablespoons olive oil

1   lb uncooked large shrimp, peeled (with tail shells left on), deveined

½   lb smoked chorizo sausage, sliced

1   medium red bell pepper, chopped (1 cup)

1   medium green bell pepper, chopped (1 cup)

1   medium yellow bell pepper, chopped (1 cup)

2   cloves garlic, finely chopped

2   cups cooked long-grain white rice

1   cup frozen baby sweet peas

1   cup water

1   teaspoon salt

½   teaspoon ground turmeric

¼   teaspoon pepper

½   cup pimiento-stuffed manzanilla olives

1 In 12-inch nonstick skillet, heat 1 tablespoon of the oil over medium-high heat. Cook shrimp and sausage in oil 3 to 5 minutes, stirring frequently, until shrimp are pink and sausage is browned. Remove to plate; cover to keep warm.

2 In same skillet, heat remaining 1 tablespoon oil over medium-high heat. Cook bell peppers and garlic in oil 2 to 3 minutes, stirring occasionally, until crisp-tender. Stir in rice, peas, water, salt, turmeric and pepper; cook 2 to 4 minutes, stirring occasionally, until water is absorbed.

3 Add sausage, shrimp and olives. Cook 1 to 2 minutes, stirring constantly, just until hot.

1 Serving: Calories 390; Total Fat 21g (Saturated Fat 6g, Trans Fat 0g); Cholesterol 140mg; Sodium 1130mg; Total Carbohydrate 23g (Dietary Fiber 2g); Protein 25g **Exchanges:** 1 Starch, ½ Other Carbohydrate, ½ Vegetable, 3 Very Lean Meat, 4 Fat **Carbohydrate Choices:** 1½

USE IT UP You can use any type of pitted olives you have on hand . . . and just one or two colors of bell peppers instead of three.

Chapter Four

MEATLESS

ROASTED ROOT VEGGIE PIZZA
with BEER BREAD CRUST

6 servings | Prep Time: 30 Minutes | Start to Finish: 1 Hour 20 Minutes

VEGETABLES

- 1 medium sweet potato
- 4 medium beets with tops
- 1 tablespoon olive oil

CRUST

- 2 cups all-purpose flour
- 1 tablespoon sugar
- 1 package regular active dry yeast
- 1 teaspoon baking powder
- 1 teaspoon coarse (kosher or sea) salt
- ¾ cup lager beer, warmed to 105°F
- 1 tablespoon olive oil

TOPPINGS

- ¾ cup ricotta cheese
- 1½ cups shredded Gruyère cheese (6 oz)
- 1 tablespoon chopped fresh rosemary leaves

USE IT UP Beets and sweet potato make a terrific combination with the flavors of this pizza, but if you have any leftover roasted veggies, feel free to swap in those instead.

1 Heat oven to 425°F. Peel sweet potato; cut lengthwise in half, then cut each half into ½-inch pieces. Peel beets; cut into ¾- to 1-inch cubes. Chop ½ to 1 cup beet greens; set aside for topping.

2 Spray 2 cookie sheets with cooking spray. Place sweet potatoes and beets on cookie sheets; brush with 1 tablespoon oil. Roast 30 minutes or until tender when pierced with fork. Cool.

3 Meanwhile, in medium bowl, mix 1 cup of the flour, the sugar, yeast, baking powder and salt. Stir in beer and 1 tablespoon oil. Stir in remaining 1 cup flour to make a soft dough. On lightly floured surface, knead dough until smooth and elastic, about 5 minutes. Cover; let rest 30 minutes.

4 Spray large cookie sheet with cooking spray. On cookie sheet, press dough evenly into 13-inch round, patting and using heel of hand to push crust out from center; build up ½-inch rim.

5 Spread ricotta cheese evenly over crust. Sprinkle with Gruyère cheese. Top with roasted vegetables; sprinkle with rosemary.

6 Bake at 425°F for 15 to 18 minutes or until crust is golden and cheese is melted. Sprinkle with reserved beet greens; press lightly. Cut into wedges.

1 Serving: Calories 410; Total Fat 17g (Saturated Fat 8g, Trans Fat 0g); Cholesterol 40mg; Sodium 760mg; Total Carbohydrate 46g (Dietary Fiber 4g); Protein 18g
Exchanges: 3 Starch, ½ Vegetable, 1 Medium-Fat Meat, 2 Fat **Carbohydrate Choices:** 3

WHITE BEAN AND SPINACH PIZZA

8 servings | Prep Time: 10 Minutes | Start to Finish: 30 Minutes

½ cup dry-pack sun-dried tomato halves

1 can (15 to 16 oz) great northern or navy beans, drained, rinsed

2 cloves garlic, peeled

1 package (10 oz) prebaked thin Italian pizza crust (12 inch)

¼ teaspoon dried oregano leaves

1 cup firmly packed fresh spinach leaves, shredded

½ cup shredded reduced-fat Colby–Monterey Jack cheese blend (2 oz)

1 Heat oven to 425°F. In small bowl, place sun-dried tomatoes. Pour enough boiling water over tomatoes to cover; let stand 10 minutes. Drain. Cut into thin strips; set aside.

2 In food processor, place beans and garlic. Cover; process until smooth. Place pizza crust on ungreased cookie sheet. Spread bean mixture over crust. Sprinkle with oregano, tomatoes, spinach and cheese.

3 Bake about 10 minutes or until cheese is melted.

1 Serving: Calories 190; Total Fat 4g (Saturated Fat 1g, Trans Fat 0g); Cholesterol 0mg; Sodium 410mg; Total Carbohydrate 30g (Dietary Fiber 4g); Protein 8g **Exchanges:** 2 Other Carbohydrate, ½ Vegetable, 1 Very Lean Meat, ½ Fat **Carbohydrate Choices:** 2

USE IT UP You could use baby kale or arugula instead of the spinach—if that's what's in your fridge!

MAKE A MEAL The crunch of a crispy green salad next to a slice of pizza will fill your plate and fill you up.

POTATO AND CHIVE TAQUITOS

6 servings | Prep Time: 20 Minutes | Start to Finish: 45 Minutes

1½ cups mashed potatoes

¾ cup shredded Cheddar cheese (3 oz)

⅓ cup sour cream

3 tablespoons chopped fresh chives

12 flour tortillas (6 inch)

2 tablespoons butter, melted

Salsa or sour cream, if desired

Additional chopped fresh chives, if desired

1 Heat oven to 375°F. Line cookie sheet with cooking parchment paper or spray with cooking spray.

2 In medium bowl, stir together potatoes, cheese, sour cream and 3 tablespoons chives. Place tortillas on microwavable plate; cover with damp microwavable paper towel. Microwave on High 45 to 60 seconds just until warm.

3 Spread about 3 tablespoons potato mixture on each tortilla to within ¼ inch of edge; roll up tightly. Place, seam side down, on cookie sheet. Brush with melted butter.

4 Bake 18 to 22 minutes or until tortillas begin to brown and crisp. Serve with salsa; sprinkle with additional chives.

1 Serving (**2 Taquitos**): Calories 330; Total Fat 16g (Saturated Fat 8g, Trans Fat 1g); Cholesterol 30mg; Sodium 590mg; Total Carbohydrate 38g (Dietary Fiber 2g); Protein 9g **Exchanges:** 2 Starch, ½ Other Carbohydrate, ½ High-Fat Meat, 2 Fat **Carbohydrate Choices:** 2½

USE IT UP Got leftover mashed sweet potatoes? Go ahead and substitute them for the regular mashed potatoes.

Chopped green onions can be used instead of chives.

MEDITERRANEAN FLATBREAD WRAPS

6 servings | Prep Time: 15 Minutes | Start to Finish: 45 Minutes

1   package (8.5 oz) seven-grain pilaf

1   cup chopped (peeled and seeded, if desired) cucumber

1   cup chopped seeded tomato (1 medium)

¼   cup crumbled feta cheese (1 oz)

2   tablespoons fresh lemon juice

1   tablespoon olive oil

¼   teaspoon freshly ground pepper

1   container (7 oz) plain hummus

3   whole-grain white flatbread wraps (2.8 oz each)

1 Prepare pilaf as directed on package; cool. Meanwhile, in medium bowl, mix cucumber, tomato, cheese, lemon juice, oil and pepper. Stir in pilaf.

2 Spread hummus evenly over half of each flatbread wrap. Spoon pilaf mixture over half of each wrap; fold wrap over filling. Cut each sandwich in half to serve.

1 Serving (½ **Sandwich**): Calories 310; Total Fat 9g (Saturated Fat 1g, Trans Fat 0g); Cholesterol 0mg; Sodium 820mg; Total Carbohydrate 48g (Dietary Fiber 8g); Protein 10g **Exchanges:** 3 Starch, 1½ Fat **Carbohydrate Choices:** 3

USE IT UP
If whole-grain brown rice is what you have on hand, feel free to use it in place of the seven-grain pilaf.

This is the perfect thing to make for dinner when you find yourself with a bounty of fresh cucumbers and tomatoes.

WAY TO USE ➤ HERBS

- **Toss Them** Add chopped fresh herbs to green salads, pasta salads, rice or potato dishes. A little can go a long way and will build flavor as the dish sits. Start with a tablespoon of herbs for 2 to 3 cups salad, rice or potatoes, then taste and add more if you like.

- **Smell Them** Add stems of fresh herbs to flower bouquets. The fresh, earthy aroma blends nicely with the scent of flowers and is a natural air freshener!

- **Butter Them Up** Melt a tablespoon or two of butter and mix with one small, finely chopped garlic clove and a tablespoon of finely chopped fresh herbs to brush over ready-to-bake rolls or French bread.

- **Infuse Them** Add a few sprigs or leaves of fresh herbs and fresh fruit or cucumbers to a pitcher of water and chill. Let the flavors blend 30 minutes to 2 hours before serving (the longer the water sits, the more intense the flavor). Try strawberry-basil, lemon-rosemary or cucumber-mint.

- **Freeze Them** Place chopped herbs in ice cube trays and cover with olive or vegetable oil, chicken broth or water. When frozen, pop out the cubes and transfer them to a freezer-storage bag. Store in the freezer to add while making soups, broths and sauces for fresh-picked flavor any time.

OPEN-FACE CHILE-CHEESE QUESADILLAS

5 servings | Prep Time: 10 Minutes | Start to Finish: 20 Minutes

5   flour tortillas (8 inch)
    Olive oil

2   cups shredded pepper
    Jack or Monterey Jack
    cheese (8 oz)

½   cup roasted red bell
    peppers (from a jar),
    drained, finely chopped

½   cup pitted ripe olives,
    drained, chopped

1   to 2 chipotle chiles in
    adobo sauce (from 7-oz
    can), chopped

1   teaspoon adobo
    sauce (from can of
    chipotle chiles)

¼   cup finely chopped fresh
    cilantro

1 Heat oven to 400°F. Place tortillas on 2 large cookie sheets. Brush tortillas lightly with oil; prick several times with fork. Bake 5 minutes or until lightly browned and puffed. Cool.

2 Meanwhile, in medium bowl, mix cheese and the remaining ingredients. Sprinkle cheese mixture evenly over tortillas. Bake 6 to 8 minutes or until cheese is melted. Cut into wedges; serve warm.

1 Serving: Calories 390; Total Fat 26g (Saturated Fat 10g, Trans Fat 0g); Cholesterol 0mg; Sodium 1102mg; Total Carbohydrate 27g (Dietary Fiber 2g); Protein 14g **Exchanges:** 2 Starch, 1 High-Fat Meat, 3½ Fat **Carbohydrate Choices:** 2

USE IT UP
Top these yummy quesadillas with fresh pico de gallo or your favorite salsa and sour cream.

You can add your leftover chiles in adobo sauce to so many things! Try adding a tablespoon or so of finely chopped chiles to meatloaf while mixing, or to softened butter with a tablespoon of chopped chives for a special spread for rolls.

CABBAGE–BLACK BEAN ENCHILADAS

4 servings | Prep Time: 25 Minutes | Start to Finish: 1 Hour 30 Minutes

1   can (10 oz) mild or hot enchilada sauce

8   large cabbage leaves

1   cup cooked quinoa

1   cup black beans (from 15-oz can), drained, rinsed

1½ cups shredded Cheddar cheese (6 oz)

¾   cup crumbled Cotija (white Mexican) cheese (3 oz)

½   teaspoon ground cumin

1   tablespoon chopped fresh cilantro

USE IT UP Make your favorite coleslaw using the remaining cabbage.

MAKE A MEAL Garnish these enchiladas with your favorite taco toppings, such as sour cream, chopped avocado and chopped tomatoes. Serve Mexican rice on the side.

1 Heat oven to 375°F. Spray 8-inch square (2-quart) glass baking dish with cooking spray. Pour ½ cup of the enchilada sauce into baking dish; set aside.

2 Fill 5- to 6-quart Dutch oven or stockpot half full of water; heat to boiling. Add cabbage leaves; boil 3 to 5 minutes or until wilted. Drain.

3 Meanwhile, in medium bowl, stir together quinoa, beans, ½ cup of the Cheddar cheese, ½ cup of the Cotija cheese and the cumin until well blended. Spoon about ⅓ cup mixture on thick end of each cabbage leaf. Roll up, tucking sides in. Place cabbage rolls, seam side down, in sauce in baking dish. Pour remaining enchilada sauce over rolls. Sprinkle with remaining 1 cup Cheddar cheese.

4 Cover with foil; bake 45 minutes. Uncover; bake 15 to 20 minutes longer or until cabbage is tender. Sprinkle with remaining ¼ cup Cotija cheese and the cilantro.

1 Serving (**2 Enchiladas**): Calories 420; Total Fat 23g (Saturated Fat 13g, Trans Fat 1g); Cholesterol 65mg; Sodium 1180mg; Total Carbohydrate 29g (Dietary Fiber 8g); Protein 23g **Exchanges:** ½ Starch, 1½ Other Carbohydrate, 1 Very Lean Meat, 1 Medium-Fat Meat, 1 High-Fat Meat, 2 Fat **Carbohydrate Choices:** 2

WHOLE BEET TABBOULEH

6 servings | Prep Time: 25 Minutes | Start to Finish: 1 Hour 25 Minutes

- 2 cups boiling water
- 1 cup uncooked bulgur
- 3 medium fresh beets with tops
- 4 small fresh carrots with tops
- 6 medium stalks celery, sliced (2 cups)
- 8 medium green onions, sliced (½ cup)
- 1 teaspoon salt
- ½ teaspoon pepper
- ⅓ cup lemon juice
- ¼ cup olive oil
- 3 cloves garlic, finely chopped

1 In medium bowl, pour boiling water over bulgur. Let stand while preparing vegetables.

2 Chop beet tops and carrot tops. Peel beets; cut into julienne strips. Thinly slice carrots. In large bowl, toss beets and carrots with their tops, the celery, onions, salt and pepper.

3 Drain bulgur if necessary; stir into vegetable mixture.

4 In tightly covered container, shake lemon juice, oil and garlic. Add to bulgur mixture; toss well. Cover; refrigerate at least 1 hour or up to 3 days. Stir before serving.

1 Serving (1⅓ Cups): Calories 220; Total Fat 10g (Saturated Fat 1.5g, Trans Fat 0g); Cholesterol 0mg; Sodium 480mg; Total Carbohydrate 28g (Dietary Fiber 7g); Protein 4g **Exchanges:** 1 Starch, ½ Other Carbohydrate, 1 Vegetable, 2 Fat **Carbohydrate Choices:** 2

IN A SNAP The smaller you cut the beets and the longer you let the salad sit, the more it takes on the rosy-glow beet color.

USE IT UP Carrot greens work great in recipes, but the part between the carrot and the leaves can be stringy and hard to chew, so it's best to compost or throw out that portion. The beet tops, however, are completely edible and one of the most vitamin-packed parts of this colorful root vegetable.

Here are some other ingredients you can stir into your tabbouleh: chick peas (garbanzo beans), grape or cherry tomatoes (cut cherry tomatoes in half) or chopped bell peppers (any color).

Don't forget the leaves! Chop up the celery leaves as well as the stalks for this recipe.

GLUTEN-FREE QUINOA SALAD– STUFFED TOMATOES

6 servings | Prep Time: 35 Minutes | Start to Finish: 35 Minutes

6 large tomatoes (about 3 inches diameter)

1 tablespoon olive oil

2 tablespoons fresh lime juice

1 teaspoon ground cumin

1 teaspoon ground coriander

½ teaspoon ground red pepper (cayenne)

¼ teaspoon salt

3 green onions, thinly sliced (3 tablespoons)

1 medium red bell pepper, diced (about 1 cup)

½ cup black beans (from 15-oz can), drained, rinsed

½ cup white shoepeg corn (from 11-oz can), drained, rinsed

1 cup cooked quinoa

¾ cup crumbled feta cheese (3 oz)

¼ cup chopped fresh cilantro

1 Cut tops off tomatoes. Gently scoop out seeds and pulp; discard. Pat insides of tomatoes dry with paper towels; set aside.

2 In large bowl, beat oil and lime juice with whisk. Beat in cumin, coriander, cayenne and salt. Stir in onions, bell pepper, beans, corn and quinoa. Gently stir in cheese.

3 Evenly spoon mixture into tomatoes; top with cilantro.

1 Serving: Calories 180; Total Fat 7g (Saturated Fat 2.5g, Trans Fat 0g); Cholesterol 15mg; Sodium 370mg; Total Carbohydrate 23g (Dietary Fiber 5g); Protein 7g **Exchanges:** 1 Other Carbohydrate, 1½ Vegetable, ½ Medium-Fat Meat, 1 Fat **Carbohydrate Choices:** 1½

USE IT UP
If you aren't in the mood for a meatless meal and have some cooked chicken in the fridge, stir in ¾ cup shredded chicken along with the feta cheese.

COOKING GLUTEN FREE?
Always read labels to make sure *each* recipe ingredient is gluten free. Products and ingredient sources can change.

MEDITERRANEAN BULGUR AND LENTILS

8 servings | Prep Time: 15 Minutes | Start to Finish: 3 Hours 30 Minutes

- 1 cup uncooked bulgur or cracked wheat
- ½ cup dried lentils, sorted, rinsed
- 1 teaspoon ground cumin
- ¼ teaspoon salt
- 3 cloves garlic, finely chopped
- 1 can (15.25 oz) whole kernel corn, drained
- 2 cans (14 oz each) vegetable broth
- 2 medium tomatoes, chopped (1½ cups)
- 1 can (2¼ oz) sliced ripe olives, drained
- 1 cup crumbled feta cheese (4 oz)

1 Spray 3- to 4-quart slow cooker with cooking spray. In slow cooker, mix bulgur, lentils, cumin, salt, garlic, corn and broth.

2 Cover; cook on Low heat setting 3 to 4 hours.

3 Stir in tomatoes and olives. Increase heat setting to High; cook 15 minutes longer. Sprinkle individual servings with cheese.

1 Serving: Calories 200; Total Fat 4.5g (Saturated Fat 2.5g, Trans Fat 0g); Cholesterol 15mg; Sodium 810mg; Total Carbohydrate 31g (Dietary Fiber 6g); Protein 8g **Exchanges:** 1 Starch, 1 Other Carbohydrate, ½ Vegetable, ½ Medium-Fat Meat, ½ Fat **Carbohydrate Choices:** 2

IN A SNAP Quickly sort lentils by spreading them out in a single layer in a pan with sides. Pull out any small stones, discolored lentils or grains, and discard before cooking.

USE IT UP If you have chicken broth in your cupboard, feel free to use it instead of the vegetable broth if you like. Omit the salt, as chicken broth is a lot saltier than vegetable broth.

MAKE A MEAL Toasted wedges of pita bread, spread with your choice of hummus, would be a great accompaniment to this Mediterranean dish.

BOW-TIES WITH BROCCOLI PESTO

6 servings | Prep Time: 30 Minutes | Start to Finish: 30 Minutes

PESTO

- 1 bag (12 oz) frozen broccoli cuts
- ½ cup lightly packed fresh basil leaves
- ¼ cup walnut pieces
- 1 clove garlic, peeled
- ¼ cup shredded Parmesan cheese (1 oz)
- ¼ teaspoon salt
- ⅛ teaspoon pepper
- ⅓ cup olive oil
- 2 tablespoons water
- 1 teaspoon lemon juice

PASTA

- 4 cups uncooked multigrain bow-tie (farfalle) pasta (8 oz)
- 1 medium yellow bell pepper, cut into bite-size strips
- 1 medium plum (Roma) tomato, seeded, chopped

  Additional shredded Parmesan cheese, if desired

1 Cook broccoli as directed on package until crisp-tender; drain. Set aside 1½ cups.

2 Place remaining broccoli and remaining pesto ingredients in food processor. Cover; process until smooth, stopping occasionally to scrape down side with rubber spatula. Set aside.

3 In 4-quart saucepan, cook pasta as directed on package, adding reserved 1½ cups broccoli and the bell pepper during last 1 minute of cooking time. Drain; place in serving bowl. Add tomato and pesto; toss to coat. Serve with additional cheese.

1 Serving: Calories 320; Total Fat 17g (Saturated Fat 3g, Trans Fat 0g); Cholesterol 0mg; Sodium 180mg; Total Carbohydrate 33g (Dietary Fiber 5g); Protein 9g **Exchanges:** 2 Starch, 1 Vegetable, 3 Fat **Carbohydrate Choices:** 2

USE IT UP The broccoli pesto makes 1¼ cups. Try it—mixed with mayo—as a spread on sandwiches or in other recipes calling for pesto.

Other pasta shapes, such as penne or macaroni, can be used in this recipe. Use what you have . . . or buy what's on sale!

VEGETABLE-CASHEW NOODLE BOWLS

4 servings | Prep Time: 30 Minutes | Start to Finish: 30 Minutes

8　oz uncooked Japanese udon noodles (from 10-oz package)

1　medium red bell pepper, cut into 2x¼-inch strips

1　medium yellow bell pepper, cut into 2x¼-inch strips

2　small carrots, thinly sliced

2　cups fresh cilantro leaves

1　tablespoon grated lemon peel

3　cloves garlic, peeled

1　teaspoon lemon juice

½　teaspoon salt

⅛　teaspoon pepper

¼　cup olive oil

1　medium green onion, sliced (1 tablespoon)

¼　cup lightly salted roasted cashews

1 In 6- to 8-quart Dutch oven or stockpot, heat 4 quarts water to boiling. Add noodles; return to boiling. Reduce heat; boil 13 to 14 minutes or until noodles are tender. During last 4 minutes of cooking time, add bell peppers and carrots. Drain; place in large bowl.

2 Meanwhile, in food processor, place cilantro, lemon peel and garlic and process until very finely chopped. Add lemon juice, salt, pepper and oil; process until mixture forms a smooth puree.

3 Pour cilantro mixture over noodle-vegetable mixture; toss to coat. Divide among 4 individual bowls. Garnish with onion and cashews.

1 Serving (1¼ Cups): Calories 410; Total Fat 18g (Saturated Fat 2.5g, Trans Fat 0g); Cholesterol 0mg; Sodium 140mg; Total Carbohydrate 53g (Dietary Fiber 6g); Protein 8g **Exchanges:** 3 Starch, 1 Vegetable, 3 Fat **Carbohydrate Choices:** 3½

USE IT UP
Udon noodles are wheat noodles that are popular in Asia. They are readily available now at many larger grocery stores and at stores that specialize in Asian cuisines. If you have linguine or fettuccine on hand, you can substitute that if you like.

Green bell pepper can be used for the yellow pepper; or substitute a 1-pound bag of frozen stir-fry vegetables for all the fresh vegetables.

Chop those cilantro stems with the leaves so nothing goes to waste. In this recipe, you'll never notice the stems.

CHICK PEA AND TOMATO CURRY

6 servings | Prep Time: 25 Minutes | Start to Finish: 25 Minutes

1 tablespoon olive or vegetable oil

1 medium onion, chopped (½ cup)

3 cloves garlic, finely chopped

1 tablespoon finely chopped gingerroot

1 tablespoon curry powder

2 cans (15 to 19 oz each) chick peas or garbanzo beans, drained, rinsed

2 cans (14.5 oz each) fire roasted diced tomatoes, undrained

½ cup finely chopped fresh cilantro

1 tablespoon fresh lemon juice

½ teaspoon coarse (kosher or sea) salt

Hot cooked rice, if desired

Plain yogurt, if desired

1 In 3-quart saucepan, heat oil over medium heat. Cook onion, garlic, gingerroot and curry powder in oil about 2 minutes, stirring frequently, until onion is tender.

2 Stir in chick peas and tomatoes. Heat to boiling; reduce heat. Simmer uncovered 15 minutes, stirring occasionally. Stir in cilantro, lemon juice and salt.

3 Serve over rice. Top individual servings with yogurt.

1 Serving (1 Cup): Calories 190; Total Fat 5g (Saturated Fat 0.5g, Trans Fat 0g); Cholesterol 0mg; Sodium 590mg; Total Carbohydrate 29g (Dietary Fiber 7g); Protein 8g **Exchanges:** 1½ Other Carbohydrate, 1 Vegetable, 1 Very Lean Meat, 1 Fat **Carbohydrate Choices:** 2

USE IT UP
If you have leftover takeout rice, this would be a great way to put it to use! Place the rice in a microwavable bowl and sprinkle lightly with water if it looks dry. Cover with microwavable plastic wrap and heat on High 1 minute to 1 minute 30 seconds for 1 cup of rice.

MAKE A MEAL
Serve with Indian flatbread, or whatever bread you have on hand, to soak up the yummy goodness.

RICE AND MORE

- **Make a Wrap** Spoon leftover cooked rice into sturdy leaves of lettuce or cabbage. Top with leftover Asian-seasoned chicken or beef (if it isn't already seasoned with Asian flavors, reheat first while tossing with a tablespoon or two of an Asian condiment from your fridge—teriyaki, sweet-and-sour or soy sauce). Add some hot cooked veggies and a sprinkling of sesame oil and chopped peanuts or sesame seed; roll up and enjoy.

- **Toss a Salad** Make a salad for lunch tomorrow by combining ½ cup leftover cooked rice, quinoa or other grains with 2 cups torn lettuce, 1 cup chopped veggies and a tablespoon or two of chopped cilantro. Mix together 1 tablespoon fresh lemon or lime juice, 1 teaspoon miso paste, ½ teaspoon toasted sesame oil, a few drops of sriracha and a pinch of salt. If dressing is too thick, add a teaspoon or two of water until desired consistency. Toss the dressing with the salad just before serving.

- **Sneak It In** Use up that container of oats sitting in your pantry by adding it to smoothies. About ¼ cup per 3 cups of smoothie mixture adds nutrition that you won't even know is there.

- **Dump It In** Add cooked rice, quinoa, couscous or other grains to homemade or prepared soups during the last few minutes of cooking time.

VEGETABLE CURRY WITH COUSCOUS

6 servings | Prep Time: 40 Minutes | Start to Finish: 5 Hours 45 Minutes

CURRY

- 2 teaspoons vegetable oil
- 1 medium onion, chopped (½ cup)
- 2 cloves garlic, finely chopped
- 2 teaspoons curry powder
- ½ teaspoon ground turmeric
- ¼ teaspoon ground cinnamon
- ⅛ teaspoon ground red pepper (cayenne)
- 3 cups cubed (¾ to 1 inch) peeled eggplant
- 2 medium tomatoes, coarsely chopped (1 cup)
- 1 medium red bell pepper, coarsely chopped (1 cup)
- 1 cup sliced (¼ inch) ready-to-eat baby-cut carrots
- 1 can (15 to 19 oz) chick peas or garbanzo beans, drained, rinsed
- ½ teaspoon salt
- ¼ teaspoon pepper
- 2 cups fresh baby spinach leaves
- 2 cups uncooked whole wheat couscous

SAUCE

- ½ cup plain fat-free yogurt
- ¼ cup chopped fresh cilantro
- 1½ teaspoons lime juice
- 1 clove garlic, finely chopped
- Dash salt
- Dash freshly ground black pepper

1 Spray 5- to 6-quart slow cooker with cooking spray. In 10-inch nonstick skillet, heat oil over medium heat. Cook onion in oil about 5 minutes, stirring occasionally, until translucent. Add garlic; cook and stir until softened. Stir in curry powder, turmeric, cinnamon and red pepper; cook and stir 30 seconds.

2 Spoon onion mixture into slow cooker. Stir in eggplant, tomatoes, bell pepper, carrots, chick peas, salt and pepper.

3 Cover; cook on Low heat setting 5 to 6 hours. Stir in spinach. Cover; cook 5 to 10 minutes longer or until slightly wilted.

4 Meanwhile, cook couscous as directed on package. While couscous cooks, in small bowl, mix sauce ingredients. Serve curry over couscous; top with sauce.

1 Serving: Calories 350; Total Fat 3.5g (Saturated Fat 0g, Trans Fat 0g); Cholesterol 0mg; Sodium 370mg; Total Carbohydrate 67g (Dietary Fiber 9g); Protein 13g **Exchanges:** 1 Starch, 3 Other Carbohydrate, 1½ Vegetable, 1 Very Lean Meat, ½ Fat **Carbohydrate Choices:** 4½

ITALIAN ZUCCHINI STRATA

6 servings | Prep Time: 20 Minutes | Start to Finish: 1 Hour 30 Minutes

- 6 cups cubes (1 inch) day-old Italian or French bread
- 1½ cups shredded Italian cheese blend (6 oz)
- 2 tablespoons olive oil
- 1 medium onion, chopped (½ cup)
- 2 cloves garlic, finely chopped
- 2 medium zucchini, chopped (2 cups)
- 2 medium tomatoes, cut into small chunks (1 cup)
- 5 whole eggs
- 2 egg yolks
- 2 cups milk
- 1 tablespoon red pepper sauce
- 1 teaspoon Italian seasoning
- ¼ teaspoon salt
- ¼ teaspoon pepper

1 Heat oven to 325°F. Spray 11x7-inch (2-quart) glass baking dish with cooking spray. Place bread cubes in baking dish; sprinkle with 1 cup of the cheese.

2 In 10-inch skillet, heat oil over medium-high heat. Cook onion, garlic, zucchini and tomatoes in oil 5 to 6 minutes, stirring frequently, until lightly browned. Spoon vegetables over bread and cheese.

3 In medium bowl, beat eggs, egg yolks, milk, pepper sauce, Italian seasoning, salt and pepper with fork or whisk; pour evenly over vegetables. Top with remaining ½ cup cheese.

4 Bake uncovered 50 to 60 minutes or until knife inserted in center comes out clean. Let stand 10 minutes before cutting.

1 Serving: Calories 380; Total Fat 20g (Saturated Fat 8g, Trans Fat 0g); Cholesterol 245mg; Sodium 640mg; Total Carbohydrate 30g (Dietary Fiber 2g); Protein 20g **Exchanges:** 2 Starch, ½ Vegetable, 1 Medium-Fat Meat, 1 High-Fat Meat, 1 Fat **Carbohydrate Choices:** 2

IN A SNAP This strata makes a great do-ahead recipe. Prepare as directed through Step 3. Cover and refrigerate up to 24 hours. When ready to bake, heat oven to 325°F, uncover and bake as directed.

USE IT UP Add the unused egg whites to your scrambled eggs for an extra boost of protein.

MAKE A MEAL Serve the strata with fresh fruit and muffins or bagels for a delicious brunch.

ITALIAN FRITTATA WITH VINAIGRETTE TOMATOES

6 servings | Prep Time: 35 Minutes | Start to Finish: 35 Minutes

1 can (14 oz) chicken broth

¾ cup uncooked bulgur

1 medium zucchini, halved lengthwise, sliced (1½ cups)

1 cup sliced fresh mushrooms (3 oz)

1 small red bell pepper, chopped (½ cup)

1 small onion, chopped (⅓ cup)

½ teaspoon dried oregano leaves

½ teaspoon dried basil leaves

6 eggs

⅓ cup fat-free (skim) milk

¼ teaspoon salt

¼ teaspoon pepper

½ cup shredded mozzarella cheese (2 oz)

3 medium plum (Roma) tomatoes, chopped, drained (1 cup)

2 tablespoons balsamic vinaigrette dressing

1 Heat oven to 350°F. In 12-inch ovenproof nonstick skillet, heat broth to boiling over high heat. Stir in bulgur; reduce heat to low. Top bulgur with zucchini, mushrooms, bell pepper and onion. Sprinkle with oregano and basil. Cover; cook 12 minutes. Fluff bulgur with spatula, mixing with vegetables.

2 Meanwhile, in medium bowl, beat eggs, milk, salt and pepper with whisk until well blended.

3 Pour egg mixture evenly over bulgur mixture. Increase heat to medium-low. Cover; cook 5 minutes. Sprinkle with cheese. Transfer to oven and bake uncovered 5 to 7 minutes or until sharp knife inserted in center of egg mixture comes out clean.

4 Meanwhile, in medium microwavable bowl, mix tomatoes and dressing. Microwave uncovered on High 30 to 60 seconds to blend flavors.

5 Cut frittata into wedges (bulgur will form a "crust" on the bottom); use spatula to lift wedges out of skillet. Top with tomato mixture.

1 Serving: Calories 230; Total Fat 10g (Saturated Fat 3.5g, Trans Fat 0g); Cholesterol 215mg; Sodium 560mg; Total Carbohydrate 20g (Dietary Fiber 4g); Protein 14g **Exchanges:** 1 Other Carbohydrate, 1 Vegetable, 1½ Very Lean Meat, 2 Fat **Carbohydrate Choices:** 1

IN A SNAP For a truly meatless dish, simply swap out the chicken broth for vegetable broth and increase the salt to ½ teaspoon.

FIVE-VEGETABLE SPAGHETTI CASSEROLE

8 servings | Prep Time: 25 Minutes | Start to Finish: 1 Hour

2 tablespoons olive oil

2 cups shredded zucchini

1 cup chopped fresh kale or spinach leaves

1 medium onion, chopped (½ cup)

1 package (8 oz) sliced fresh mushrooms (about 3 cups)

1¼ cups chopped tomatoes; or 1 can (14.5 oz) diced tomatoes, drained

1 jar (24 oz) marinara or tomato pasta sauce (any meatless variety)

4 oz (from 8-oz package) cream cheese, cubed

3 cups cooked spaghetti

3 tablespoons chopped fresh chives

1 cup shredded mozzarella cheese (4 oz)

1 Heat oven to 350°F. Spray 11x7-inch (2-quart) glass baking dish or 2-quart casserole with cooking spray.

2 In 3- to 4-quart saucepan, heat oil over medium-high heat. Cook zucchini, kale, onion and mushrooms in oil 4 to 6 minutes, stirring frequently, until onion is crisp-tender; drain well. Return vegetables to saucepan. Stir in tomatoes and marinara sauce; heat until hot.

3 In large microwavable bowl, microwave cream cheese on Medium (50%) 1 to 2 minutes, stirring once, until melted. Add spaghetti and 2 tablespoons of the chives; mix well. Spread spaghetti evenly in baking dish. Spoon vegetable mixture over spaghetti.

4 Bake uncovered about 30 minutes or until bubbly. Sprinkle with mozzarella cheese; bake 5 minutes longer or until cheese is melted. Sprinkle with remaining 1 tablespoon chives.

1 Serving: Calories 290; Total Fat 13g (Saturated Fat 5g, Trans Fat 0g); Cholesterol 25mg; Sodium 460mg; Total Carbohydrate 31g (Dietary Fiber 3g); Protein 10g **Exchanges:** 1 Starch, ½ Other Carbohydrate, 1½ Vegetable, ½ Medium-Fat Meat, 2 Fat **Carbohydrate Choices:** 2

USE IT UP Any leftover cooked pasta can be used in this casserole. And other greens—such as collard greens, beet greens or mustard greens—can be substituted for the kale or spinach.

Not in the mood for meatless? If you have extra cooked ground beef, chicken or sausage, just stir it in with the pasta sauce.

RIGATONI WITH SPICY TOMATO SAUCE

8 servings | Prep Time: 45 Minutes | Start to Finish: 45 Minutes

1 tablespoon olive oil

1 cup sliced red onion (1 large)

8 oz fresh shiitake mushrooms, sliced

3 cloves garlic, sliced

¼ cup spicy harissa

1 can (28 oz) fire roasted diced tomatoes, undrained

4 cups water

1 box (16 oz) rigatoni pasta

¼ cup pitted kalamata olives, chopped

1 cup shredded fresh basil leaves

½ cup shredded Parmesan cheese (2 oz)

1 In 5-quart Dutch oven or stockpot, heat oil over medium heat. Cook onion in oil 3 to 4 minutes or until translucent. Add mushrooms; cook 5 to 7 minutes, stirring frequently, until mushrooms are browned and liquid is evaporated.

2 Stir in garlic, harissa and tomatoes; heat just to simmering. Stir in water; heat to boiling. Add pasta; return to simmering.

3 Reduce heat to medium-low; cook 15 to 20 minutes, stirring frequently, until pasta is cooked to desired tenderness. Stir in olives. Top with basil and cheese.

1 Serving (1½ Cups): Calories 340; Total Fat 6g (Saturated Fat 2g, Trans Fat 0g); Cholesterol 0mg; Sodium 460mg; Total Carbohydrate 59g (Dietary Fiber 5g); Protein 13g **Exchanges:** 3½ Starch, 1 Vegetable, 1 Fat **Carbohydrate Choices:** 4

IN A SNAP To make this dish vegan, sprinkle 1 tablespoon nutritional yeast over each serving in place of the Parmesan cheese.

USE IT UP If you have oil-cured black olives, try them in place of the kalamatas for a different flavor.

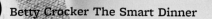

VEGGIE POT PIE STEW

4 servings | Prep Time: 25 Minutes | Start to Finish: 7 Hours 25 Minutes

3 **cups reduced-sodium chicken broth**

2 **medium sweet potatoes (about ¾ lb), peeled, cubed (about 2½ cups)**

1 **medium baking potato (about ½ lb), peeled, cubed (about 2 cups)**

3 **medium stalks celery with leaves, chopped (1¼ cups)**

1 **medium onion, chopped (½ cup)**

2 **teaspoons finely chopped garlic**

1 **teaspoon dried thyme leaves**

½ **teaspoon salt**

¼ **teaspoon pepper**

2 **tablespoons cornstarch**

½ **cup half-and-half**

1 **cup frozen peas and carrots, thawed**

4 **dinner roll tops**

1 **tablespoon butter, melted**

1 **tablespoon finely chopped celery leaves**

1 Spray 4- to 5-quart slow cooker with cooking spray. In slow cooker, mix broth, sweet potatoes, potato, celery, onion, 1 teaspoon of the garlic, the thyme, salt and pepper.

2 Cover; cook on Low heat setting 7 to 8 hours (or High heat setting 3 to 4 hours) or until potatoes are tender.

3 In small bowl, mix cornstarch and half-and-half with whisk until smooth. Add cornstarch mixture and peas and carrots to slow cooker; stir to combine. Increase heat setting to High. Cover; cook about 20 minutes longer or until slightly thickened.

4 Meanwhile, heat oven to 350°F. Place dinner roll tops, cut sides down, on ungreased cookie sheet. In small bowl, mix melted butter, celery leaves and remaining 1 teaspoon garlic. Brush over roll tops; bake 5 minutes. Brush with any remaining butter mixture. Serve rolls on top of stew.

1 Serving: Calories 290; Total Fat 8g (Saturated Fat 4.5g, Trans Fat 0.5g); Cholesterol 20mg; Sodium 930mg; Total Carbohydrate 45g (Dietary Fiber 5g); Protein 9g **Exchanges:** 2 Starch; ½ Other Carbohydrate; 1½ Vegetable; 1 Fat **Carbohydrate Choices:** 3

USE IT UP This recipe uses just the tops of the rolls. You can crumble the bottoms into soft bread crumbs and use to make Cod Cakes with Red Pepper Aioli, page 115.

Use red garnet or dark-orange sweet potatoes for the prettiest color.

We prefer the flavor of chicken broth over vegetable broth in this recipe, but if you would like the recipe to be completely meatless, feel free to use vegetable broth instead.

PUMPKIN LASAGNA

12 servings | Prep Time: 30 Minutes | Start to Finish: 5 Hours 50 Minutes

RICOTTA FILLING

- 1 tablespoon olive oil
- 1 medium onion, chopped (½ cup)
- 2 cloves garlic, finely chopped
- 1 package (8 oz) sliced fresh mushrooms (about 3 cups)
- 1 box (9 oz) frozen chopped spinach, thawed, squeezed to drain
- 1 container (15 oz) part-skim ricotta cheese
- 1 jar (15 oz) reduced-fat Alfredo pasta sauce
- 1 egg
- ½ cup shredded reduced-fat Italian cheese blend (2 oz)
- ½ teaspoon salt

PUMPKIN FILLING

- 1 can (15 oz) pumpkin (not pumpkin pie mix)
- 1 jar (15 oz) reduced-fat Alfredo pasta sauce
- 2 tablespoons chopped fresh sage leaves

NOODLES AND CHEESE

- 9 uncooked lasagna noodles
- ½ cup shredded reduced-fat Italian cheese blend (2 oz)

1 Line 5-quart oval slow cooker with removable crock with a slow cooker liner; spray liner with cooking spray.

2 In 10-inch skillet, heat oil over medium-high heat. Cook onion, garlic and mushrooms in oil, stirring frequently, until soft and just beginning to brown. In large bowl, mix remaining ricotta filling ingredients; stir in cooked vegetables.

3 In medium bowl, mix pumpkin filling ingredients.

4 In slow cooker, spread about one-third of the pumpkin filling (about 1 cup). Break 3 noodles to fit over pumpkin, making pieces fit together. Top with one-third of the ricotta filling (about 1½ cups). Repeat layers 2 more times. Top with ½ cup Italian cheese blend.

5 Cover; cook on Low heat setting 5 to 7 hours or until thermometer inserted in center reads 165°F. Transfer ceramic insert from slow cooker to cooling rack; let stand 20 minutes uncovered. Use liner bag to lift lasagna from crock to cutting board. Cut away liner; cut lasagna into 12 pieces.

1 Serving: Calories 290; Total Fat 14g (Saturated Fat 8g, Trans Fat 0g); Cholesterol 55mg; Sodium 570mg; Total Carbohydrate 25g (Dietary Fiber 2g); Protein 15g **Exchanges:** 1 Starch, ½ Other Carbohydrate, ½ Vegetable, ½ Lean Meat, 1 Medium-Fat Meat, 1½ Fat **Carbohydrate Choices:** 1½

IN A SNAP Not only does the slow cooker liner help prevent scorching along the edges, it also allows for the lasagna to be removed for easier cutting. Plus, cleanup is a breeze!

Prep the two fillings ahead of time. Then just assemble and let the slow cooker make dinner for you.

BEER-GLAZED BRATS AND BEANS

8 servings | Prep Time: 15 Minutes | Start to Finish: 3 Hours 15 Minutes

- 2 cans (28 oz each) vegetarian beans in sauce or baked beans
- ¼ teaspoon chili powder
- 2 tablespoons butter
- 1 large sweet onion, thinly sliced
- 8 vegetarian bratwurst
- 1 tablespoon packed brown sugar
- 1 teaspoon ground mustard
- ¼ cup barbecue sauce
- ¼ cup regular or nonalcoholic beer
- 8 hot dog buns, toasted

1 Spray 6-quart slow cooker with cooking spray. In slow cooker, mix beans and chili powder.

2 In 10-inch skillet, melt butter over medium heat. Cook onion in butter 6 to 8 minutes, stirring frequently, until very tender. Using tongs or slotted spoon, remove onion from skillet and place over beans in slow cooker; do not stir onion into beans.

3 Arrange bratwurst over onion. In small bowl, mix brown sugar, mustard, barbecue sauce and beer. Pour over bratwurst; do not stir.

4 Cover; cook on Low heat setting 3 to 4 hours.

5 To serve, place bratwurst in buns. Lift onion from slow cooker with tongs; arrange over bratwurst. Serve beans as a side dish.

1 Serving: Calories 540; Total Fat 16g (Saturated Fat 5g, Trans Fat 0.5g); Cholesterol 55mg; Sodium 1530mg; Total Carbohydrate 72g (Dietary Fiber 9g); Protein 28g **Exchanges:** 4½ Starch, ½ Vegetable, 2 Very Lean Meat, 2½ Fat **Carbohydrate Choices:** 5

IN A SNAP
A perfect dish to prep before you're away for the afternoon. Vegetarian brats vary by brand, but generally, most require very short cooking times and will dry out or fall apart if overcooked. So you wouldn't want to let this one sit all day.

Don't be tempted to stir! By keeping the ingredients in layers, you can serve the brats in buns, top them with the onions, and then serve the beans alongside.

THREE-INGREDIENT MAC AND CHEESE

6 servings | Prep Time: 20 Minutes | Start to Finish: 20 Minutes

1   can (12 oz) evaporated milk

1   box (16 oz) elbow macaroni

2   cups shredded sharp Cheddar cheese (8 oz)

1 In 5-quart nonstick Dutch oven or stockpot, heat evaporated milk, macaroni and 4 cups hot water to boiling over high heat. Reduce heat to medium-high; cook 6 minutes, stirring frequently.

2 Reduce heat. Simmer uncovered 8 minutes, stirring frequently; do not drain. Remove from heat; stir in cheese until melted.

1 Serving (1½ Cups): Calories 540; Total Fat 17g (Saturated Fat 10g, Trans Fat 0g); Cholesterol 50mg; Sodium 310mg; Total Carbohydrate 71g (Dietary Fiber 4g); Protein 25g **Exchanges:** 3 Starch, 1 Other Carbohydrate, 1 Low-Fat Milk, 1 High-Fat Meat, ½ Fat **Carbohydrate Choices:** 5

USE IT UP Though the flavor of sharp Cheddar is tough to beat, substituting 8 ounces of American cheese or prepared cheese product makes a creamy, kid-friendly mac and cheese. Cut the cheese into cubes before stirring into the macaroni mixture.

MAKE A MEAL Bulk up this dish with some added veggies for a one-dish dinner. Cook frozen chopped broccoli or peas as directed on the package, and stir them in with the cheese.

CHIPOTLE RED BEANS AND RICE CASSEROLE

4 servings | Prep Time: 10 Minutes | Start to Finish: 1 Hour 25 Minutes

- 1 **cup uncooked regular long-grain white rice**
- 1 **cup frozen corn**
- 1 **can (16 oz) spicy chili beans in sauce, undrained**
- 1 **can (14.5 oz) diced tomatoes with green chiles, undrained**
- 1 **can (14 oz) vegetable broth**
- 1 **chipotle chile in adobo sauce (from 7-oz can), chopped**
- 1 **cup chili cheese–flavored corn chips**
- 1 **cup shredded Monterey Jack cheese (4 oz)**

1 Heat oven to 350°F. Spray 2-quart casserole or 8-inch square (2-quart) glass baking dish with cooking spray. In casserole, mix rice, corn, beans, tomatoes, broth and chile.

2 Cover with foil; bake 1 hour. Uncover; stir well. Sprinkle with chips and cheese. Bake 10 to 15 minutes longer or until bubbly and rice is tender.

1 Serving (1½ **Cups**): Calories 510; Total Fat 14g (Saturated Fat 6g, Trans Fat 0g); Cholesterol 25mg; Sodium 1620mg; Total Carbohydrate 82g (Dietary Fiber 8g); Protein 19g **Exchanges:** 5 ½ Starch, 2 Fat **Carbohydrate Choices:** 5

USE IT UP For extra zip, add 1 to 2 tablespoons of the adobo sauce from the can of chipotle chiles to the casserole.

Chapter Five

SOUPS

AND

SIDES

CHICKEN "FRIDGE SWEEP" CHOWDER

6 servings | Prep Time: 40 Minutes | Start to Finish: 40 Minutes

6 slices bacon, cut into 1-inch pieces

1 medium onion, chopped (½ cup)

2 cloves garlic, finely chopped

1 medium orange bell pepper, chopped (1 cup)

2 tablespoons all-purpose flour

½ teaspoon salt

¼ teaspoon pepper

1 cup whole milk

2 cups chicken broth

1 can (14¾ oz) cream-style corn

2 cups cooked broccoli

2 cups shredded or cubed cooked chicken

1 large tomato, chopped (1 cup)

1 In 4-quart Dutch oven or stockpot over medium-high heat, cook bacon 5 to 8 minutes, stirring occasionally, until crisp. Drain bacon on paper towels. Reserve 3 tablespoons drippings in Dutch oven.

2 Cook onion, garlic and bell pepper in bacon drippings 3 to 5 minutes, stirring occasionally, until onion is translucent. Stir in flour, salt and pepper. Cook over medium heat, stirring constantly, until blended.

3 Gradually stir in milk. Heat to boiling; boil 1 minute, stirring constantly. Stir in broth, corn, broccoli, chicken and tomato. Cook about 5 minutes, stirring occasionally, until thoroughly heated. Top individual servings with bacon.

1 Serving (1⅓ Cups): Calories 260; Total Fat 8g (Saturated Fat 2.5g, Trans Fat 0g); Cholesterol 55mg; Sodium 890mg; Total Carbohydrate 24g (Dietary Fiber 3g); Protein 21g **Exchanges:** ½ Starch, ½ Other Carbohydrate, 2½ Vegetable, 1 Very Lean Meat, 1 Lean Meat, 1 Fat **Carbohydrate Choices:** 1½

IN A SNAP
No tomatoes on hand? Just sub in a 14.5-ounce can of fire roasted tomatoes, which also adds extra flavor and a hint of orange color to the soup.

USE IT UP
This chunky chowder is designed to use leftover veggies, bacon, broth, chicken and on-hand pantry ingredients to make a tasty main dish in minutes. Feel free to stir in any leftover veggies you have.

CHEESY BUFFALO CHICKEN SOUP

7 servings | Prep Time: 40 Minutes | Start to Finish: 40 Minutes

1¼ lb boneless skinless chicken breasts, cut into 1-inch cubes

¼ cup red pepper sauce

½ teaspoon salt

¼ teaspoon pepper

2 tablespoons butter

1 medium onion, chopped (½ cup)

1 medium stalk celery, chopped (½ cup)

1 teaspoon finely chopped garlic

2 tablespoons all-purpose flour

1 carton (32 oz) unsalted chicken broth (4 cups)

4 cups shredded Cheddar cheese (16 oz)

Crumbled blue cheese, crushed tortilla chips and additional chopped celery, if desired

1 In medium bowl, stir together chicken, pepper sauce, salt and pepper.

2 In 5-quart Dutch oven or stockpot, melt butter over medium-high heat. Cook chicken mixture in butter 7 to 9 minutes, stirring occasionally, until chicken is no longer pink in center. Add onion, celery and garlic. Cook 2 to 3 minutes, stirring occasionally, until vegetables are softened.

3 Sprinkle flour over chicken-vegetable mixture, stirring constantly until mixture is bubbly. Slowly stir in broth. Heat to boiling; reduce heat to low. Simmer uncovered 10 minutes, stirring occasionally. Slowly add cheese, ½ cup at a time, stirring constantly with whisk until cheese is melted and soup is hot.

4 Top individual servings with blue cheese, crushed chips and additional celery. Serve with additional pepper sauce, if desired.

1 **Serving** (1 **Cup**): Calories 430; Total Fat 29g (Saturated Fat 15g, Trans Fat 1g); Cholesterol 125mg; Sodium 930mg; Total Carbohydrate 5g (Dietary Fiber 0g); Protein 39g **Exchanges:** 1 Vegetable, 3 Very Lean Meat, 2 High-Fat Meat, 2½ Fat **Carbohydrate Choices:** ½

USE IT UP Try sharp Cheddar cheese for even more kick!

LOADED POTATO SOUP

15 servings | Prep Time: 45 Minutes | Start to Finish: 45 Minutes

1 package (12 oz) bacon

1½ cups chopped onions
    (3 medium)

6 cups chicken broth

2 lb baking potatoes,
   peeled, cubed

⅔ cup butter

¾ cup all-purpose flour

4 cups milk

1 teaspoon salt

1 teaspoon freshly
   ground pepper

1 cup diced cooked ham

1 container (8 oz)
   sour cream

2½ cups shredded sharp
    Cheddar cheese (10 oz)

¾ cup sliced green onions
   (12 medium)

USE IT UP Feel free to
customize this soup with cheese
you have on hand. Swiss, or a
Mexican or Italian cheese blend,
would change up the flavor in a
fun new way!

1 In 12-inch skillet, cook bacon over medium heat 6 to 7 minutes
or until crisp; drain on paper towels. Crumble bacon; set aside.
Reserve 2 tablespoons drippings in skillet. Cook onions in
bacon drippings over medium-high heat about 6 minutes or
until almost tender.

2 Transfer the onions to a 6-quart Dutch oven or stockpot, and
add broth and potatoes; bring to boiling and reduce heat.
Cook about 10 minutes or until potatoes are very tender.

3 Meanwhile, in same skillet, melt butter over low heat.
Stir in flour with whisk until smooth. Cook and stir 1 minute.
Gradually stir in 2 cups of the milk. Pour milk mixture into
potato mixture. Add remaining 2 cups milk, the salt and pepper.
Cook over medium heat, stirring constantly with whisk, until
mixture is thickened and bubbly.

4 Stir in ham, half of the bacon, the sour cream, 2 cups of the
cheese and ½ cup of the green onions. Cook until thoroughly
heated and cheese is melted. Evenly top individual servings
with remaining bacon, ½ cup cheese and ¼ cup green onions.

1 Serving (**1 Cup**): Calories 362; Total Fat 25g (Saturated Fat 14g, Trans Fat 0g);
Cholesterol 0mg; Sodium 863mg; Total Carbohydrate 20g (Dietary Fiber 1g); Protein 13g
Exchanges: 1½ Starch, 1½ High-Fat Meat, 2½ Fat **Carbohydrate Choices:** 1½

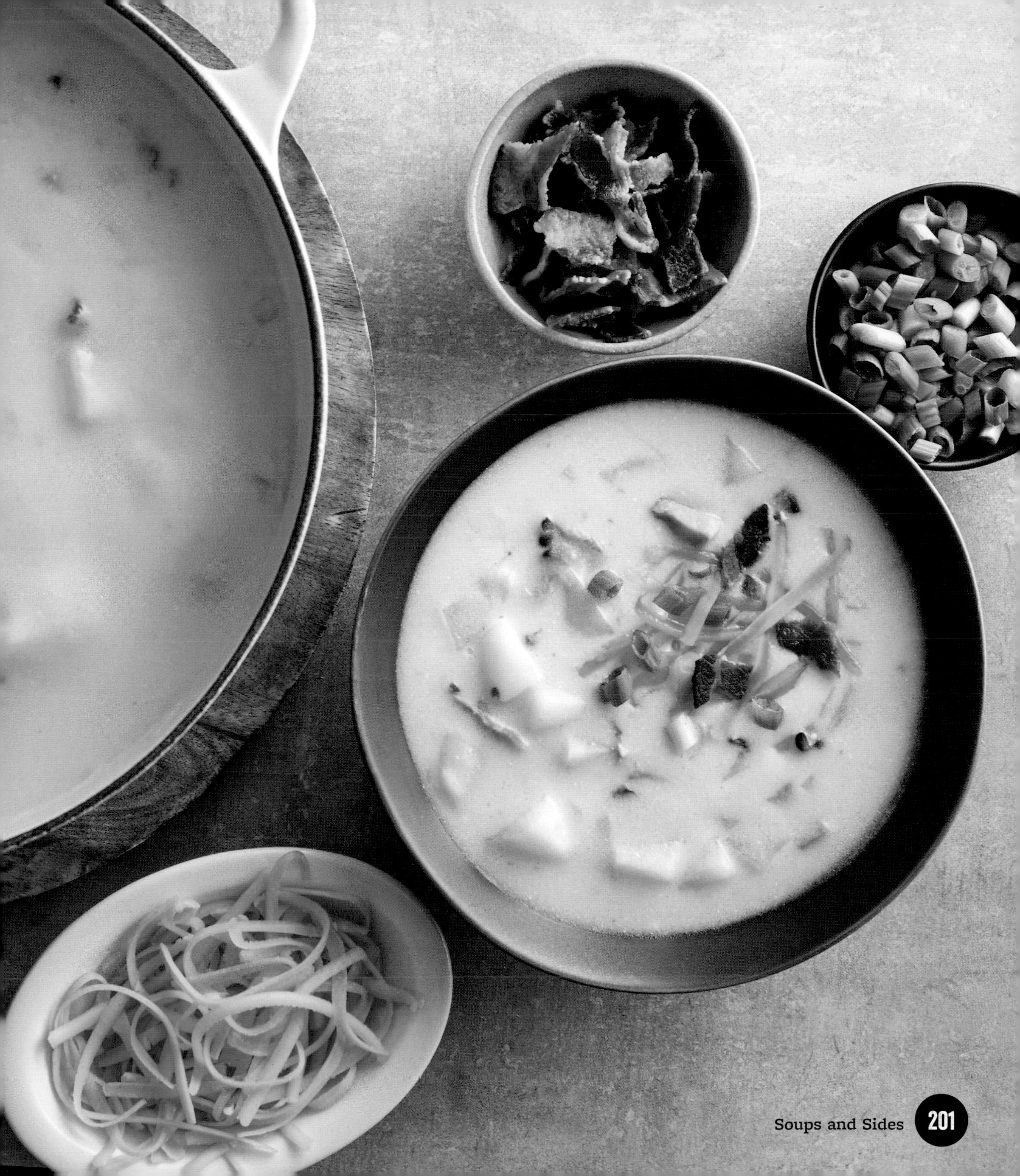

EDAMAME CORN CHOWDER

6 servings | Prep Time: 25 Minutes | Start to Finish: 40 Minutes

4 slices bacon, chopped

1 medium onion, chopped (½ cup)

2 tablespoons all-purpose flour

¾ teaspoon salt

¼ teaspoon pepper

4 cups milk

1 bag (12 oz) frozen shelled edamame (green) soybeans

1 can (14.75 oz) cream-style corn

1 can (11 oz) whole kernel corn, drained

4 cups frozen Southern-style diced hash brown potatoes (from 32-oz bag), thawed

Chopped fresh parsley, if desired

1 In 4-quart saucepan, cook bacon over medium heat until crisp; drain on paper towels. Reserve 1 tablespoon drippings in saucepan. Cook onion in bacon drippings about 2 minutes, stirring frequently, until soft.

2 Stir in flour, salt and pepper with whisk. Cook and stir over medium-high heat. Slowly stir in milk. Heat to boiling, stirring constantly; boil and stir 1 minute.

3 Stir in bacon, edamame, cream-style corn, whole kernel corn and potatoes. Heat to boiling; reduce heat to low. Cover; simmer 10 to 15 minutes or until potatoes are tender. Sprinkle individual servings with parsley.

1 Serving (1⅓ **Cups**): Calories 410; Total Fat 9g (Saturated Fat 3g, Trans Fat 0g); Cholesterol 20mg; Sodium 750mg; Total Carbohydrate 64g (Dietary Fiber 7g); Protein 18g **Exchanges:** 3½ Starch, ½ Low-Fat Milk, 1½ Vegetable, 1 Fat **Carbohydrate Choices:** 4

MAKE A MEAL Serve up some grilled cheese sandwiches with this soup for a delectable meal any night of the week.

BLACK-EYED PEA AND SAUSAGE SOUP

6 servings | Prep Time: 15 Minutes | Start to Finish: 8 Hours 30 Minutes

- 2 cans (15 to 16 oz each) black-eyed peas, drained, rinsed
- 12 oz smoked turkey kielbasa, halved lengthwise, sliced
- 4 medium carrots, chopped (2 cups)
- 4 cloves garlic, finely chopped
- 1 cup uncooked wheat berries
- 2 cups water
- 3 cans (14 oz each) reduced-sodium beef broth
- 2 cups shredded fresh spinach leaves
- 1 teaspoon dried marjoram leaves

1 Spray 3- to 4-quart slow cooker with cooking spray. In slow cooker, mix all ingredients except spinach and marjoram.

2 Cover; cook on Low heat setting 8 to 9 hours.

3 Stir in spinach and marjoram. Cover; cook about 15 minutes longer or until spinach is wilted.

1 Serving: Calories 350; Total Fat 7g (Saturated Fat 2g, Trans Fat 0g); Cholesterol 30mg; Sodium 1220mg; Total Carbohydrate 49g (Dietary Fiber 10g); Protein 23g **Exchanges:** 1 Starch, 2 Other Carbohydrate, 1 Vegetable, 1 Very Lean Meat, ½ Lean Meat, 1 Medium-Fat Meat **Carbohydrate Choices:** 3

USE IT UP Try other greens—like Swiss chard, mustard greens or turnip greens—solo or in combination with the spinach.

If you like andouille sausage, a Cajun favorite, try it in this soup instead of the kielbasa to give it a kick.

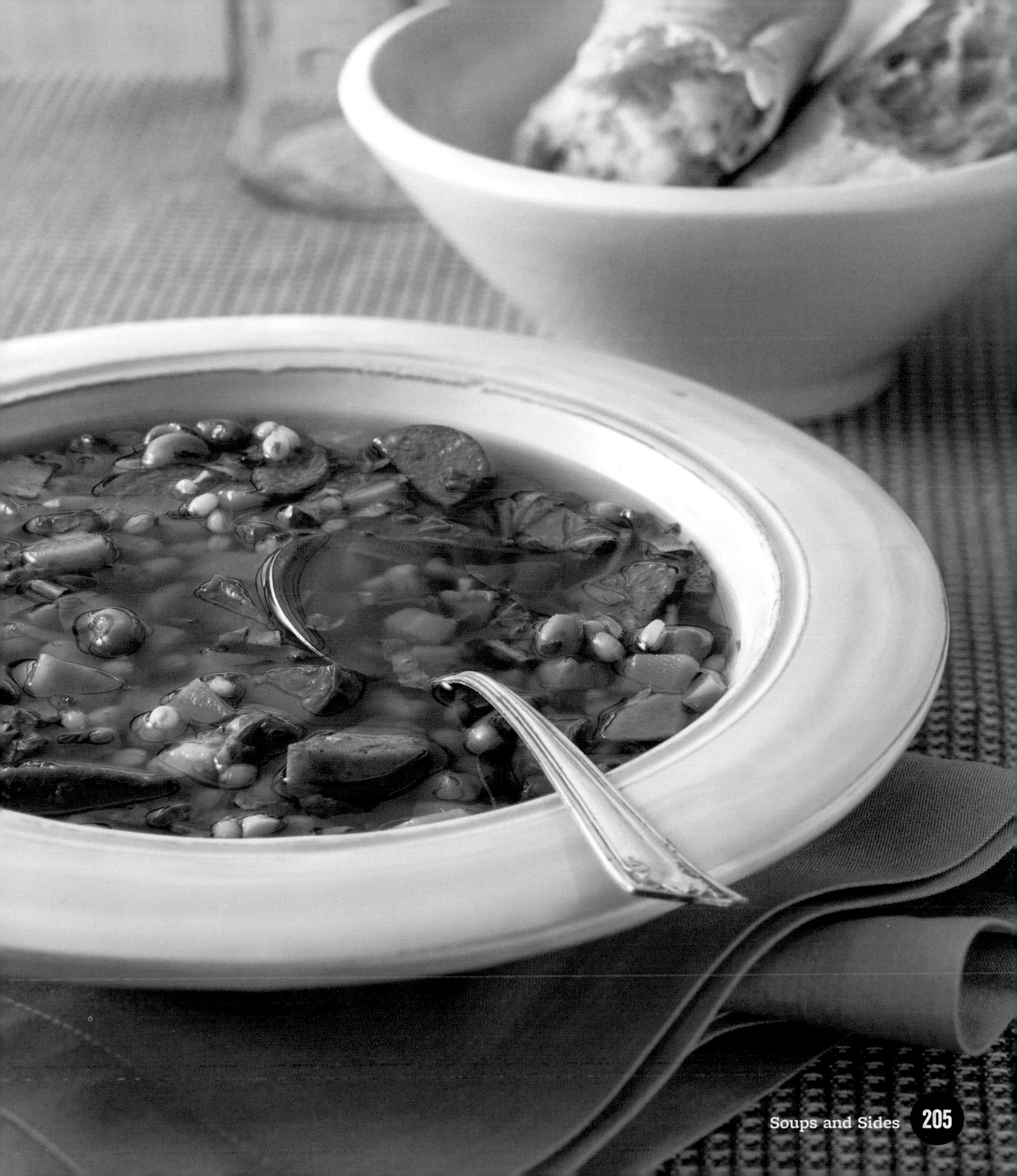

BRATWURST AND VEGETABLE SOUP

5 servings | Prep Time: 35 Minutes | Start to Finish: 35 Minutes

- 1 teaspoon caraway seed
- 1 medium baking potato, peeled, cut into ½-inch pieces (1 cup)
- ¾ cup fresh green beans (about 4 oz), cut into 1-inch pieces
- 1 cup ready-to-eat baby-cut carrots
- ¼ cup chopped fresh parsley
- ¼ teaspoon pepper
- 2 cups reduced-sodium beef broth
- 4 smoked beef bratwurst (from 12-oz package), cut into ½-inch-thick slices (about 1½ cups)
- 1 can (15 to 16 oz) great northern beans, drained, rinsed
- 1 can (14.5 oz) diced tomatoes with garlic and onion, undrained

1 In 3-quart saucepan over medium heat, cook caraway seed 1 to 2 minutes, stirring constantly, until toasted.

2 Stir in remaining ingredients. Heat to boiling; reduce heat. Cover; simmer 15 to 20 minutes, stirring occasionally, until vegetables are tender.

1 Serving (1⅓ Cups): Calories 320; Total Fat 13g (Saturated Fat 5g, Trans Fat 0g); Cholesterol 20mg; Sodium 1560mg; Total Carbohydrate 33g (Dietary Fiber 8g); Protein 16g **Exchanges:** 2 Starch, 1 Vegetable, 1 Medium-Fat Meat, 1½ Fat **Carbohydrate Choices:** 2

MAKE A MEAL This simple-to-prepare soup becomes a

comforting homemade meal when you pair it with a salad and dinner rolls—either hearty rye or pretzel rolls would be delicious.

ITALIAN SAUSAGE SOUP

6 servings | Prep Time: 30 Minutes | Start to Finish: 30 Minutes

1 lb pork or turkey Italian sausage links, casings removed and cut into 1-inch pieces

2 cups fresh broccoli florets

1 cup uncooked mostaccioli pasta (3 oz)

2½ cups water

½ teaspoon dried basil leaves

¼ teaspoon fennel seed, crushed

¼ teaspoon pepper

1 can (28 oz) organic whole peeled tomatoes with basil, undrained

1 can (18.5 oz) vegetable classics French onion soup

1 In 4-quart saucepan or Dutch oven, cook sausage over medium-high heat, stirring occasionally, until no longer pink; drain.

2 Stir in remaining ingredients, breaking up tomatoes. Heat to boiling; reduce heat to medium-low. Cover; cook about 15 minutes, stirring occasionally, until pasta is tender.

1 Serving (1½ **Cups**): Calories 230; Total Fat 8g (Saturated Fat 2g, Trans Fat 0g); Cholesterol 30mg; Sodium 1260mg; Total Carbohydrate 23g (Dietary Fiber 3g); Protein 16g **Exchanges:** ½ Starch, ½ Other Carbohydrate, 1 Vegetable, 2 Lean Meat, ½ Fat **Carbohydrate Choices:** 1½

USE IT UP
If you've got bratwurst, substitute it for the Italian sausage. If it is fully cooked, skip Step 1 and heat the bratwurst with the remaining ingredients.

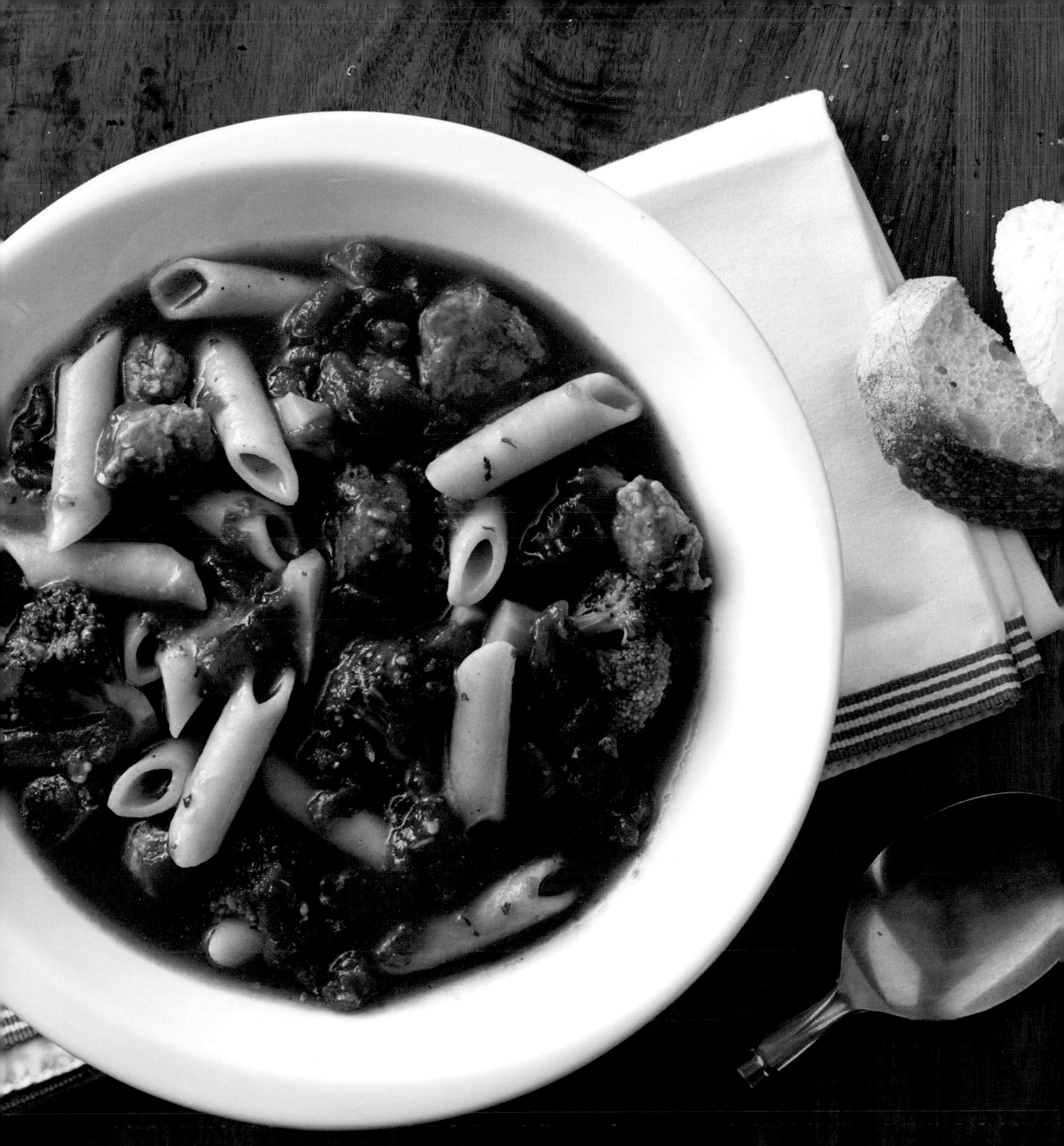

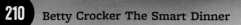

SMOKY BEANS AND GREENS SOUP

8 servings | Prep Time: 20 Minutes | Start to Finish: 35 Minutes

2 tablespoons olive oil

1 ring (14 oz) fully cooked
   smoked sausage, cut into
   ¼-inch slices

1 small onion, sliced

2 cloves garlic,
   finely chopped

2 cans (15 oz each)
   cannellini beans, drained,
   rinsed

1 can (14.5 oz) fire
   roasted diced tomatoes,
   undrained

2 teaspoons chopped fresh
   thyme leaves

½ teaspoon freshly
   ground pepper

¼ teaspoon salt

1 carton (32 oz) chicken
   broth (4 cups)

1 bag (6 oz) fresh
   baby spinach leaves,
   coarsely chopped

1 cup finely shredded
   Parmesan cheese (4 oz)

1 In 4-quart Dutch oven or stockpot, heat oil over medium-high heat. Cook sausage and onion in oil 6 to 8 minutes, stirring frequently, until lightly browned. Add garlic; cook 1 minute.

2 Stir in beans, tomatoes, thyme, pepper and salt. Add broth. Heat to boiling; reduce heat. Simmer uncovered 15 minutes.

3 Divide spinach among 8 soup bowls. Ladle soup over spinach. Sprinkle each serving with 2 tablespoons cheese.

1 Serving: Calories 340; Total Fat 22g (Saturated Fat 8g, Trans Fat 0g); Cholesterol 0mg; Sodium 1460mg; Total Carbohydrate 20g (Dietary Fiber 5g); Protein 17g **Exchanges:** 1 Starch, 1 Vegetable, ½ Very Lean Meat, 1 Medium-Fat Meat, 1 High-Fat Meat, 2 Fat **Carbohydrate Choices:** 1

HAM AND WILD RICE SOUP

6 servings | Prep Time: 15 Minutes | Start to Finish: 7 Hours 25 Minutes

2 cups diced cooked ham

1 cup julienne-cut carrots (from 10-oz bag)

¾ cup uncooked wild rice

1 medium onion, chopped (½ cup)

1¾ cups chicken broth

1 can (10¾ oz) condensed reduced-sodium cream of celery soup

¼ teaspoon pepper

3 cups water

1 cup half-and-half

¼ cup sliced almonds

2 tablespoons dry sherry, if desired

¼ cup chopped fresh parsley

1 Spray 3- to 4-quart slow cooker with cooking spray. In slow cooker, stir together ham, carrots, wild rice, onion, broth, soup, pepper and water.

2 Cover; cook on Low heat setting 7 to 8 hours.

3 Stir in remaining ingredients. Increase heat setting to High; cook 10 to 15 minutes or until hot.

1 Serving (1½ Cups): Calories 290; Total Fat 12g (Saturated Fat 4.5g, Trans Fat 0g); Cholesterol 45mg; Sodium 1180mg; Total Carbohydrate 28g (Dietary Fiber 3g); Protein 16g **Exchanges:** 1½ Other Carbohydrate, ½ Vegetable, 1 Lean Meat, 1 Medium-Fat Meat, 1 Fat **Carbohydrate Choices:** 2

USE IT UP
This is a great recipe when you have leftover holiday ham. But if you don't, look for packages of diced ham near the packaged deli meats and bacon at the grocery store.

MISO CUP

1 serving | Prep Time: 10 Minutes | Start to Finish: 10 Minutes

¾ cup chicken broth

1 teaspoon white miso paste

1 tablespoon finely diced firm tofu

1 tablespoon finely chopped green onion

1 In 1½-quart saucepan, heat all ingredients to boiling over high heat. Reduce heat to low; simmer 5 minutes, stirring occasionally.

2 Pour into mug. Serve immediately.

1 Serving: Calories 40; Total Fat 1g (Saturated Fat 0g, Trans Fat 0g); Cholesterol 0mg; Sodium 850mg; Total Carbohydrate 3g (Dietary Fiber 0g); Protein 4g **Exchanges:** ½ Lean Meat **Carbohydrate Choices:** 0

IN A SNAP Prep the tofu and green onions on the weekend so it's even easier to stir together this quick soup whenever the mood strikes throughout the week.

USE IT UP Red miso paste works well in this recipe, too.

TEXAS CHILI

8 servings | Prep Time: 55 Minutes | Start to Finish: 2 Hours 10 Minutes

CHILI

2 lb beef stew meat, cut into ¾-inch pieces

1 teaspoon salt

4 tablespoons butter

2 cups diced onions

2 red bell peppers, diced

1 serrano chile, finely chopped

3 cloves garlic, finely chopped

2 teaspoons ground cumin

1 teaspoon ground coriander

1 can (28 oz) fire roasted diced tomatoes, undrained

½ cup water

1 to 2 tablespoons chopped chipotle chiles in adobo sauce (from 7-oz can)

2 tablespoons yellow cornmeal

2 tablespoons lime juice

1 tablespoon packed brown sugar

FOR SERVING, IF DESIRED

1 cup shredded sharp Cheddar cheese (4 oz)

Plain yogurt or sour cream

Chopped fresh cilantro

1 Heat oven to 325°F. Pat beef dry; rub salt into beef. In 5-quart ovenproof Dutch oven, melt 2 tablespoons of the butter over medium-high heat. In two batches, brown beef in single layer without moving, 5 to 7 minutes, then turn and brown 5 to 7 minutes longer. Using slotted spoon, transfer beef to medium bowl.

2 Add remaining 2 tablespoons butter to Dutch oven. Cook onions and bell peppers in butter 5 to 7 minutes, stirring occasionally, until soft. Stir in serrano chile, garlic, cumin and coriander; cook 30 seconds. Stir in beef, tomatoes, water and chipotle chiles; heat to simmering.

3 In small bowl, stir together cornmeal, lime juice and brown sugar. Stir into beef mixture.

4 Bake uncovered 1 hour to 1 hour 15 minutes or until beef is tender.

5 Top individual servings with cheese; serve with yogurt and cilantro.

1 Serving: Calories 360; Total Fat 23g (Saturated Fat 11g, Trans Fat 1g); Cholesterol 90mg; Sodium 570mg; Total Carbohydrate 13g (Dietary Fiber 2g); Protein 26g **Exchanges:** ½ Other Carbohydrate, 1 Vegetable, 3 Lean Meat, ½ High-Fat Meat, 2 Fat **Carbohydrate Choices:** 1

USE IT UP Don't toss the tops! When you slice off the top of a bell pepper, be sure to cut around and remove the stem, then the remaining part of the top can be used too.

BOURBON CHILI

4 servings | Prep Time: 50 Minutes | Start to Finish: 50 Minutes

1   lb lean (at least 80%) ground beef

1   large onion, chopped (1 cup)

2   cloves garlic, finely chopped, or ¼ teaspoon garlic powder

⅓   cup bourbon or beef broth

2   tablespoons packed brown sugar

1   tablespoon chili powder

2   teaspoons chopped fresh or ¾ teaspoon dried oregano leaves

1   teaspoon ground cumin

½   teaspoon salt

¼   to ½ teaspoon crushed red pepper flakes

1   can (14.5 oz) diced tomatoes, undrained

1   can (15 to 16 oz) red kidney beans, undrained

1   can (8 oz) tomato sauce

    Sour cream, shredded Cheddar cheese and chopped green onions, if desired

1 In 3-quart saucepan, cook beef, onion and garlic over medium heat 8 to 10 minutes, stirring occasionally, until beef is thoroughly cooked; drain.

2 Stir in remaining ingredients except sour cream, cheese and onions. Heat to boiling; reduce heat to medium-low. Cover and cook 30 minutes, stirring occasionally.

3 Top individual servings with sour cream, cheese and onions.

1 Serving: Calories 390; Total Fat 14g (Saturated Fat 5g, Trans Fat 0.5g); Cholesterol 70mg; Sodium 990mg; Total Carbohydrate 35g (Dietary Fiber 8g); Protein 28g **Exchanges:** 1 Starch, 1 Other Carbohydrate, ½ Vegetable, 1 Very Lean Meat, 2½ Medium-Fat Meat **Carbohydrate Choices:** 2

IN A SNAP
You can make this chili ahead of time to serve when convenient. Just heat and enjoy!

MAKE A MEAL
Tortilla or corn chips, or wedges of warm cornbread, would be good alongside a bowl of this chili, with fresh fruit on the side.

THREE-GRAIN SALAD

5 servings | Prep Time: 25 Minutes | Start to Finish: 2 Hours 25 Minutes

SALAD

- 5 cups water
- ¾ cup uncooked wheat berries
- ⅓ cup uncooked regular brown rice
- ½ cup uncooked hulled or pearl barley
- ½ cup dried cherries or cranberries
- ¼ cup diced carrot
- ¼ cup diced celery
- ¼ cup chopped fresh parsley, if desired
- 1 medium unpeeled apple, chopped (1 cup)
- 4 medium green onions, chopped (¼ cup)

SWEET RED ONION DRESSING

- 3 tablespoons sugar
- 3 tablespoons vegetable oil
- ⅓ cup cider vinegar
- 2 tablespoons grated red onion
- 1 tablespoon Worcestershire sauce
- 2 cloves garlic, finely chopped

1 In 2-quart saucepan, heat water and wheat berries to boiling. Reduce heat to low. Cover; simmer 10 minutes. Stir in brown rice and barley. Cover; simmer about 50 minutes longer or until grains are tender. Drain if necessary.

2 In small bowl, mix dressing ingredients.

3 In large bowl, mix cooked grains and remaining salad ingredients. Pour dressing over salad; toss. Cover; refrigerate 1 to 2 hours or until chilled.

1 Serving (1⅓ Cups): Calories 400; Total Fat 9g (Saturated Fat 0.5g, Trans Fat 0g); Cholesterol 0mg; Sodium 210mg; Total Carbohydrate 71g (Dietary Fiber 10g); Protein 7g **Exchanges:** 2½ Starch, 2 Other Carbohydrate, 1½ Fat **Carbohydrate Choices:** 5

IN A SNAP Make this whole-grain salad in the morning or the night before you want to serve it, allowing the flavors to meld. It will be ready when you are hungry! Or chop the veggies and cook the grains the night before to get a jump on dinner.

USE IT UP Keep a stash! If you like cooking with whole grains, stock up and keep them in your pantry up to 3 months or in the freezer up to 6 months.

NUTS AND SEEDS

- **Sprinkle Them** Chopped nuts or seeds (such as pumpkin seeds or poppy seed) sprinkled into muffin, quick-bread or pancake batter before baking add flavor and crunch.

- **Whirl Them** Add a small handful of nuts or a tablespoon of seeds such as flaxseed or chia seeds to smoothies for added nutrition.

- **Mix and Match** Rather than use one type of nut in a dish, why not do a mash-up of those you have on hand? Try making brownies using a mixture of chopped walnuts, pecans and slivered almonds, for example.

- **Coat Meat** Ground nuts add texture and flavor when coating chicken, beef or pork. Enlist your coffee grinder to grind pecans, peanuts or cashews. Then dip the meat in egg or mustard and roll in the ground nuts; mix in fresh herbs if you like.

- **Toss for Crunch** For an extra punch of crunch, add a small handful of nuts or a tablespoon or two of pumpkin or sunflower seeds to your green salad either instead of croutons or in addition to them.

- **Think Breakfast** Top your hot oatmeal or yogurt with chopped nuts or a sprinkling of seeds. While you're at it, add those small amounts of raisins or dried cranberries lurking in your pantry as well.

GREENS

- **Whirl Them** You can use up a lot of greens in smoothies. Get used to the subtle grassy flavor by gradually building up the amount of greens you add each time you make smoothies. For 2 large or 4 small smoothies, place ½ cup water in blender. Add up to 3 cups spinach, kale leaves, romaine or lettuce or juicing blends. Add a cupful of frozen berries, a banana, other fixings such as a small handful of nuts or 2 tablespoons chia seeds or flaxseed, a scoop of protein powder and another ½ cup or so of water or juice. Cover and blend until smooth, starting on the lowest speed and working your way up to the highest speed.

- **Wilt Them** When tossing hot pasta with a sauce and other ingredients, add a handful or two of spinach, arugula or baby kale leaves and toss just until wilted.

- **Fill Them** Instead of bread, use large green leaves such as cabbage or romaine as sandwich wraps. Arrange your favorite luncheon meat and cheese, or spoon tuna, egg or pasta salad into a leaf and roll up. Secure with a wooden toothpick to serve immediately, or wrap tightly with plastic wrap for lunch on the go.

GREEN RICE WITH TOASTED PUMPKIN SEEDS

10 servings | Prep Time: 20 Minutes | Start to Finish: 40 Minutes

PUMPKIN SEEDS

- ⅓ cup raw unsalted hulled pumpkin seeds (pepitas), pine nuts or slivered almonds
- 1 tablespoon olive oil

RICE

- ½ cup tightly packed fresh cilantro (stems and leaves)
- ½ cup tightly packed fresh parsley (stems and leaves)
- 1 medium green bell pepper, coarsely chopped (1 cup)
- 1 small onion, chopped (⅓ cup)
- 2 cloves garlic, finely chopped
- 1 jalapeño chile, seeded
- 1½ teaspoons salt
- ¼ teaspoon ground cumin
- 2¾ cups water
- 3 tablespoons olive oil
- 1½ cups uncooked regular long-grain rice

1 In 8-inch skillet, heat pumpkin seeds and 1 tablespoon oil over medium heat about 3 minutes, stirring occasionally, until seeds are lightly toasted. (Watch carefully—they can burn quickly.) Use slotted spoon to remove pumpkin seeds from pan and cool on paper towel–lined plate.

2 In food processor or blender, puree cilantro, parsley, bell pepper, onion, garlic, chile, salt, cumin and water until smooth; set aside.

3 In 3-quart saucepan, heat 3 tablespoons oil over medium heat until hot. Add rice and cook 3 minutes, stirring occasionally, until slightly translucent around edges. Add pureed liquid and heat to boiling. Reduce heat to low; cover and simmer 20 minutes or until all liquid is absorbed. Fluff with fork and stir in pumpkin seeds. Serve hot.

1 Serving (½ **Cup**): Calories 210; Total Fat 9g (Saturated Fat 1.5g, Trans Fat 0g); Cholesterol 0mg; Sodium 360mg; Total Carbohydrate 27g (Dietary Fiber 1g); Protein 5g **Exchanges:** 1½ Starch, 1 Vegetable, 1½ Fat **Carbohydrate Choices:** 2

CREAMY LEMON ORZO SALAD

6 servings | Prep Time: 30 Minutes | Start to Finish: 1 Hour 30 Minutes

1¼ cups uncooked orzo or rosamarina pasta (8 oz)

1 cup frozen sweet peas

¾ cup plain yogurt

¼ cup mayonnaise

¼ cup milk

2 tablespoons chopped fresh mint leaves

1 tablespoon grated lemon peel

1 teaspoon salt

½ teaspoon pepper

1 medium red bell pepper, chopped (1 cup)

¼ cup chopped green onions (4 medium)

½ cup sliced almonds, toasted*

1 Cook orzo as directed on package, adding frozen peas for last 3 minutes of cooking time. Drain; rinse with cool water.

2 Meanwhile, in large bowl, stir together yogurt, mayonnaise, milk, mint, lemon peel, salt and pepper.

3 Stir in orzo and peas, bell pepper and onions. Cover; refrigerate 1 hour to blend flavors. Stir in almonds.

*To toast almonds, sprinkle in ungreased skillet. Cook over medium heat 5 to 7 minutes, stirring frequently until almonds begin to brown, then stirring constantly until nuts are light brown.

1 Serving: Calories 320; Total Fat 12g (Saturated Fat 2g, Trans Fat 0g); Cholesterol 5mg; Sodium 640mg; Total Carbohydrate 41g (Dietary Fiber 4g); Protein 11g **Exchanges:** 2½ Starch, 1 Vegetable, 2 Fat **Carbohydrate Choices:** 3

USE IT UP You can use other pasta you have in your pantry. Try rotini, macaroni, or small or medium shells.

MAKE A MEAL For a main-dish salad, add cubed cooked ham or chicken.

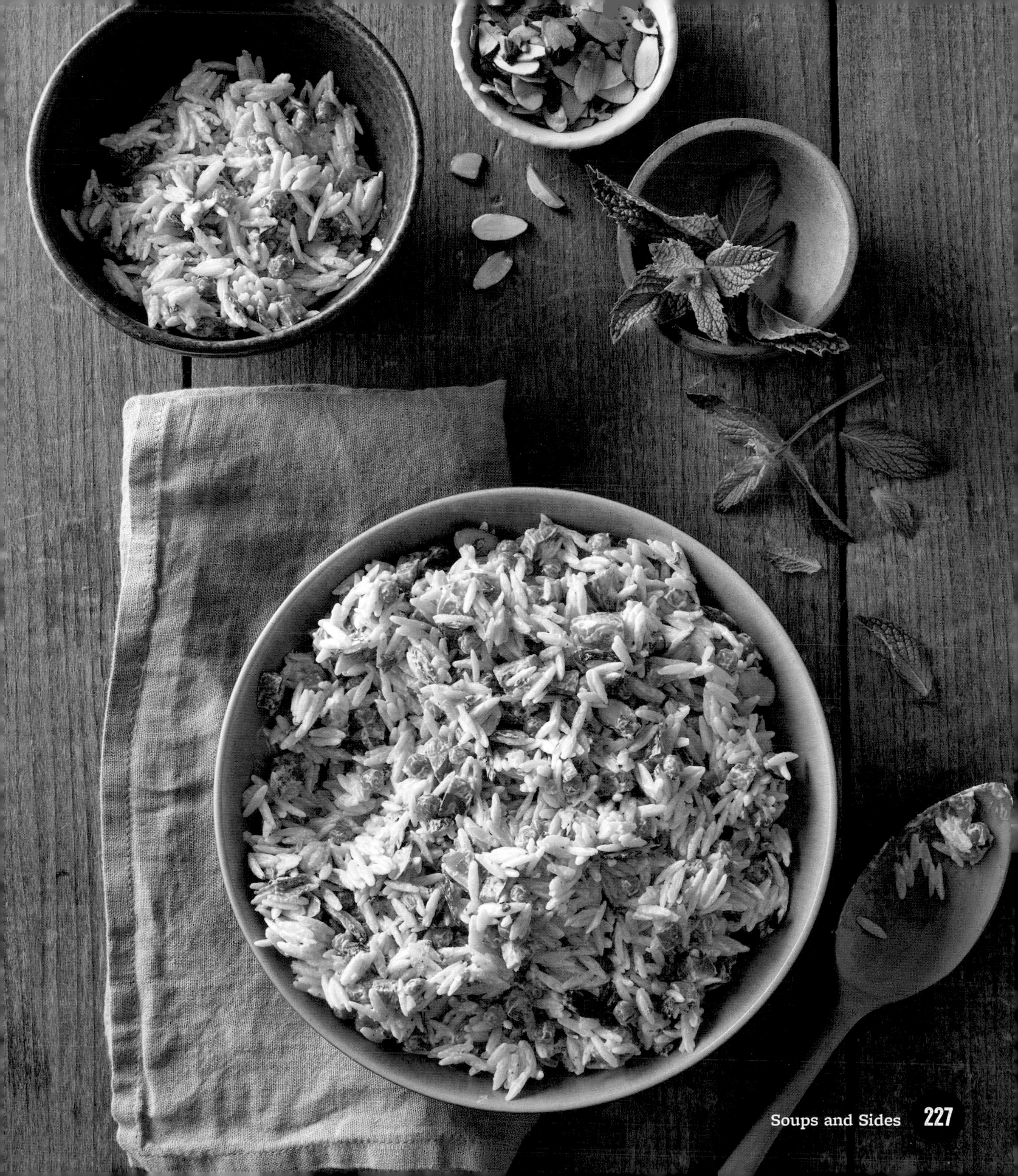

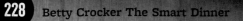

FRUITED TABBOULEH
WITH WALNUTS AND FETA

10 servings | Prep Time: 20 Minutes | Start to Finish: 3 Hours 20 Minutes

1 cup uncooked bulgur

1 cup boiling water

¼ cup orange juice

¼ cup olive oil

½ medium cucumber, peeled and seeded if desired, chopped (about 1 cup)

½ cup chopped red onion

½ cup sweetened dried cranberries

⅓ cup loosely packed fresh Italian (flat-leaf) parsley, finely chopped

⅓ cup loosely packed fresh mint leaves, finely chopped

1 tablespoon grated orange peel

½ teaspoon salt

1 orange, peeled, divided into sections and chopped

½ cup chopped walnuts, toasted*

½ cup crumbled feta cheese (2 oz)

1 Place bulgur in large heatproof bowl. Pour boiling water over bulgur; stir. Let stand about 1 hour or until water is absorbed.

2 Stir in orange juice, oil, cucumber, onion, cranberries, parsley, mint, orange peel and salt; toss well. Cover; refrigerate 2 to 3 hours or overnight until well chilled.

3 Just before serving, stir in chopped orange; sprinkle with walnuts and cheese.

*To toast walnuts, sprinkle in ungreased skillet. Cook over medium heat 5 to 7 minutes, stirring frequently until walnuts begin to brown, then stirring constantly until nuts are light brown.

1 Serving (½ Cup): Calories 200; Total Fat 11g (Saturated Fat 2.5g, Trans Fat 0g); Cholesterol 5mg; Sodium 210mg; Total Carbohydrate 21g (Dietary Fiber 4g); Protein 4g **Exchanges:** 1 Starch, ½ Other Carbohydrate, 2 Fat **Carbohydrate Choices:** 1½

USE IT UP What flavor-packed cheese do you have on hand?
You could experiment with crumbled chèvre (goat) cheese or blue cheese instead of the feta.

This is a kitchen-sweep salad. It uses up small amounts of several ingredients most likely in your fridge and pantry. Feel free to substitute whichever dried fruits and nuts you have on hand.

Use the remaining cucumber tossed in a green salad, sliced in a sandwich or cut into sticks for a quick snack with hummus.

RED HARVEST QUINOA

8 servings | Prep Time: 20 Minutes | Start to Finish: 40 Minutes

1 tablespoon butter

1 cup uncooked red quinoa, rinsed, well drained

½ cup coarsely chopped apple

⅓ cup chopped celery

¼ cup chopped red onion

1½ cups roasted vegetable stock (from 32-oz carton) or chicken broth

½ cup orange juice

½ cup sweetened dried cranberries or cherries

1 jar (1¾ oz) pine nuts (about ⅓ cup), toasted*

¼ cup shredded Parmesan cheese (1 oz)

¼ teaspoon salt

2 tablespoons finely chopped fresh parsley

1 In 2-quart saucepan, melt butter over medium heat. Cook quinoa, apple, celery and onion in butter 5 minutes, stirring occasionally.

2 Stir in stock and orange juice. Heat to boiling; reduce heat. Cover; simmer 15 to 20 minutes or until liquid is absorbed and quinoa is tender.

3 Fluff with fork; stir in cranberries, nuts, cheese and salt. Sprinkle with parsley.

*To toast pine nuts, sprinkle in ungreased skillet. Cook over medium heat 5 to 7 minutes, stirring frequently until pine nuts begin to brown, then stirring constantly until nuts are light brown.

1 Serving (½ **Cup**): Calories 190; Total Fat 7g (Saturated Fat 2g, Trans Fat 0g); Cholesterol 5mg; Sodium 190mg; Total Carbohydrate 25g (Dietary Fiber 3g); Protein 5g **Exchanges:** 1 Starch, ½ Other Carbohydrate, 1½ Fat **Carbohydrate Choices:** 1½

IN A SNAP
Quinoa, pronounced *KEEN-wah*, was a staple grain of the Incas of South America. It's very mild in flavor and loaded with nutrients. Before cooking, it needs to be thoroughly rinsed to remove its natural bitter coating. Place it in a fine-mesh strainer and hold under cold running water until the water runs clear.

USE IT UP
Chopped walnuts, pecans or slivered almonds can be substituted for the pine nuts.

FATTOUSH SALAD

4 servings | Prep Time: 25 Minutes | Start to Finish: 25 Minutes

¾ cup fresh lemon juice

¼ cup olive oil

¼ teaspoon salt

½ teaspoon pepper

4 cloves garlic,
finely chopped

3 cups thinly sliced
red cabbage

1 cup diced (peeled and
seeded, if desired)
cucumber

3 medium plum (Roma)
tomatoes, diced
(1¾ cups)

½ medium red bell pepper,
diced (½ cup)

½ cup chopped fresh
Italian (flat-leaf) parsley

¼ cup chopped fresh
mint leaves

2 pita (pocket) breads
(6 inch), toasted, torn
into 1-inch chunks

1 In large bowl, beat lemon juice, oil, salt, pepper and garlic
with whisk. Add remaining ingredients except pita; toss well
to combine.

2 Divide salad among 4 shallow bowls or plates. Top with
pita pieces.

1 Serving: Calories 250; Total Fat 14g (Saturated Fat 2g, Trans Fat 0g); Cholesterol 0mg;
Sodium 290mg; Total Carbohydrate 25g (Dietary Fiber 3g); Protein 4g **Exchanges:** 1 Other
Carbohydrate, 1½ Vegetable, 3 Fat **Carbohydrate Choices:** 1½

IN A SNAP As a convenient alternative to squeezing fresh lemons,
look for the bright yellow plastic bottles of frozen fresh lemon juice
(7.5 ounces) in the freezer aisle of your grocery store.

ROASTED VEGETABLES

10 servings | Prep Time: 15 Minutes | Start to Finish: 40 Minutes

3 tablespoons olive or vegetable oil

½ teaspoon salt

⅛ teaspoon pepper

1 clove garlic, finely chopped

1 cup baby-cut carrots

6 small red potatoes, cut into quarters

2 small onions, cut into ½-inch wedges

1 small red bell pepper, cut into 1-inch pieces

1 medium zucchini, cut lengthwise in half, then cut crosswise into 1-inch slices

1 cup grape tomatoes or cherry tomatoes

1 Heat oven to 450°F.

2 In small bowl, stir oil, salt, pepper and garlic until well mixed. In 15x10x1-inch pan, toss carrots, potatoes, onions, bell pepper and zucchini with oil mixture until coated.

3 Roast uncovered 20 minutes, stirring once.

4 Stir in tomatoes. Roast about 5 minutes longer or until vegetables are tender and starting to brown.

1 Serving: Calories 110; Total Fat 4.5g (Saturated Fat 0.5g, Trans Fat 0g); Cholesterol 0mg; Sodium 130mg; Total Carbohydrate 16g (Dietary Fiber 3g); Protein 2g **Exchanges:** ½ Starch, 1 Vegetable, 1 Fat **Carbohydrate Choices:** 1

IN A SNAP Pick packaged baby-cut carrots that are all about the same size so they cook evenly and are done at the same time.

LOADED SMASHED SWEET POTATOES

6 servings | Prep Time: 10 Minutes | Start to Finish: 1 Hour 30 Minutes

3 large sweet potatoes (about 1 lb each), cut into quarters

¼ cup olive oil

½ teaspoon salt

¼ teaspoon pepper

½ cup sour cream

1 cup shredded Cheddar cheese (4 oz)

4 slices thick-sliced bacon, crisply cooked, crumbled

1 tablespoon chopped fresh chives

1 Heat oven to 350°F. Spray 15x10x1-inch pan with cooking spray.

2 In large bowl, toss potatoes, oil, salt and pepper until well coated. Place in single layer in pan.

3 Bake 55 to 60 minutes or until potatoes are tender when pierced with knife. Using fork, slightly mash potatoes. Bake 15 to 20 minutes longer or until slightly crisp.

4 Top each potato quarter with sour cream, cheese, bacon and chives.

1 Serving: Calories 290; Total Fat 21g (Saturated Fat 8g, Trans Fat 0g); Cholesterol 35mg; Sodium 460mg; Total Carbohydrate 16g (Dietary Fiber 2g); Protein 8g **Exchanges:** 1 Starch, ½ Vegetable, ½ High-Fat Meat, 3½ Fat **Carbohydrate Choices:** 1

USE IT UP Don't have chives? Substitute sliced green onions or chopped fresh cilantro.

OVEN-FRIED VEGGIE FRITTERS
WITH RANCH-DILL SAUCE

4 servings | Prep Time: 25 Minutes | Start to Finish: 25 Minutes

FRITTERS

2 cups chopped seasoned cooked vegetables (such as broccoli, carrots, cauliflower, peas or corn), cooled

1 egg, slightly beaten

¾ cup panko crispy bread crumbs

2 tablespoons butter, melted

RANCH-DILL SAUCE

¼ cup ranch dressing

2 teaspoons chopped fresh dill weed

½ teaspoon grated lemon peel

1 teaspoon lemon juice

1 Heat oven to 400°F. Line cookie sheet with cooking parchment paper or spray with cooking spray.

2 In medium bowl, stir together vegetables and egg. Stir in bread crumbs.

3 For each fritter, tightly pack vegetable mixture into ¼-cup measuring cup, then place on cookie sheet 2 inches apart; flatten slightly. Brush with melted butter. Bake 15 to 18 minutes or until golden brown.

4 Meanwhile, in small bowl, mix sauce ingredients. Serve fritters hot with sauce.

1 Serving (2 Fritters and 1 Tablespoon Sauce): Calories 230; Total Fat 14g (Saturated Fat 5g, Trans Fat 0g); Cholesterol 65mg; Sodium 430mg; Total Carbohydrate 19g (Dietary Fiber 1g); Protein 5g **Exchanges:** 1 Starch, 1 Vegetable, 2½ Fat **Carbohydrate Choices:** 1

IN A SNAP One 12-ounce bag of frozen vegetables is enough for this recipe. Just cook, season as desired and cool them before chopping.

USE IT UP Offer family members their favorite condiments instead of making the Ranch-Dill Sauce. Salsa, tartar sauce, ketchup or barbecue sauce would all be great.

MAKE A MEAL For a kid-pleasing supper, serve these fritters with chicken fingers and a wedge of watermelon.

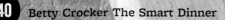

ROASTED CURRIED CAULIFLOWER

8 servings | Prep Time: 15 Minutes | Start to Finish: 35 Minutes

1 tablespoon olive oil

1 teaspoon curry powder

½ teaspoon coarse (kosher or sea) salt

¼ teaspoon freshly ground pepper

1 medium head cauliflower (2 lb), separated into florets

1½ teaspoons olive oil

¼ to ½ teaspoon grated lemon peel

2 teaspoons lemon juice

3 tablespoons dried currants

3 tablespoons sliced almonds, toasted*

1 tablespoon chopped fresh parsley

1 Heat oven to 450°F. Spray 15x10x1-inch pan with cooking spray.

2 In large bowl, mix 1 tablespoon oil, the curry powder, salt and pepper. Add cauliflower; toss to coat. Spread cauliflower in single layer in pan.

3 Roast uncovered 15 to 20 minutes, stirring once, until cauliflower is golden brown and just tender when pierced with fork.

4 In small bowl, mix 1½ teaspoons oil, the lemon peel and lemon juice. In serving bowl, stir together cauliflower, currants and almonds. Drizzle with oil mixture; toss gently. Sprinkle with parsley.

*To toast almonds, sprinkle in ungreased skillet. Cook over medium heat 5 to 7 minutes, stirring frequently until almonds begin to brown, then stirring constantly until nuts are light brown.

1 Serving: Calories 70; Total Fat 4g (Saturated Fat 0.5g, Trans Fat 0g); Cholesterol 0mg; Sodium 150mg; Total Carbohydrate 9g (Dietary Fiber 3g); Protein 3g **Exchanges:** 1 Vegetable, ½ Fat **Carbohydrate Choices:** 0

MAKE A MEAL Serve up this flavorful dish next time you've got plain chicken, beef or pork. The perky flavors make it a great sidekick.

CILANTRO-LIME COLESLAW

8 servings | Prep Time: 20 Minutes | Start to Finish: 20 Minutes

2 teaspoons grated lime peel

1 tablespoon lime juice

3 tablespoons dill pickle juice

3 tablespoons olive oil

½ teaspoon salt

6 cups finely chopped cabbage (green cabbage or mixture of green and red cabbage)

1 cup shredded carrot (1½ to 2 medium)

5 medium green onions, sliced (⅓ cup)

¼ cup chopped fresh cilantro

2 tablespoons chopped fresh carrot greens or parsley

1 In large bowl, mix lime peel, lime juice, pickle juice, oil and salt. Add remaining ingredients; toss well.

2 Serve immediately, or cover and refrigerate up to 24 hours. Stir before serving.

1 Serving (¾ **cup**): Calories 70; Total Fat 5g (Saturated Fat 0.5g, Trans Fat 0g); Cholesterol 0mg; Sodium 200mg; Total Carbohydrate 6g (Dietary Fiber 2g); Protein 1g **Exchanges:** 1 Vegetable, 1 Fat **Carbohydrate Choices:** ½

IN A SNAP
Save time by purchasing preshredded cabbage or coleslaw mix, sold in bags in the produce department of most grocery stores.

USE IT UP
If you have sweet pickle juice and like a little sweeter salad, substitute it for the dill pickle juice.

AVOCADO-CAESAR PANZANELLA SALAD

6 servings | Prep Time: 15 Minutes | Start to Finish: 45 Minutes

1 ripe avocado, pitted, peeled

3 tablespoons Caesar dressing

3 tablespoons water

2 tablespoons cider vinegar

4 cups torn romaine lettuce

2 cups cubes (1 inch) day-old French bread

1½ cups halved grape tomatoes or quartered cherry tomatoes

½ cup chopped green onions (8 medium)

3 hard-cooked eggs, chopped

¼ cup salted sunflower nuts

1 In small bowl, mash half of the avocado with fork. Add dressing, water and vinegar; stir until smooth.

2 In large bowl, toss lettuce and bread cubes with avocado dressing. Chop remaining half of avocado; sprinkle over lettuce. Top with tomatoes, onions, eggs and nuts. Cover; refrigerate 30 minutes. Toss just before serving.

1 Serving (1¼ Cups): Calories 200; Total Fat 13g (Saturated Fat 2.5g, Trans Fat 0g); Cholesterol 95mg; Sodium 210mg; Total Carbohydrate 14g (Dietary Fiber 4g); Protein 7g **Exchanges:** ½ Starch, ½ Other Carbohydrate, ½ Vegetable, ½ Medium-Fat Meat, 2 Fat **Carbohydrate Choices:** 1

IN A SNAP Purchase hard-cooked eggs from the dairy or salad bar section of the grocery store, or cook a few extra when making them for another recipe.

USE IT UP Toss in your favorite nuts instead of the sunflower nuts. Dry-roasted peanuts, pecans, walnuts or pine nuts would all add flair to the salad.

MAKE A MEAL Make a hearty main-dish salad by stirring in chopped cooked chicken or cooked shrimp.

Chapter Six

BREAKFAST
FOR
DINNER

SPINACH-MUSHROOM EGGS BENEDICT ENCHILADAS

6 servings | Prep Time: 25 Minutes | Start to Finish: 45 Minutes

1 tablespoon butter

2 cups sliced fresh mushrooms (about 5 oz)

6 eggs

⅓ cup water

¼ teaspoon salt

⅛ teaspoon pepper

¾ cup diced cooked ham

6 flour tortillas (6 inch)

1 package (1.25 oz) hollandaise sauce mix

1 cup water

¼ cup butter

3 cups fresh baby spinach leaves, chopped

1 tablespoon water

½ cup shredded Monterey Jack cheese (2 oz)

¼ cup chopped tomato

IN A SNAP We cook the eggs and mushrooms separately so the eggs retain their pretty yellow color, but you can stir the egg mixture into the mushrooms and scramble it all together.

1 Heat oven to 350°F. Spray 11x7-inch (2-quart) glass baking dish with cooking spray. In 10-inch nonstick skillet, melt 1 tablespoon butter over medium heat. Cook mushrooms in butter 3 minutes, stirring frequently; remove from skillet.

2 In medium bowl, beat eggs, ⅓ cup water, the salt and pepper with fork or whisk. Pour egg mixture into same skillet; sprinkle with ham. Cook over medium heat. As mixture begins to set on bottom and side, gently lift cooked portions so that thin, uncooked portion can flow to bottom. Avoid constant stirring. Cook 3 to 4 minutes or until eggs are thickened throughout but still moist. Remove from heat.

3 For each enchilada, spoon slightly less than ½ cup egg mixture down center of tortilla; top with about 2 tablespoons mushrooms. Roll up; place enchiladas, seam sides down, in baking dish. Cover; bake 15 minutes.

4 Meanwhile, make hollandaise sauce as directed on package using 1 cup water and ¼ cup butter.

5 Wipe out skillet. On high heat, toss spinach and 1 tablespoon water 1 to 2 minutes or until spinach is wilted.

6 Pour hollandaise sauce over enchiladas. Spoon spinach, cheese and tomatoes down center of enchiladas. Bake uncovered 5 minutes or until cheese is melted.

1 Serving: Calories 340; Total Fat 21g (Saturated Fat 10g, Trans Fat 1g); Cholesterol 230mg; Sodium 940mg; Total Carbohydrate 21g (Dietary Fiber 1g); Protein 16g **Exchanges:** 1 Starch, 1 Vegetable, ½ Lean Meat, 1 Medium-Fat Meat, 3 Fat **Carbohydrate Choices:** 1½

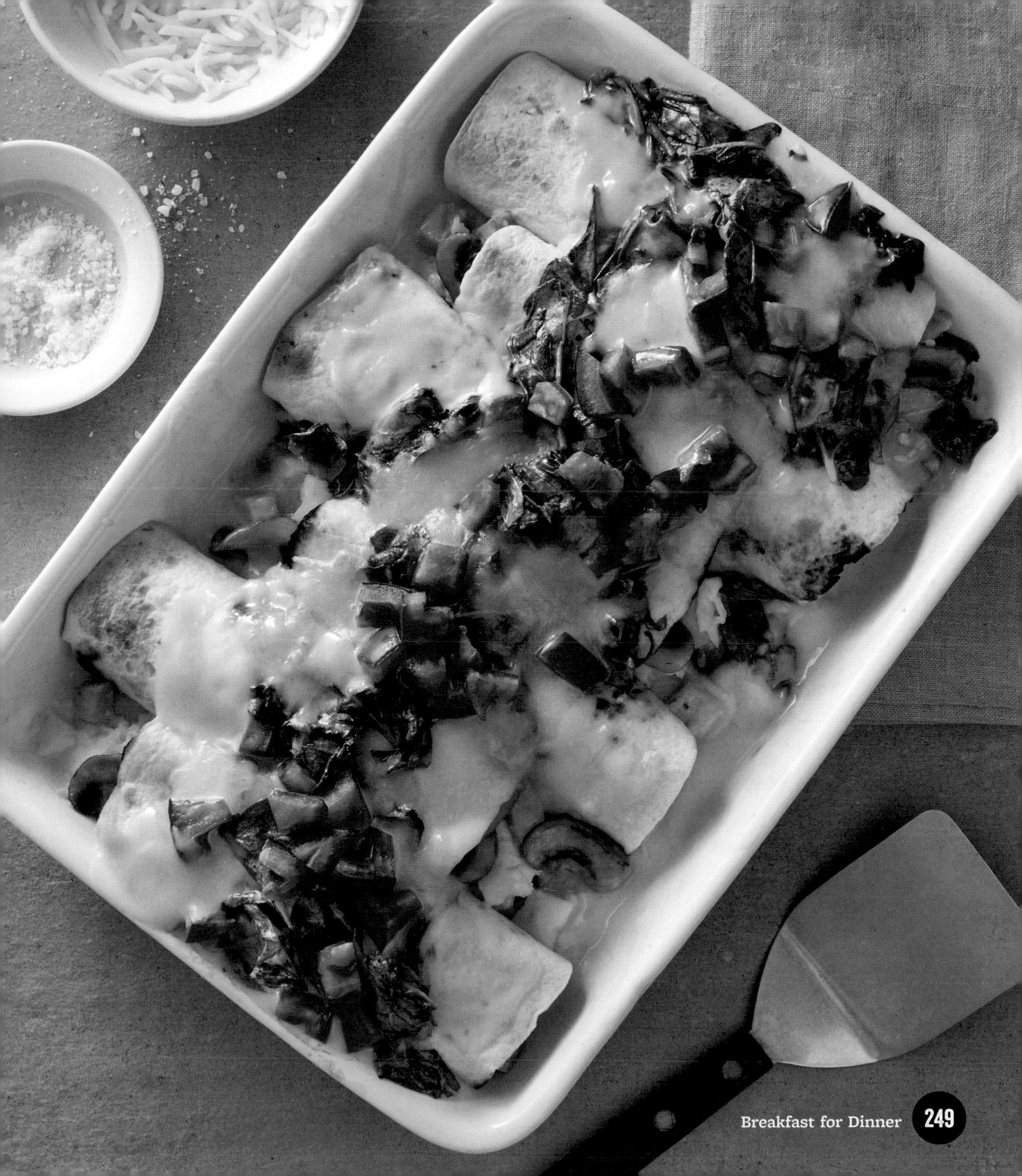

BACON, EGG AND BLACK BEAN QUESADILLAS

6 servings | Prep Time: 35 Minutes | Start to Finish: 35 Minutes

6 eggs

⅓ cup milk

½ teaspoon salt

¼ teaspoon pepper

1 cup fresh spinach leaves

6 flour tortillas (8 inch)

6 slices bacon, crisply cooked, crumbled

¾ cup black beans (from 15-oz can), drained, rinsed

¾ cup shredded sharp Cheddar cheese (3 oz)

Salsa and sour cream, if desired

1 Heat 8-inch nonstick skillet over medium heat. In medium bowl, beat eggs, milk, salt and pepper with whisk until well combined. Add eggs to skillet; cook about 3 minutes, stirring frequently, until eggs are nearly cooked. Add spinach; cook 2 to 3 minutes longer or until spinach is wilted and eggs are cooked through.

2 Spoon egg mixture onto half of each tortilla. Top each with 1 slice bacon, 2 tablespoons black beans and 2 tablespoons shredded cheese. Fold in half.

3 Heat 12-inch nonstick skillet over medium heat. Cook 2 quesadillas at a time 3 to 4 minutes, turning once, until golden brown and thoroughly heated. Cut into wedges. Serve with salsa and sour cream.

1 Serving: Calories 340; Total Fat 17g (Saturated Fat 7g, Trans Fat 1g); Cholesterol 210mg; Sodium 910mg; Total Carbohydrate 27g (Dietary Fiber 2g); Protein 18g **Exchanges:** 1 Starch, ½ Other Carbohydrate, ½ Vegetable, ½ Very Lean Meat, 1 Medium-Fat Meat, ½ High-Fat Meat, 1½ Fat **Carbohydrate Choices:** 2

USE IT UP Swap out the black beans with white beans or kidney beans. Or, spread a small amount of refried beans or refried black beans onto each tortilla before adding the eggs.

BREAKFAST BURGERS

6 burgers | Prep Time: 30 Minutes | Start to Finish: 30 Minutes

1 package (19.5 oz) refrigerated hot Italian turkey sausage links

1 medium onion, finely chopped (½ cup)

½ cup finely chopped red bell pepper

1½ cups frozen country-style shredded hash brown potatoes (from 30-oz bag), thawed

2 teaspoons vegetable oil

6 slices (1 oz each) pepper Jack cheese

6 English muffins, split, toasted

1 Remove casings from sausages; crumble sausages into medium bowl. Add onion, bell pepper and potatoes; mix well. Shape mixture into 6 patties, about 1 inch thick.

2 In 12-inch nonstick skillet, heat oil over medium heat. Cook patties in oil 13 to 16 minutes, turning once or twice, until thermometer inserted in center of patties reads 165°F.

3 Top each patty with cheese slice. Cover; let stand 1 minute until cheese is melted. Serve on toasted English muffins.

1 Burger: Calories 470; Total Fat 22g (Saturated Fat 9g, Trans Fat 0g); Cholesterol 80mg; Sodium 1010mg; Total Carbohydrate 40g (Dietary Fiber 3g); Protein 27g **Exchanges:** 1½ Starch, 1 Other Carbohydrate, ½ Vegetable, 2 Medium-Fat Meat, 1 High-Fat Meat, ½ Fat **Carbohydrate Choices:** 2½

IN A SNAP Refrigerate patties before cooking for easier handling.

USE IT UP Mild turkey sausage or pork sausage can be substituted for the hot turkey sausage.

OPEN-FACE SCRAMBLED EGG SANDWICHES

4 servings | Prep Time: 20 Minutes | Start to Finish: 20 Minutes

10 eggs

2 tablespoons milk

2 tablespoons butter

5 oz Canadian bacon, finely chopped (about 1 cup)

2 cups lightly packed fresh baby spinach leaves

4 oz Brie cheese, rind removed, cut into ½-inch pieces

4 English muffins, split, toasted

1 In large bowl, beat eggs and milk with fork or whisk. Set aside.

2 In 12-inch nonstick skillet, melt butter over medium heat. Cook bacon and spinach in butter 1 minute, stirring constantly, just until spinach begins to wilt.

3 Pour egg mixture over spinach mixture; top with cheese. Cook 3 to 5 minutes, stirring occasionally, until eggs are set but slightly moist. Spoon ½ cup egg mixture onto each muffin half.

1 Serving: Calories 520; Total Fat 30g (Saturated Fat 14g, Trans Fat 0g); Cholesterol 525mg; Sodium 1090mg; Total Carbohydrate 28g (Dietary Fiber 2g); Protein 34g **Exchanges:** 2 Starch, 1 Very Lean Meat, 3 Medium-Fat Meat, 2½ Fat **Carbohydrate Choices:** 2

USE IT UP No English muffins? No problem! Just serve the egg mixture atop slices of toasted wheat bread or your favorite bread.

MAKE A MEAL Bulk up the sandwiches by topping them with chopped tomatoes. Add some fruit and dinner is done!

BACON-AND-EGG PANCAKE TACOS

6 servings | Prep Time: 45 Minutes | Start to Finish: 45 Minutes

EGGS

- 6 eggs
- ⅓ cup milk
- 1 tablespoon butter

PANCAKES

- 2 cups Original Bisquick mix
- 1 cup milk
- 2 eggs
- ¼ cup sliced green onions (4 medium)

TOPPINGS

- ¾ cup shredded Cheddar cheese (3 oz)
- ⅓ cup crumbled crisply cooked bacon
- ¾ cup pico de gallo salsa
- ⅓ cup diced avocado
- Chopped fresh cilantro and additional sliced green onions, if desired

1 In medium bowl, beat 6 eggs and ⅓ cup milk with whisk until well combined. In 10-inch nonstick skillet, melt butter over medium heat. Add egg mixture; cook 3 to 4 minutes, stirring occasionally, until eggs are thickened throughout but still moist and creamy. Cover to keep warm.

2 Heat nonstick griddle or skillet over medium-high heat (375°F); brush lightly with vegetable oil if necessary. In medium bowl, beat Bisquick mix, 1 cup milk and 2 eggs with whisk until well combined. Stir in ¼ cup onions.

3 For each pancake, pour slightly less than ¼ cup batter onto hot griddle. Cook until edges are dry and bubbles begin to form on top. Turn; cook other side until golden brown. Keep warm in 200°F oven until serving time.

4 Spoon 2 heaping tablespoons scrambled eggs onto center of each pancake; top each with 1 tablespoon cheese, 1 heaping teaspoon bacon, 1 tablespoon salsa and 1 heaping teaspoon avocado. Top with cilantro and additional onions.
Fold up sides of pancake to eat.

1 Serving (2 Tacos): Calories 400; Total Fat 21g (Saturated Fat 8g, Trans Fat 0g); Cholesterol 275mg; Sodium 770mg; Total Carbohydrate 34g (Dietary Fiber 1g); Protein 18g **Exchanges:** 1 Starch, 1 Other Carbohydrate, 1½ Medium-Fat Meat, ½ High-Fat Meat, 2 Fat **Carbohydrate Choices:** 2

IN A SNAP Cooking and crumbling the bacon ahead of time means you'll have everything ready when you want to cook. Or, buy precooked bacon at the grocery store.

Make these tacos quickly by investing in a taco holder to serve them up, or serve them open face.

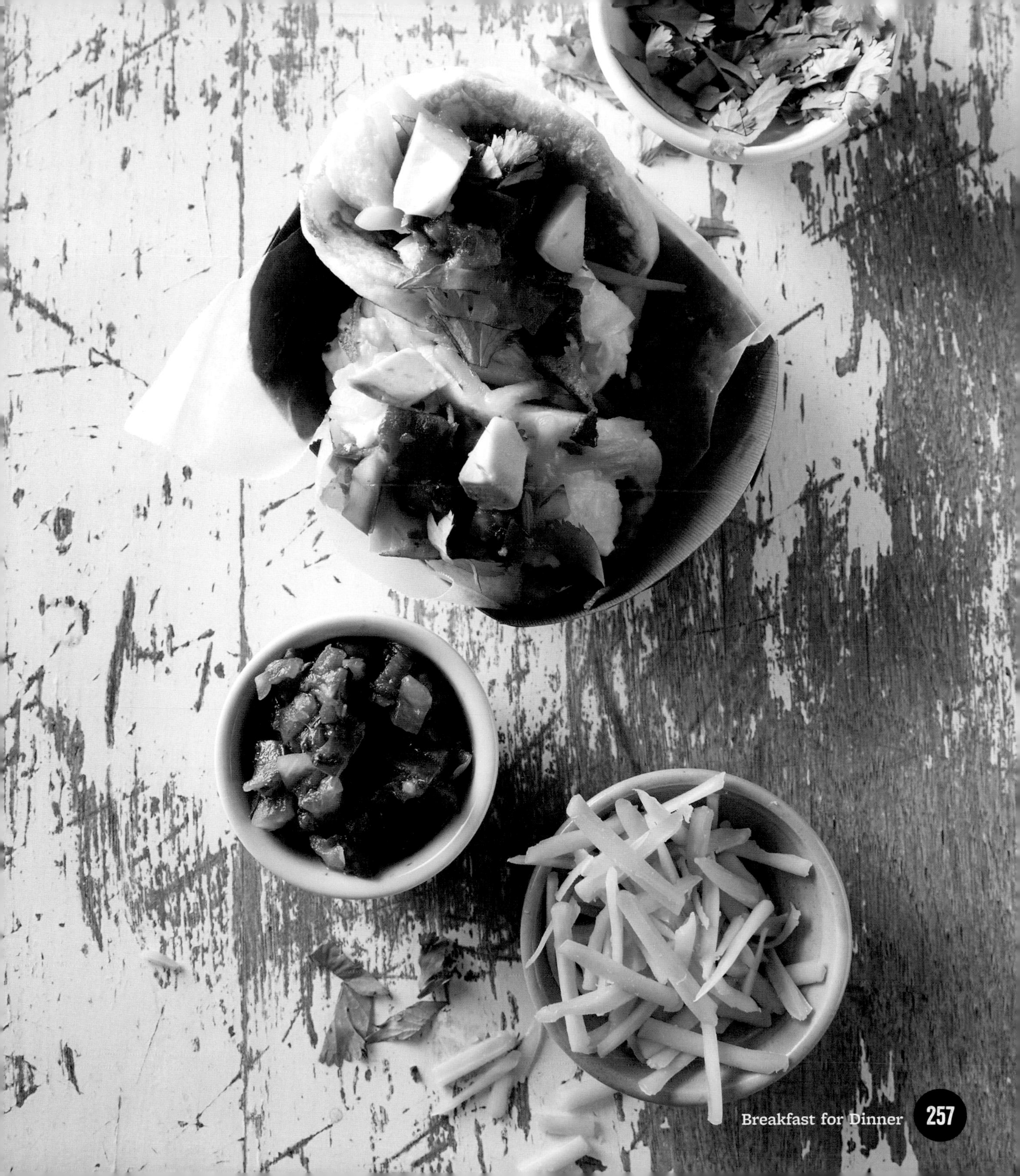

VEGGIE PANCAKES

4 servings | Prep Time: 30 Minutes | Start to Finish: 30 Minutes

2   tablespoons butter

2   **medium carrots,
    shredded** (1½ cups)

2   **medium stalks celery,
    chopped** (1 cup)

1   **medium red bell pepper,
    chopped** (1 cup)

1   **medium yellow onion,
    chopped** (½ cup)

2   **cups fresh baby spinach
    leaves, chopped**

1   cup Original
    Bisquick mix

2   eggs

¾   teaspoon salt

¼   teaspoon pepper

1   cup tomato pasta sauce,
    warmed

1 In 12-inch nonstick skillet, melt butter over medium-high heat. Cook carrots, celery, bell pepper and onion in butter 2 to 3 minutes, stirring frequently, until crisp-tender. Add spinach; cook 1 to 2 minutes, stirring constantly, until wilted. Cool slightly.

2 In medium bowl, stir Bisquick mix and eggs. Add vegetables, salt and pepper; stir well.

3 Heat same skillet over medium heat. For each pancake, pour ¼ cup batter into skillet; flatten slightly with spatula. Cook 3 to 4 minutes, turning once, until golden brown. Serve pancakes with pasta sauce.

1 Serving (3 Pancakes): Calories 300; Total Fat 15g (Saturated Fat 7g, Trans Fat 0g); Cholesterol 110mg; Sodium 1170mg; Total Carbohydrate 34g (Dietary Fiber 4g); Protein 8g **Exchanges:** ½ Starch, 1½ Other Carbohydrate, 1½ Vegetable, ½ Medium-Fat Meat, 2½ Fat **Carbohydrate Choices:** 2

USE IT UP
Any leftover cooked veggies would be great in the pancakes. Chop them so they are fairly small, then heat up instead of cooking in the first step; continue as directed.

What condiments do you have in your fridge that need some love? The pancakes would also be good with salsa, marinara, barbecue sauce, cheese sauce or dip.

READY-TO-EAT CEREAL

- **Coat Ice Cream** Make ice cream balls or pops by rolling scoops of ice cream in cereal and inserting a craft stick or straw. Place in a single layer on a parchment-lined tray and freeze until firm. Or roll the sides of ice cream sandwiches in cereal and freeze as directed for the ice cream balls.

- **Make a Mix** Use up leftover bits of cereal by making an on-the-go trail mix. Mix and match different cereals and add other snacking delights such as small pretzels, marshmallows, chocolate chips, small crackers or dried fruit. Pour into snack- or quart-size resealable food-storage plastic bags and take along with you when heading out.

- **Sprinkle It** Ditch the syrup on pancakes and instead top with whipped cream and sprinkle with cereal. It's quick, crunchy and fun.

- **Parfait It** Layer yogurt or pudding with cereal and fruit for a fun take on breakfast or dessert.

- **Coat Bananas** Peel bananas, spread them with creamy peanut butter, melted chocolate or hazelnut spread and roll in your favorite cereal; push a craft stick into the bottom end. (Be sure to refrigerate the chocolate-coated bananas on a parchment-lined cookie sheet until the chocolate sets up.)

- **Decorate Cake** Sprinkle leftover cereal on top of cake or cupcakes immediately after frosting them (so the cereal sticks to the frosting). You can also crush or grind crunchy cereal and use it like decorating sugar on cake or cupcakes.

FRUIT

- **Make Dressing** Puree enough peeled and pitted cut-up fruit in a food processor to equal about ¼ cup. Whisk in ¼ cup of your favorite vinegar, ⅓ to ½ cup olive or vegetable oil, 1 teaspoon sugar or honey and ¼ teaspoon each salt and pepper. Or use ¼ cup citrus juice (grapefruit or orange) instead of the pureed fruit and vinegar.

- **Pop It** Make fro-yo pops by stirring bite-size pieces of fruit into yogurt in paper cups or popsicle molds. Freeze 30 minutes to an hour or until partially frozen; insert craft sticks into center of pops. Freeze 4 hours longer or until solid. Remove from cups or molds.

- **Toss It** Add bite-size pieces of fresh fruit to salad greens. Top with blue cheese crumbles and nuts for a deliciously different salad.

- **Fold It In** Add finely chopped (well-drained and patted dry with paper towels, if juicy) fruit or blueberries to muffin, pancake or waffle batter during the last few strokes of mixing the batter. Do not over mix.

- **Freeze It** Place bite-size pieces of fruit in fruit juice or water in ice cube trays to add to beverages. If you like, add fresh herbs, submerging them completely in the juice for a unique flavor twist.

HAM AND SWISS WAFFLES

7 servings | Prep Time: 25 Minutes | Start to Finish: 25 Minutes

2 cups Original Bisquick mix

1⅓ cups milk

2 tablespoons vegetable oil

1 egg

1 cup diced cooked ham

1 cup shredded Swiss cheese (4 oz)

⅓ cup sour cream

Chopped fresh chives, if desired

1 Heat waffle maker; lightly brush with vegetable oil if necessary. In medium bowl, stir Bisquick mix, milk, oil and egg until blended. Stir in ham and cheese.

2 Pour batter onto center of hot waffle maker. Use about ½ cup, but waffle makers vary in size, so check manufacturer's directions for recommended amount. Close lid of waffle maker. Bake according to manufacturer's directions until steaming stops and waffle is golden brown; carefully remove waffle. Repeat with remaining batter. Keep waffles warm in a 200°F oven until you've finished making all the waffles. Top each waffle with a dollop of sour cream; sprinkle with chives.

1 Serving: Calories 310; Total Fat 16g (Saturated Fat 6g, Trans Fat 0g); Cholesterol 60mg; Sodium 680mg; Total Carbohydrate 27g (Dietary Fiber 0g); Protein 13g **Exchanges:** 1 Starch, 1 Other Carbohydrate, 1 Lean Meat, ½ High-Fat Meat, 1½ Fat **Carbohydrate Choices:** 2

MAKE A MEAL
These are great as a portable "sandwich" for those nights dinner is on-the-go.

For heartier appetites, serve these with fried eggs—yum!

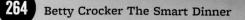

SPICY CORNMEAL WAFFLES

6 servings | Prep Time: 25 Minutes | Start to Finish: 35 Minutes

WAFFLES

- 2 cups Original Bisquick mix
- ¼ cup yellow cornmeal
- 1½ cups buttermilk
- 2 tablespoons vegetable oil
- 1 egg
- 2 teaspoons chili powder
- 1 teaspoon ground cumin
- ¾ cup shredded Cheddar cheese (3 oz)

TOPPINGS

- 1½ cups pico de gallo salsa
- 1 large avocado, pitted, peeled, thinly sliced (18 slices)
- ½ cup chopped fresh cilantro
- ½ cup crumbled queso fresco cheese (2 oz)

1 In medium bowl, stir Bisquick mix, cornmeal, buttermilk, oil, egg, chili powder and cumin until blended. Stir in Cheddar cheese. Let stand 10 minutes, allowing cornmeal to soften.

2 Heat waffle maker; lightly brush with vegetable oil if necessary. Pour batter onto center of hot waffle maker. Use about ½ cup, but waffle makers vary in size, so check manufacturer's directions for recommended amount. Close lid of waffle maker. Bake according to manufacturer's directions or until steaming stops and waffle is golden brown; carefully remove waffle. Repeat with remaining batter. Keep waffles warm in a 200°F oven until you've finished making all the waffles.

3 Top each waffle with ¼ cup salsa, 3 slices avocado, 1 heaping tablespoon cilantro and 1 heaping tablespoon queso fresco.

1 Serving: Calories 400; Total Fat 21g (Saturated Fat 7g, Trans Fat 0g); Cholesterol 55mg; Sodium 840mg; Total Carbohydrate 41g (Dietary Fiber 3g); Protein 13g **Exchanges:** 1 Starch, 1½ Other Carbohydrate, ½ Vegetable, 1 High-Fat Meat, 2½ Fat **Carbohydrate Choices:** 3

USE IT UP
Have some Sriracha sauce on hand? Add a few drops, or to taste, to the batter to increase the spicy heat.

CORN, CHEDDAR AND TOMATO QUICHE

6 servings | Prep Time: 10 Minutes | Start to Finish: 55 Minutes

1   cup milk

4   eggs or 1 cup fat-free
     egg product

¼   cup chopped
     fresh cilantro

½   teaspoon chili powder

¼   teaspoon salt

¼   teaspoon pepper

1   cup frozen corn, thawed

¾   cup shredded reduced-
     fat Cheddar cheese
     (3 oz)

1   medium tomato, seeded,
     chopped (¾ cup)

1 Heat oven to 350°F. Spray 9-inch glass pie plate with cooking spray.

2 In medium bowl, beat milk, eggs, cilantro, chili powder, salt and pepper with fork or whisk until blended. Stir in corn, cheese and tomato. Pour into pie plate.

3 Bake 30 to 35 minutes or until knife inserted in center comes out clean. Let stand 10 minutes before cutting.

1 Serving: Calories 140; Total Fat 7g (Saturated Fat 3.5g, Trans Fat 0g); Cholesterol 140mg; Sodium 260mg; Total Carbohydrate 9g (Dietary Fiber 1g); Protein 10g **Exchanges:** ½ Other Carbohydrate, ½ Lean Meat, 1 Medium-Fat Meat **Carbohydrate Choices:** ½

USE IT UP Add a cup of leftover cooked veggies or canned black beans instead of the corn.

MAKE A MEAL Partner this delicious quiche with a mixed-greens salad dressed with your favorite vinaigrette.

CHEESY BROCCOLI FRITTATA

4 servings | Prep Time: 15 Minutes | Start to Finish: 25 Minutes

4   eggs

¼   cup milk

1   tablespoon chopped fresh parsley

¼   teaspoon salt

¼   teaspoon red pepper sauce

1   tablespoon vegetable oil

1   cup broccoli florets

1   medium carrot, shredded (½ cup)

1   medium onion, chopped (½ cup)

1   cup shredded Cheddar cheese (4 oz)

1   tablespoon grated Parmesan cheese

1 In medium bowl, beat eggs, milk, parsley, salt and pepper sauce with whisk until well blended; set aside.

2 In 10-inch nonstick skillet, heat oil over medium-high heat. Cook broccoli, carrot and onion in oil about 5 minutes, stirring frequently, until vegetables are crisp-tender.

3 Pour egg mixture over vegetables. Sprinkle with cheeses; reduce heat to low. Cover; cook about 10 minutes or until eggs are set in center. Cut into wedges to serve.

1 Serving: Calories 260; Total Fat 19g (Saturated Fat 8g, Trans Fat 0g); Cholesterol 220mg; Sodium 450mg; Total Carbohydrate 7g (Dietary Fiber 1g); Protein 15g **Exchanges:** ½ Other Carbohydrate, 1 Medium-Fat Meat, 1 High-Fat Meat, 1 Fat **Carbohydrate Choices:** ½

IN A SNAP Substitute 1½ cups broccoli slaw mix for the broccoli florets and carrot.

HASH BROWN BREAKFAST CASSEROLE

8 servings | Prep Time: 20 Minutes | Start to Finish: 1 Hour 20 Minutes

1 lb bulk spicy
 pork sausage

1 small onion, chopped
 (⅓ cup)

2½ cups frozen
 Southern-style diced
 hash brown potatoes
 (from 32-oz bag)

5 eggs

1¾ cups milk

1 cup Original
 Bisquick mix

¼ teaspoon salt

¼ teaspoon pepper

2 cups shredded sharp
 Cheddar cheese (8 oz)

 Picante sauce or green
 pepper sauce, if desired

 Sour cream, if desired

1 Heat oven to 350°F. Spray 13x9-inch (3-quart) glass baking dish with cooking spray. In 10-inch nonstick skillet, cook sausage and onion over medium-high heat 5 minutes, stirring occasionally. Add potatoes. Cook 5 to 7 minutes, stirring occasionally, until sausage is no longer pink and potatoes are lightly browned. Drain mixture on paper towels; spoon into baking dish.

2 In medium bowl, stir eggs, milk, Bisquick mix, salt and pepper with fork or whisk until blended. Stir in cheese. Pour over sausage mixture; stir well.

3 Cover casserole with foil; bake 45 minutes. Uncover and bake 5 to 10 minutes longer or until knife inserted in center comes out clean. Let stand 5 minutes. Serve with picante sauce and sour cream.

1 Serving: Calories 451; Total Fat 30g (Saturated Fat 13g, Trans Fat 0g); Cholesterol 0g; Sodium 895mg; Total Carbohydrate 22g (Dietary Fiber 1g); Protein 22g **Exchanges:** 1½ Starch, 2½ High-Fat Meat, 2 Fat **Carbohydrate Choices:** 1½

MAKE AHEAD In Step 2, refrigerate covered casserole up to 24 hours. In Step 3, increase second bake time to 10 to 15 minutes.

HUEVOS RANCHEROS TARTS

4 servings | Prep Time: 40 Minutes | Start to Finish: 40 Minutes

1 can (8 oz) refrigerated crescent dinner rolls

½ teaspoon dried oregano leaves

½ teaspoon chipotle chili pepper powder

¼ teaspoon coarse (kosher or sea) salt

4 eggs

1 can (14.5 oz) fire roasted tomatoes, undrained

1 small onion, chopped (⅓ cup)

1 clove garlic, peeled

4 tablespoons chopped fresh cilantro

1 can (15 oz) black beans, drained, rinsed

½ cup crumbled queso fresco cheese (2 oz)

Avocado slices, if desired

USE IT UP Queso fresco is a creamy, white Mexican cheese that crumbles easily and can be found in the refrigerated cheese section of most supermarkets. Shredded Monterey Jack or Cheddar cheese can be substituted.

1 Heat oven to 375°F. Line cookie sheet with cooking parchment paper. Separate dough into 4 rectangles on cookie sheet. Firmly press perforations to seal. For each rectangle, roll edges toward center to form 3½-inch-diameter round with ½-inch rim; press rim firmly to seal.

2 In small bowl, mix oregano, ¼ teaspoon of the chili powder and the salt. Sprinkle over dough rounds. Break 1 egg in center of each dough round (egg may run over slightly). Bake 16 to 18 minutes or until egg whites and yolks are firm, not runny.

3 Meanwhile, in blender, place tomatoes, onion, garlic, 2 tablespoons of the cilantro and the remaining ¼ teaspoon chili powder. Cover; blend until smooth. In 2-quart saucepan, heat tomato mixture over medium-high heat 4 to 5 minutes or until hot.

4 Remove ¾ cup tomato mixture to small bowl; cover to keep warm. Add beans to remaining mixture in saucepan. Cook over medium-high heat 5 minutes, stirring frequently and mashing beans slightly with back of spoon, until slightly thickened.

5 Place egg tarts on individual plates; spoon about ⅓ cup bean mixture alongside each tart. Top evenly with cheese and remaining 2 tablespoons cilantro. Serve with avocado and reserved tomato mixture.

1 Serving: Calories 450; Total Fat 22g (Saturated Fat 9g, Trans Fat 0g); Cholesterol 195mg; Sodium 1330mg; Total Carbohydrate 45g (Dietary Fiber 5g); Protein 18g **Exchanges:** 2½ Starch, ½ Other Carbohydrate, 1 Very Lean Meat, ½ Medium-Fat Meat, 3½ Fat **Carbohydrate Choices:** 3

IN A SNAP Short on time? Serve the egg tarts with purchased salsa and refried beans or refried black beans.

BREAKFAST PIZZA

6 servings | Prep Time: 20 Minutes | Start to Finish: 35 Minutes

1 can refrigerated artisan pizza crust with whole grain

½ cup coarsely chopped bacon

6 eggs, beaten

4 oz (half of 8-oz package) cream cheese, cut into small pieces

2 cups shredded pepper Jack cheese (8 oz)

½ cup sliced red bell pepper

¼ cup thinly sliced red onion

Chopped fresh cilantro, if desired

Salsa, if desired

1 Heat oven to 425°F (400°F for dark or nonstick pan). Spray 14-inch pizza pan with cooking spray. Unroll dough on pan; starting at center, press out dough to edge of pan. Bake about 8 minutes or until crust edge begins to set.

2 Meanwhile, in 10-inch skillet, cook bacon 4 to 6 minutes over medium-high heat, stirring frequently, just until crisp. Drain bacon on paper towels. Reserve 1 teaspoon drippings in skillet. Cook eggs in bacon drippings 2 to 3 minutes, stirring frequently, until firm but still moist.

3 Spoon and spread eggs over partially baked crust. Top with cream cheese, pepper Jack cheese, bell pepper, onion and bacon.

4 Bake 9 to 13 minutes or until crust is golden brown and cheese is melted. Sprinkle with cilantro. Cut into wedges; serve with salsa.

1 Serving: Calories 490; Total Fat 29g (Saturated Fat 14g, Trans Fat 0g); Cholesterol 245mg; Sodium 760mg; Total Carbohydrate 33g (Dietary Fiber 2g); Protein 23g **Exchanges:** 2 Starch, 2½ Medium-Fat Meat, 3 Fat
Carbohydrate Choices: 2

IN A SNAP Don't have a pizza pan? Make a rectangular pizza in a 15x10x1-inch pan and cut into squares.

USE IT UP You can use flavored cream cheese if you like . . . and Monterey Jack or Cheddar cheese instead of pepper Jack.

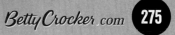

METRIC CONVERSION GUIDE

VOLUME

U.S. UNITS	CANADIAN METRIC	AUSTRALIAN METRIC
¼ teaspoon	1 mL	1 ml
½ teaspoon	2 mL	2 ml
1 teaspoon	5 mL	5 ml
1 tablespoon	15 mL	20 ml
¼ cup	50 mL	60 ml
cup	75 mL	80 ml
½ cup	125 mL	125 ml
cup	150 mL	170 ml
¾ cup	175 mL	190 ml
1 cup	250 mL	250 ml
1 quart	1 liter	1 liter
1½ quarts	1.5 liters	1.5 liters
2 quarts	2 liters	2 liters
2½ quarts	2.5 liters	2.5 liters
3 quarts	3 liters	3 liters
4 quarts	4 liters	4 liters

WEIGHT

U.S. UNITS	CANADIAN METRIC	AUSTRALIAN METRIC
1 ounce	30 grams	30 grams
2 ounces	55 grams	60 grams
3 ounces	85 grams	90 grams
4 ounces (¼ pound)	115 grams	125 grams
8 ounces (½ pound)	225 grams	225 grams
16 ounces (1 pound)	455 grams	500 grams
1 pound	455 grams	0.5 kilogram

MEASUREMENTS

INCHES	CENTIMETERS
1	2.5
2	5.0
3	7.5
4	10.0
5	12.5
6	15.0
7	17.5
8	20.5
9	23.0
10	25.5
11	28.0
12	30.5
13	33.0

TEMPERATURES

FAHRENHEIT	CELSIUS
32°	0°
212°	100°
250°	120°
275°	140°
300°	150°
325°	160°
350°	180°
375°	190°
400°	200°
425°	220°
450°	230°
475°	240°
500°	260°

Note: The recipes in this cookbook have not been developed or tested using metric measures. When converting recipes to metric, some variations in quality may be noted.

INDEX

Page numbers in *italics* indicate illustrations

A

Aioli, Red Pepper, Cod Cakes with, *114, 115*

Alfredo, Easy Chicken, with Biscuits, *22, 22*

Almond-Crusted Cod with Veggies, *122, 123*

Amazing Bacon-Cheeseburger Tacos, *80, 81*

Angel Hair Pasta, in Asian Beef Noodle Bowls, 78, *79*

Artichokes
  Chicken with Tomatoes and, *45, 45*
  cooking chart, 10
  Parmesan-Chicken Ziti with Spinach and, *30, 31*

Asian Beef Noodle Bowls, 78, *79*

Asian Salmon Sheet Pan Dinner, *134, 135*

Asparagus, cooking chart, 10

Asparagus, Quinoa Pilaf with Salmon and, *128, 129*

Avocado
  Bacon, and Tomato Grilled Cheese, 106, *107*
  -Caesar Panzanella Salad, *244, 245*
  Guacamole, Chunky, Salmon Tacos with, *130, 131*
  -Onion Slaw, Fajita Pulled-Pork Wraps with, *90, 91*

B

Bacon
  -Cheeseburger Tacos, Amazing, *80, 81*
  and Chicken Pasta Bake, Cheesy No-Boil, *54, 55*
  Egg and Black Bean Quesadillas, *250, 251*
  Grilled Cheese Sandwiches, Beer-Battered, *108, 109*
  Grilled Cheese, Tomato, Avocado and, 106, *107*
  Pancake Tacos, -and-Egg, *256, 257*
  Pizza, Breakfast, *274, 275*
  Pork Loin Sheet Pan Dinner, Roasted, *92, 93*
  Potato Soup, Loaded, *200, 201*
  Sweet Potatoes, Loaded Smashed, *236, 237*

Baked Greek Tilapia, 126

Baked Lemon-Pepper Fish, *118, 119*

Bananas, cereal-coated, 260

Barbecue
  Beef Biscuit Stacks, BBQ, *82, 83*
  Chicken–Cheddar Sliders, BBQ Chipotle, *46, 47*
  Sauce, Fruity BBQ, 120
  Sauce, Korean, 85

Barley, in Three-Grain Salad, *220, 221*

BBQ Beef Biscuit Stacks, *82, 83*

BBQ Chipotle Chicken–Cheddar Sliders, *46, 47*

Bean(s). *See also* Black Bean(s); Chick Pea(s)
  Black-Eyed Pea and Sausage Soup, *204, 205*
  and Brats, Beer-Glazed, *190, 191*
  canned, way to use, 87
  Chili, Bourbon, *218, 219*
  Edamame Corn Chowder, *202, 203*
  fresh, cooking chart, 10
  and Greens Soup, Smoky, *210, 211*
  Red, and Rice Casserole, Chipotle, *193, 193*
  White, and Spinach Pizza, *156, 157*

Beef
  Biscuit Stacks, BBQ, *82, 83*
  Burger, Cheddar, and Veggie Packets, Grilled, *74, 75*
  Burgers, Greek, with Tzatziki Sauce, *72, 73*
  Cheeseburger-Bacon Tacos, Amazing, *80, 81*

Recipe Testing and Calculating Nutrition Information

RECIPE TESTING:

- Large eggs and 2% milk were used unless otherwise indicated.

- No fat-free, low-fat, low-sodium or lite products were used unless indicated.

- No nonstick cookware and bakeware were used unless otherwise indicated. No dark-colored, black or insulated bakeware was used.

- When a pan is specified, a metal pan was used; a baking dish or pie plate means ovenproof glass was used.

- An electric hand mixer was used for mixing only when mixer speeds are specified.

CALCULATING NUTRITION:

- The first ingredient was used wherever a choice is given, such as ⅓ cup sour cream or plain yogurt.

- The first amount was used wherever a range is given, such as 3- to 3½-pound whole chicken.

- The first serving number was used wherever a range is given, such as 4 to 6 servings.

- "If desired" ingredients were not included.

- Only the amount of a marinade or frying oil that is absorbed was included.

- Diabetic exchanges are not calculated in recipes containing uncooked alcohol due to its effect on blood sugar levels.

Beef, *continued*
    Chili, Bourbon, *218, 219*
    Chili, Texas, *216, 217*
    and Kasha Mexicana, *66, 66*
    Noodle Bowls, Asian, *78, 79*
    Pasta Bolognese, *68, 69*
    Sloppy Joes, Steakhouse, *70, 71*
    Steak Bibimbap, *84, 85*
Beefed-Up Grilled Cheese, 9
Beer
    -Battered Grilled Cheese
        Sandwiches, *108, 109*
    in BBQ Beef Biscuit Stacks, *82, 83*
    Bread Crust, Roasted Root Veggie
        Pizza with, *154, 155*
    -Glazed Brats and Beans, *190, 191*
Beets
    cooking chart, 10
    Root Veggie Pizza, Roasted, with
        Beer Bread Crust, *154, 155*
    Tabbouleh, Whole Beet, *166, 167*
Bell Peppers
    Cod, Almond-Crusted, with
        Veggies, *122, 123*
    cooking chart, 11
    Red Pepper Aioli, Cod Cakes with,
        114, 115
    Roasted Vegetables, *234, 235*
    Shrimp Burrito Bowls, Chili-Lime,
        Gluten-Free, *144, 145*
    Shrimp Paella, Easy, *150, 151*
    Steak Bibimbap, *84, 85*
    Vegetable-Cashew Noodle Bowls,
        172, 173
    Vegetable Curry with Couscous,
        176, 177
Bibimbap, Steak, *84, 85*
Biscuits
    BBQ Beef Biscuit Stacks, *82, 83*
    Cheese, 82
    Chicken Alfredo with, Easy, *22, 22*
Black Bean(s)
    Bacon and Egg Quesadillas, *250,
        251*
    Burritos, Homemade Takeout,
        52, 53
    –Cabbage Enchiladas, *164, 165*
    Chicken Enchilada Pasta, Cheesy,
        38, 39

Fried Rice, Cuban, 98, *99*
Huevos Rancheros Tarts, *272, 273*
Quinoa Salad–Stuffed Tomatoes,
    Gluten-Free, *168,* 168
Shrimp Burrito Bowls, Chili-Lime,
    Gluten-Free, *144, 145*
Black-Eyed Pea and Sausage Soup,
    204, 205
Blue Cheese Dipping Sauce, Buffalo
    Chicken Bites with, *44, 44*
Bolognese Pasta, *68, 69*
Bourbon Chili, *218, 219*
Bow-Ties with Broccoli Pesto, *170, 171*
Brats and Beans, Beer-Glazed, *190, 191*
Bratwurst and Vegetable Soup, *206,
    207*
Bread(s)
    Beer Bread Crust, Roasted Root
        Veggie Pizza with, *154, 155*
    Biscuits, Cheese, 82
    Cheesy Toast, 33
    Croutons, 67
    French Bread Taco Pizza, *76, 77*
    French Toast, 67
    Panzanella Salad, Avocado-Caesar,
        244, 245
    Pizza Pockets, Pineapple-Chicken,
        56, 57
    in Pot Pie Stew, Veggie, *186, 187*
    way to use, 67
    Zucchini Strata, Italian, *178, 179*
Bread Crumbs, 67
Breakfast Burgers, *252, 253*
Breakfast Pizza, *274, 275*
Broccoli
    cooking chart, 10
    Fettuccine with Chicken and
        Vegetables, *32,* 32
    Frittata, Cheesy, *268, 269*
    General Tso's Chicken, Easy, 48,
        49
    Pesto, Bow-Ties with, *170, 171*
    Salmon Sheet Pan Dinner, Asian,
        134, 135
Brown Sugar–Soy–Glazed Chicken
    Thighs, *26, 27*
Brussels Sprouts
    cooking chart, 10
    Pork Chop Skillet, Citrusy, *94, 95*

Pork Loin Sheet Pan Dinner,
    Roasted, *92, 93*
Buckwheat Groats, Beef and Kasha
    Mexicana, *66, 66*
Buffalo Chicken Bites with Blue
    Cheese Dipping Sauce, *44, 44*
Buffalo Chicken Soup, Cheesy, *198,
    199*
Buffalo Pasta Salad, 120
Buffalo Sauce, Quick, 120
Bulgur
    and Lentils, Mediterranean, *169, 169*
    Tabbouleh, Beet, Whole, *166, 167*
    Tabbouleh, Fruited, with Walnuts
        and Feta, *228, 229*
Burger(s)
    Breakfast, *252, 253*
    Cheddar, and Veggie Packets,
        Grilled, *74, 75*
    Greek, with Tzatziki Sauce, *72, 73*
Burrito Bowls, Shrimp, Chili-Lime,
    Gluten-Free, *144, 145*
Burritos, Homemade Takeout, *52, 53*

C

Cabbage. *See also* Red Cabbage
    –Black Bean Enchiladas, *164, 165*
    Coleslaw, Creamy, *82, 83*
    Coleslaw, Cilantro-Lime, *242, 243*
Caesar-Avocado Panzanella Salad,
    244, 245
Cajun Catfish, *121,* 121
Calzones, Spinach, Ricotta and
    Sausage, *100, 101*
Campanelle, in Creamy Pulled-Pork
    Pasta, *88, 89*
Carrots
    Beet Tabbouleh, Whole, *166, 167*
    Cheddar Burger and Veggie
        Packets, Grilled, *74, 75*
    cooking chart, 10
    Pancakes, Veggie, *258, 259*
    Roasted Vegetables, *234, 235*
    Steak Bibimbap, *84, 85*
    Vegetable Curry with Couscous,
        176, 177

Cashew-Vegetable Noodle Bowls, 172,
173
Casserole(s)
cracker crumb topping, 141
Hash Brown Breakfast, 270, 271
Red Beans and Rice, Chipotle, 193,
193
Spaghetti, Five-Vegetable, 182, 183
Catfish, Cajun, 121, 121
Cauliflower
cooking chart, 10
Pan-Roasted, Chicken with Orzo
and, 42, 43
Roasted Curried, 240, 241
Cereal, way to use, 260
Cheddar
Biscuits, 82, 83
Broccoli Frittata, Cheesy, 268, 269
Burger and Veggie Packets,
Grilled, 74, 75
Cabbage–Black Bean Enchiladas,
164, 165
Chicken Enchilada Pasta, Cheesy,
38, 39
–Chicken Sliders, BBQ Chipotle,
46, 47
Chicken Soup, Cheesy Buffalo,
198, 199
Grilled Cheese, Bacon, Tomato
and Avocado, 106, 107
Grilled Cheese Sandwiches, Beer-
Battered, 108, 109
Hash Brown Breakfast Casserole,
270, 271
Mac and Cheese, Three-
Ingredient, 192, 192
Potato Soup, Loaded, 200, 201
Quiche, Corn, Tomato and, 266,
267
Sweet Potatoes, Loaded Smashed,
236, 237
Taquitos, Potato and Chive, 158,
159
Cheese. See also Cheesy; specific
cheese
Cabbage–Black Bean Enchiladas,
164, 165
Chicken Breasts, Mexican Stuffed,
24, 25

Grilled, Bacon, Tomato and
Avocado, 106, 107
Grilled, Beefed-Up, 9
Grilled, Beer-Battered, 108, 109
Pizza, Breakfast, 274, 275
Quesadillas, Chicken-Pesto, 58, 59
Quesadillas, Chile-, Open-Face,
162, 163
Root Veggie Pizza, Roasted, with
Beer Bread Crust, 154, 155
Sauce, 33
Tuna Melts, 138, 139
way to use, 33
Zucchini Strata, Italian, 178, 179
Cheeseburger-Bacon Tacos, Amazing,
80, 81
Cheesy
Broccoli Frittata, 268, 269
Buffalo Chicken Soup, 198, 199
Chicken and Bacon No-Boil Pasta
Bake, 54, 55
Chicken Enchilada Pasta, 38, 39
Chicken and Sausage, 36, 37
Toast, 33
Cherry Tomatoes
Cheddar Burger and Veggie
Packets, Grilled, 74, 75
Mediterranean Chicken, Easy, 18,
19
Roasted Vegetables, 234, 235
Sausage-Pizza Quinoa, 102, 103
Shrimp Sheet Pan Dinner, Spicy,
148, 149
Chicken
Alfredo with Biscuits, Easy, 22,
22
and Bacon Pasta Bake, Cheesy No-
Boil, 54, 55
Bites, Buffalo, with Blue Cheese
Dipping Sauce, 44, 44
Boat Tacos, Ten-Minute, 16, 17
Breasts, Mexican Stuffed, 24, 25
Burritos, Homemade Takeout,
52, 53
–Cheddar Sliders, BBQ Chipotle,
46, 47
Chowder, "Fridge Sweep," 196,
197
Enchilada Pasta, Cheesy, 38, 39

Fettuccine with Vegetables and,
32, 32
General Tso's, Easy, 48, 49
Grilled Sriracha, with Garlic-
Cilantro Rice, 14, 15
Mediterranean, Easy, 18, 19
and Orzo with Pan-Roasted
Cauliflower, 42, 43
Packets, Honey-Sriracha, 50, 51
-Parmesan Ziti with Artichokes
and Spinach, 30, 31
Pizza Pockets, -Pineapple, 56, 57
Quesadillas, -Pesto, 58, 59
and Sausage, Cheesy, 36, 37
Singapore Noodles with, 20, 21
Spaghetti-Pizza Bake, White, 40,
41
taco coating, 23
Tetrazzini, Gluten-Free, 28, 29
Thai Peanut Pasta, 34, 35
Thighs, Soy–Brown Sugar–Glazed,
26, 27
with Tomatoes and Artichokes,
45, 45
Chick Pea(s)
Shrimp Sheet Pan Dinner, Spicy,
148, 149
and Tomato Curry, 174, 174
Vegetable Curry with Couscous,
176, 177
Chile(s)
Beef and Kasha Mexicana, 66, 66
-Cheese Quesadillas, Open-Face,
162, 163
Chicken Breasts, Mexican Stuffed,
24, 25
Chipotle Chicken–Cheddar
Sliders, BBQ, 46, 47
Chipotle Red Beans and Rice
Casserole, 193, 193
Chili, Bourbon, 218, 219
Chili, Texas, 216, 217
Chipotle Chicken–Cheddar Sliders,
BBQ, 46, 47
Chipotle Red Beans and Rice
Casserole, 193, 193
Chowder, Chicken "Fridge Sweep,"
196, 197
Chowder, Edamame Corn, 202, 203

Cilantro
    -Garlic Rice, Grilled Sriracha
        Chicken with, 14, *15*
    Green Rice with Toasted Pumpkin
        Seeds, *224, 225*
    -Lime Coleslaw, *242, 243*
Citrusy Pork Chop Skillet, 94, *95*
Coconut Shrimp, Crispy, 146, *147*
Cod
    Almond-Crusted, with Veggies,
        122, 123
    Cakes with Red Pepper Aioli, 114,
        115
    Crunchy Panko Fish Nuggets with
        Lemon-Dill Sauce, 116, *117*
    Lemon-Pepper Fish, Baked, *118, 119*
Coleslaw, Creamy, 82, *83*
Coleslaw, Cilantro-Lime, *242, 243*
Colorful Ham Salad Sandwiches, *96,
    97*
Condiments, way to use, 120
Cooking chart, fresh veggie, 10–11
Corn
    Beef and Kasha Mexicana, *66, 66*
    Bulgur and Lentils,
        Mediterranean, *169, 169*
    Chicken Enchilada Pasta, Cheesy,
        38, *39*
    Chowder, Edamame, *202, 203*
    cooking chart, 11
    Quiche, Cheddar, Tomato and,
        266, *267*
    Quinoa Salad–Stuffed Tomatoes,
        Gluten-Free, *168, 168*
Cornmeal Waffles, Spicy, *264, 265*
Couscous, Israeli, Risotto with
    Caramelized Onions and
    Sausage, *104, 105*
Couscous, Vegetable Curry with, 176,
    177
Cracker crumbs, way to use, 141
Creamy
    Coleslaw, 82, *83*
    Lemon Orzo Salad, *226, 227*
    Pulled-Pork Pasta, 88, *89*
Crispy Coconut Shrimp, 146, *147*
Croutons, 67
Crunchy Panko Fish Nuggets with
    Lemon-Dill Sauce, 116, *117*

Cuban Fried Rice, 98, *99*
Cucumber, in Tzatziki Sauce, *72, 73,*
    126, 127
Curry(ied)
    Cauliflower, Roasted, *240, 241*
    Chick Pea and Tomato, *174, 174*
    Vegetable, with Couscous, 176, *177*

D

Dill-Lemon Sauce, Crunchy Panko
    Fish Nuggets with, 116, *117*
Dill-Ranch Sauce, 238
Dip, Sour Cream, Seasoned, 120
Dipping Sauce, *146, 147*
    Blue Cheese, Buffalo Chicken Bites
        with, *44, 44*

E

Easy Chicken Alfredo with Biscuits,
    22, 22
Easy General Tso's Chicken, 48, *49*
Easy Mediterranean Chicken, 18, *19*
Easy Shrimp Paella, *150, 151*
Edamame Corn Chowder, *202, 203*
Egg(s)
    Bacon and Black Bean Quesadillas,
        250, 251
    Benedict Enchiladas, Spinach-
        Mushroom, 248, *249*
    French Toast, 67
    Fried Rice, Cuban, 98, *99*
    Frittata, Broccoli, Cheesy, *268, 269*
    Frittata, Italian, with Vinaigrette
        Tomatoes, *180, 181*
    Huevos Rancheros Tarts, *272, 273*
    Pancake Tacos, Bacon-and-, *256,
        257*
    Pizza, Breakfast, *274, 275*
    Scrambled, Sandwiches, Open-
        Face, *254, 255*
    Zucchini Strata, Italian, 178, *179*
Eggplant, in Vegetable Curry with
    Couscous, 176, *177*

Enchilada(s)
    Cabbage–Black Bean, 164, *165*
    Eggs Benedict, Spinach-
        Mushroom, 248, *249*
    Pasta, Cheesy Chicken, 38, *39*

F

Fajita Pulled-Pork Wraps with
    Avocado-Onion Slaw, 90, *91*
Fattoush Salad, *232, 233*
Feta
    Bulgur and Lentils,
        Mediterranean, *169, 169*
    Burgers, Greek, with Tzatziki
        Sauce, *72, 73*
    Flatbread Wraps, Mediterranean,
        160, 160
    Quinoa Salad–Stuffed Tomatoes,
        Gluten-Free, *168, 168*
    Shrimp Sheet Pan Dinner, Spicy,
        148, *149*
    Tabbouleh, Fruited, with Walnuts
        and, *228, 229*
Fettuccine with Chicken and
    Vegetables, *32, 32*
Fish
    Catfish, Cajun, *121, 121*
    coating, 23
    Cod, Almond-Crusted, with
        Veggies, *122, 123*
    Cod Cakes with Red Pepper Aioli,
        114, 115
    Lemon-Pepper, Baked, *118, 119*
    Nuggets, Crunchy Panko, with
        Lemon-Dill Sauce, 116, *117*
    Salmon, Honey-Mustard Glazed,
        132, 133
    Salmon, Quinoa Pilaf with
        Asparagus and, *128, 129*
    Salmon Sheet Pan Dinner, Asian,
        134, 135
    Salmon, Soba with, *136, 137*
    Salmon Tacos with Chunky
        Guacamole, *130, 131*
    Tacos, Soft and Crunchy, *124, 125*
    Tilapia, Greek, Baked, 126

Tilapia Gyros, 126, 127
Tuna Melts, 138, 139
Tuna-Noodle Skillet Supper, 140, 140
Five-Vegetable Spaghetti Casserole, 182, 183
Flatbread Wraps, Mediterranean, 160, 160
French Bread Taco Pizza, 76, 77
French Toast, 67
Frittata, Broccoli, Cheesy, 268, 269
Frittata, Italian, with Vinaigrette Tomatoes, 180, 181
Fritters, Oven-Fried Veggie, with Ranch-Dill Sauce, 238, 239
Fro-yo pops, 261
Fruit, way to use, 261
Fruited Tabbouleh with Walnuts and Feta, 228, 229
Fruity BBQ Sauce, 120

G

Garbanzo Bean(s). See Chick Pea(s)
Garlic
  Aioli, Red Pepper, Cod Cakes with, 114, 115
  Bread, 67
  -Chili Shrimp Pasta, Spicy, 142, 143
  -Cilantro Rice, Grilled Sriracha Chicken with, 14, 15
General Tso's Chicken, Easy, 48, 49
Gluten-Free Chicken Tetrazzini, 28, 29
Gluten-Free Chili-Lime Shrimp Burrito Bowls, 144, 145
Gluten-Free Quinoa Salad–Stuffed Tomatoes, 168, 168
Grain Salad, 175
  Three-Grain, 220, 221
Greek Burgers with Tzatziki Sauce, 72, 73
Greek Tilapia, Baked, 126
Green beans, cooking chart, 10
Green Rice with Toasted Pumpkin Seeds, 224, 225

Greens
  and Beans Soup, Smoky, 210, 211
  cooking chart, 11
  way to use, 223
Grilled Cheddar Burger and Veggie Packets, 74, 75
Grilled Cheese Sandwiches. See Cheese, Grilled
Grilled Sriracha Chicken with Garlic-Cilantro Rice, 14, 15
Guacamole, Chunky, 130, 131
Gyros, Tilapia, 126, 127

H

Haddock, Lemon-Pepper Fish, Baked, 118, 119
Ham
  Eggs Benedict Enchiladas, Spinach-Mushroom, 248, 249
  Fried Rice, Cuban, 98, 99
  Potato Soup, Loaded, 200, 201
  Salad Sandwiches, Colorful, 96, 97
  and Swiss Waffles, 262, 263
  and Wild Rice Soup, 212, 213
Hash Brown Breakfast Casserole, 270, 271
Herbs, way to use, 161
Honey-Mustard Glazed Salmon, 132, 133
Honey-Sriracha Chicken Packets, 50, 51
Hot Dogs, Kansas City Dogs, 110, 111
Huevos Rancheros Tarts, 272, 273
Hummus, in Mediterranean Flatbread Wraps, 160, 160

I

Ingredients, pantry, 67
Israeli Couscous Risotto with Caramelized Onions and Sausage, 104, 105
Italian Frittata with Vinaigrette Tomatoes, 180, 181

Italian Sausage Soup, 208, 209
Italian Zucchini Strata, 178, 179

J–K

Jerusalem artichokes, cooking chart, 10
Kansas City Dogs, 110, 111
Kasha and Beef Mexicana, 66, 66
Korean Barbecue Sauce, 85

L

Lasagna, Pumpkin, 188, 189
Lemon
  -Dill Sauce, Crunchy Panko Fish Nuggets with, 116, 117
  Orzo Salad, Creamy, 226, 227
  -Pepper Fish, Baked, 118, 119
Lentils and Bulgur, Mediterranean, 169, 169
Lettuce Wraps, Thai Turkey, 62, 63
Lime-Cilantro Coleslaw, 242, 243
Linguine, Thai Peanut Chicken Pasta, 34, 35
Loaded Potato Soup, 200, 201
Loaded Smashed Sweet Potatoes, 236, 237

M

Mac and Cheese, Three-Ingredient, 192
Make-ahead dishes
  Calzones, Spinach, Ricotta and Sausage, 100, 101
  Chili, Bourbon, 218, 219
  Coleslaw, Cilantro Lime, 242, 243
  Grain Salad, Three-, 220, 221
  Hash Brown Breakfast Casserole, 270, 271
  Orzo Salad, Creamy Lemon, 226, 227

Make-ahead dishes, *continued*
  Pulled Pork, Oven-Roasted, 86, 86
  Tabbouleh, Beet, Whole, 166, 167
  Tabbouleh, Fruited, with Walnuts and Feta, 228, 229
  Zucchini Strata, Italian, 178, 179
Marinades, 120
Meal planning, 67
Meat Loaf, Turkey, Tastiest, 60, 61
Mediterranean
  Bulgur and Lentils, 169, 169
  Chicken, Easy, 18, 19
  Flatbread Wraps, 160, 160
Mexicana, Beef and Kasha, 66, 66
Mexican Stuffed Chicken Breasts, 24, 25
Microwave, fresh veggie cooking chart, 10–11
Miso Cup, 214, 215
Mozzarella
  Calzones, Spinach, Ricotta and Sausage, 100, 101
  Chicken Breasts, Mexican Stuffed, 24, 25
  Frittata, Italian, with Vinaigrette Tomatoes, 180, 181
  Sausage-Pizza Quinoa, 102, 103
  Spaghetti Casserole, Five-Vegetable, 182, 183
  Spaghetti-Pizza Bake, White, 40, 41
Mushroom(s)
  Chicken Tetrazzini, Gluten-Free, 28, 29
  cooking chart, 11
  Lasagna, Pumpkin, 188, 189
  Pulled-Pork Pasta, Creamy, 88, 89
  Sausage-Pizza Quinoa, 102, 103
  Sloppy Joes, Steakhouse, 70
  Spaghetti Casserole, Five-Vegetable, 182, 183
  -Spinach Eggs Benedict Enchiladas, 248, 249
Mustard-Honey Glazed Salmon, 132, 133
MYO Pasta, 8

N

Noodles
  Beef Noodle Bowls, Asian, 78, 79
  Singapore, with Chicken, 20, 21
  Soba with Salmon, 136, 137
  Tuna-Noodle Skillet Supper, 140, 140
  Vegetable-Cashew Noodle Bowls, 172, 173
Nuts, way to use, 222

O

One-pot dishes
  Beans and Greens Soup, Smoky, 210, 211
  Beef and Kasha Mexicana, 66, 66
  Bratwurst and Vegetable Soup, 206, 207
  Chicken Alfredo with Biscuits, Easy, 22, 22
  Chicken Enchilada Pasta, Cheesy, 38, 39
  Chicken "Fridge Sweep" Chowder, 196, 197
  Chicken and Orzo with Pan-Roasted Cauliflower, 42, 43
  Chicken Pasta, Thai Peanut, 34, 35
  Chicken Soup, Cheesy Buffalo, 198, 199
  Chicken Tetrazzini, Gluten-Free, 28, 29
  Chicken Ziti, Parmesan-, with Artichokes and Spinach, 30, 31
  Chick Pea and Tomato Curry, 174, 174
  Chili, Texas, 216, 217
  Edamame Corn Chowder, 202, 203
  Israeli Couscous Risotto with Caramelized Onions and Sausage, 104, 105
  Mac and Cheese, Three-Ingredient, 192, 192
  Noodle Bowls, Vegetable-Cashew, 172, 173

Pasta Bolognese, 68, 69
Pork Chop Skillet, Citrusy, 94, 95
Pork Loin Sheet Pan Dinner, Roasted, 92, 93
Rigatoni with Spicy Tomato Sauce, 184, 185
Sausage-Pizza Quinoa, 102, 103
Shrimp Pasta, Chili-Garlic, Spicy, 142, 143
Soba with Salmon, 136, 137
Onion(s)
  -Avocado Slaw, Fajita Pulled-Pork Wraps with, 90, 91
  Caramelized, Israeli Couscous Risotto with Sausage and, 104, 105
  Red Onion Dressing, Sweet, 220
Open-Face Chile-Cheese Quesadillas, 162, 163
Open-Face Scrambled Egg Sandwiches, 254, 255
Orzo, Chicken with Pan-Roasted Cauliflower and, 42, 43
Orzo Salad, Creamy Lemon, 226, 227
Oven-Fried Veggie Fritters with Ranch-Dill Sauce, 238, 239
Oven-Roasted Pulled Pork, 86, 86

P

Packets, Cheddar Burger and Veggie, Grilled, 74, 75
Packets, Chicken, Honey-Sriracha, 50, 51
Paella, Shrimp, Easy, 150, 151
Pancakes, Veggie, 258, 259
Pancake Tacos, Bacon-and-Egg, 256, 257
Panko Fish Nuggets, Crunchy, with Lemon-Dill Sauce, 116, 117
Pantry ingredients, 67
Panzanella Salad, Avocado-Caesar, 244, 245
Parmesan-Chicken Ziti with Artichokes and Spinach, 30, 31
Parsnips, cooking chart, 11

Pasta. *See also* Noodles
    Bolognese, *68*, 69
    Bow-Ties with Broccoli Pesto, *170*, *171*
    Buffalo Pasta Salad, 120
    Chicken and Bacon Pasta Bake, Cheesy No-Boil, *54*, 55
    Chicken Enchilada, Cheesy, *38*, *39*
    Chicken Tetrazzini, Gluten-Free, *28*, *29*
    Fettuccine with Chicken and Vegetables, *32*, 32
    Italian Sausage Soup, *208*, *209*
    Lasagna, Pumpkin, *188*, *189*
    Mac and Cheese, Three-Ingredient, *192*, 192
    MYO, 8
    Orzo, Chicken with Pan-Roasted Cauliflower and, *42*, *43*
    Orzo Salad, Creamy Lemon, *226*, *227*
    Pulled-Pork, Creamy, *88*, 89
    Rigatoni with Spicy Tomato Sauce, *184*, *185*
    Shrimp, Chili-Garlic, Spicy, *142*, 143
    Spaghetti Casserole, Five-Vegetable, *182*, *183*
    Spaghetti-Pizza Bake, White, *40*, 41
    Thai Peanut Chicken, *34*, *35*
    Ziti, Parmesan-Chicken, with Artichokes and Spinach, *30*, 31
Peanut Chicken Pasta, Thai, *34*, *35*
Peas, cooking chart, 11
Peppers. *See* Bell Peppers; Chile(s)
Pesto, Broccoli, Bow-Ties with, *170*, *171*
Pesto-Chicken Quesadillas, *58*, 59
Pie crust, cracker crumb, 141
Pilaf, in Mediterranean Flatbread Wraps, *160*, 160
Pilaf, Quinoa, with Salmon and Asparagus, *128*, 129
Pineapple-Chicken Pizza Pockets, *56*, 57
Pita, in Fattoush Salad, *232*, *233*
Pita, Tilapia Gyros, *126*, *127*

Pizza
    beans on, 87
    Breakfast, *274*, *275*
    Calzones, Spinach, Ricotta and Sausage, *100*, 101
    French Bread Taco, *76*, 77
    Pockets, Pineapple-Chicken, *56*, 57
    Quinoa, Sausage-, *102*, *103*
    Root Veggie with Beer Bread Crust, *154*, *155*
    -Spaghetti Bake, White, *40*, 41
    tortilla crust for, 23
    White Bean and Spinach, *156*, 157
Pork. *See also* Bacon; Ham; Sausage, Pork
    Chop Skillet, Citrusy, *94*, 95
    Loin Sheet Pan Dinner, Roasted, *92*, 93
    Pulled, Oven-Roasted, *86*, 86
    Pulled-Pork Pasta, Creamy, *88*, 89
    Pulled-Pork Wraps, Fajita, with Avocado-Onion Slaw, *90*, 91
Potato(es)
    Burgers, Breakfast, *252*, *253*
    Cheddar Burger and Veggie Packets, Grilled, *74*, 75
    cooking chart, 11
    Hash Brown Breakfast Casserole, *270*, 271
    Pork Loin Sheet Pan Dinner, Roasted, *92*, 93
    Pot Pie Stew, Veggie, *186*, 187
    Roasted Vegetables, *234*, 235
    Salmon Sheet Pan Dinner, Asian, *134*, 135
    Soup, Loaded, *200*, 201
    Taquitos, Chive and, *158*, 159
Pot Pie Stew, Veggie, *186*, 187
Pumpkin Lasagna, *188*, *189*
Pumpkin Seeds, Toasted, Green Rice with, *224*, 225

Q

Quesadillas, 23
    Bacon, Egg and Black Bean, *250*, 251

    Chicken-Pesto, *58*, 59
    Chile-Cheese, Open-Face, *162*, *163*
Quiche, Corn, Cheddar and Tomato, *266*, *267*
Quick Buffalo Sauce, 120
Quick-fix dishes
    Chicken–Cheddar Sliders, BBQ Chipotle, *46*, 47
    Chicken-Pesto Quesadillas, *58*, 59
    Dogs, Kansas City, *110*, 111
    Fajita Pulled-Pork Wraps with Avocado-Onion Slaw, *90*, *91*
    Grilled Cheese, Bacon, Tomato and Avocado, *106*, *107*
    Grilled Cheese Sandwiches, Beer-Battered, *108*, 109
    Ham Salad Sandwiches, Colorful, *96*, 97
    Miso Cup, *214*, 215
    Tuna Melts, *138*, 139
Quinoa
    Cabbage–Black Bean Enchiladas, *164*, *165*
    Pilaf with Salmon and Asparagus, *128*, 129
    Red Harvest, *230*, 231
    Salad–Stuffed Tomatoes, Gluten-Free, *168*, 168
    Sausage-Pizza, *102*, *103*

R

Ranch-Dill Sauce, 238
Red Beans and Rice Casserole, Chipotle, *193*, 193
Red Cabbage
    Fattoush Salad, *232*, 233
    Pork Chop Skillet, Citrusy, *94*, 95
    in Salmon Tacos with Chunky Guacamole, *130*, 131
Red Harvest Quinoa, *230*, 231
Red Onion Dressing, Sweet, 220
Red Pepper Aioli, Cod Cakes with, *114*, 115
Rice
    beans and, 87
    Bowls, 8

Rice, *continued*
 Burritos, Homemade Takeout,
  52, 53
 Chicken Packets, Honey-Sriracha,
  50, 51
 Fried, Cuban, 98, 99
 Garlic-Cilantro, Grilled Sriracha
  Chicken with, 14, 15
 Green, with Toasted Pumpkin
  Seeds, 224, 225
 and Red Beans Casserole,
  Chipotle, 193, 193
 Salad, Three-Grain, 220, 221
 Shrimp Burrito Bowls, Chili-Lime,
  Gluten-Free, 144, 145
 Shrimp Paella, Easy, 150, 151
 way to use, 175
 Wild, and Ham Soup, 212, 213
Ricotta
 Lasagna, Pumpkin, 188, 189
 Root Veggie Pizza, Roasted, with
  Beer Bread Crust, 154, 155
 Spinach and Sausage Calzones,
  100, 101
Rigatoni with Spicy Tomato Sauce,
 184, 185
Risotto, Israeli Couscous, with
 Caramelized Onions and
 Sausage, 104, 105
Roasted Curried Cauliflower, 240, 241
Roasted Pork Loin Sheet Pan Dinner,
 92, 93
Roasted Root Vegetable Pizza with
 Beer Bread Crust, 154, 155
Roasted Vegetables, 234, 235
Roasting, fresh veggie cooking chart,
 10–11

S

Salad(s). *See also* Slaw(s)
 Buffalo Pasta, 120
 dressing, fruit in, 261
 Fattoush, 232, 233
 Grain, 175
 Grain, Three-, 220, 221
 Orzo, Creamy Lemon, 226, 227

 Panzanella, Avocado-Caesar, 244,
  245
 Quinoa, –Stuffed Tomatoes,
  Gluten-Free, 168, 168
 "Taco," 9
Salmon
 Honey-Mustard Glazed, 132, 133
 Quinoa Pilaf with Asparagus and,
  128, 129
 Sheet Pan Dinner, Asian, 134, 135
 Soba with, 136, 137
 Tacos with Chunky Guacamole,
  130, 131
Sandwich(es)
 Beef Biscuit Stacks, BBQ, 82, 83
 Burgers, Breakfast, 252, 253
 Burgers, Greek, with Tzatziki
  Sauce, 72, 73
 Chicken–Cheddar Sliders, BBQ
  Chipotle, 46, 47
 Dogs, Kansas City, 110, 111
 Fajita Pulled-Pork Wraps with
  Avocado-Onion Slaw, 90, 91
 Flatbread Wraps, Mediterranean,
  160, 160
 Grilled Cheese, Bacon, Tomato
  and Avocado, 106, 107
 Grilled Cheese, Beefed-Up, 9
 Grilled Cheese Sandwiches, Beer-
  Battered, 108, 109
 Ham Salad, Colorful, 96, 97
 Pizza Pockets, Pineapple-Chicken,
  56, 57
 Scrambled Egg, Open-Face, 254,
  255
 Sloppy Joes, Steakhouse, 70, 71
 Tilapia Gyros, 126, 127
 tortilla roll up, 23
 Tuna Melts, 138, 139
Sauce(s)
 Aioli, Red Pepper, Cod Cakes with,
  114, 115
 Barbecue, Korean, 85
 BBQ, Fruity, 120
 Blue Cheese Dipping, Buffalo
  Chicken Bites with, 44, 44
 Buffalo, Quick, 120
 Cheese, 33
 Dipping, 146, 147

 Lemon-Dill, Crunchy Panko Fish
  Nuggets with, 116, 117
 Ranch-Dill, 238
 Tomato, Spicy, Rigatoni with, 184,
  185
 Tzatziki, 72, 73, 126, 127
 Yogurt, 116
Sausage, Pork
 Beans and Greens Soup, Smoky,
  210, 211
 Bratwurst and Vegetable Soup,
  206, 207
 Calzones, Spinach and Ricotta,
  100, 101
 and Chicken, Cheesy, 36, 37
 Hash Brown Breakfast Casserole,
  270, 271
 Italian Sausage Soup, 208, 209
 -Pizza Quinoa, 102, 103
 Shrimp Paella, Easy, 150, 151
Sausage, Turkey
 and Black-Eyed Pea Soup, 204,
  205
 Breakfast Burgers, 252, 253
 Israeli Couscous Risotto with
  Caramelized Onions and, 104,
  105
 Italian Sausage Soup, 208, 209
Sausage, Vegetarian, Beer-Glazed
 Brats and Beans, 190, 191
Seafood. *See* Fish; Shrimp
Seeds, way to use, 222
Sheet Pan Dinner(s)
 Pork Loin, Roasted, 92, 93
 Salmon, Asian, 134, 135
 Shrimp, Spicy, 148, 149
Shellfish. *See* Shrimp
Shrimp
 Burrito Bowls, Chili-Lime, Gluten-
  Free, 144, 145
 Coconut, Crispy, 146, 147
 Paella, Easy, 150, 151
 Pasta, Chili-Garlic, Spicy, 142, 143
 Sheet Pan Dinner, Spicy, 148, 149
Singapore Noodles with Chicken, 20,
 21
Skewers, Grilled Sriracha Chicken
 with Garlic-Cilantro Rice, 14,
 15

Slaw(s)
    Avocado-Onion, Fajita Pulled-Pork
        Wraps with, 90, 91
    Coleslaw, Cilantro-Lime, 242, 243
    Coleslaw, Creamy, 82, 83
Sliders, BBQ Chipotle Chicken–
    Cheddar, 46, 47
Sloppy Joes, Steakhouse, 70, 71
Slow-cooker dishes
    Beef Biscuit Stacks, BBQ, 82, 83
    Brats and Beans, Beer-Glazed,
        190, 191
    Bulgur and Lentils,
        Mediterranean, 169, 169
    Chicken with Tomatoes and
        Artichokes, 45, 45
    Ham and Wild Rice Soup, 212, 213
    Lasagna, Pumpkin, 188, 189
    Pot Pie Stew, Veggie, 186, 187
    Vegetable Curry with Couscous,
        176, 177
Smoky Beans and Greens Soup, 210,
    211
Smoothies, 223
Soba with Salmon, 136, 137
Soft and Crunchy Fish Tacos, 124, 125
Soup(s)
    Beans and Greens, Smoky, 210, 211
    Black-Eyed Pea and Sausage, 204,
        205
    Bratwurst and Vegetable, 206, 207
    Chicken, Cheesy Buffalo, 198, 199
    Chicken "Fridge Sweep" Chowder,
        196, 197
    Edamame Corn Chowder, 202,
        203
    Ham and Wild Rice, 212, 213
    Italian Sausage, 208, 209
    Miso Cup, 214, 215
    Potato, Loaded, 200, 201
Sour Cream
    Potato Soup, Loaded, 200, 201
    Seasoned, 120
    Sweet Potatoes, Loaded Smashed,
        236, 237
Soy–Brown Sugar–Glazed Chicken
    Thighs, 26, 27
Spaghetti
    Casserole, Five-Vegetable, 182, 183

Chicken and Bacon Pasta Bake,
    No-Boil, Cheesy, 54, 55
Chicken Tetrazzini, Gluten-Free,
    28, 29
Pasta Bolognese, 68, 69
-Pizza Bake, White, 40, 41
Shrimp Pasta, Spicy Chili-Garlic,
    142, 143
Spicy Chili-Garlic Shrimp Pasta, 142,
    143
Spicy Cornmeal Waffles, 264, 265
Spicy Shrimp Sheet Pan Dinner, 148,
    149
Spinach
    Beans and Greens Soup, Smoky,
        210, 211
    Burgers, Greek, with Tzatziki
        Sauce, 72, 73
    Calzones, Ricotta and Sausage,
        100, 101
    cooking chart, 11
    Eggs Benedict Enchiladas,
        -Mushroom, 248, 249
    Israeli Couscous Risotto with
        Caramelized Onions and
        Sausage, 104, 105
    Lasagna, Pumpkin, 188, 189
    Pancakes, Veggie, 258, 259
    Parmesan-Chicken Ziti with
        Artichokes and, 30, 31
    Quesadillas, Chicken-Pesto, 58, 59
    Steak Bibimbap, 84, 85
    and White Bean Pizza, 156, 157
Squash, cooking chart, 11
Sriracha
    Buffalo Sauce, Quick, 120
    Chicken, Grilled, with Garlic-
        Cilantro Rice, 14, 15
    -Honey Chicken Packets, 50, 51
Steak Bibimbap, 84, 85
Steakhouse Sloppy Joes, 70, 71
Steaming, fresh veggie cooking chart,
    10–11
Stew, Veggie Pot Pie, 186, 187
Strata, Zucchini, Italian, 178, 179
Succotash, 87
Sugar Snap Peas
    Beef Noodle Bowls, Asian, 78, 79
    cooking chart, 11

Singapore Noodles with Chicken,
    20, 21
Soba with Salmon, 136, 137
Summer squash, cooking chart, 11
Sweet Potatoes
    cooking chart, 11
    Loaded Smashed, 236, 237
    Pot Pie Stew, Veggie, 186, 187
    Root Veggie Pizza, Roasted, with
        Beer Bread Crust, 154, 155
Swiss and Ham Waffles, 262, 263

T

Tabbouleh, Beet, Whole, 166, 167
Tabbouleh, Fruited, with Walnuts
    and Feta, 228, 229
Taco Pizza, French Bread, 76, 77
Tacos
    Bacon-Cheeseburger, Amazing,
        80, 81
    bean, 87
    Boat, Ten-Minute, 16, 17
    Fish, Soft and Crunchy, 124, 125
    Pancake, Bacon-and-Egg, 256, 257
    Salmon, with Chunky Guacamole,
        130, 131
    way to use, 23
"Taco" Salad, 9
Tapenade, 18
Taquitos, Potato and Chive, 158, 159
Tartar Sauce, Tasty, 120
Tarts, Huevos Rancheros, 272, 273
Tastiest Turkey Meat Loaf, 60, 61
Tasty Tartar Sauce, 120
Ten-Minute Boat Tacos, 16, 17
Texas Chili, 216, 217
Thai Peanut Chicken Pasta, 34, 35
Thai Turkey Lettuce Wraps, 62, 63
Three-Grain Salad, 220, 221
Three-Ingredient Mac and Cheese,
    192, 192
Tilapia
    Fish Tacos, Soft and Crunchy, 124,
        125
    Greek, Baked, 127
    Gyros, 126, 127

Tomato(es). *See also* Cherry
      Tomatoes
    Bacon, and Avocado Grilled
      Cheese, 106, *107*
    Chicken with Artichokes and, *45,*
      45
    and Chick Pea Curry, *174, 174*
    Corn and Cheddar Quiche, 266,
      267
    Huevos Rancheros Tarts, *272, 273*
    Pasta Bolognese, 68, *69*
    Quinoa Salad–Stuffed, Gluten-
      Free, *168, 168*
    Sauce, Spicy, Rigatoni with, 184,
      185
    Spaghetti Casserole, Five-
      Vegetable, *182, 183*
    Vegetable Curry with Couscous,
      176, *177*
    Vinaigrette, Frittata with, Italian,
      180, *181*
    Zucchini Strata, Italian, *178, 179*
Tortillas. *See also* Quesadillas
    Bacon-Cheeseburger Tacos,
      Amazing, 80, *81*
    Burritos, Homemade Takeout,
      52, 53
    Chicken and Sausage, Cheesy, *36,*
      37
    Enchiladas, Spinach-Mushroom
      Eggs Benedict, 248, *249*
    Fajita Pulled-Pork Wraps with
      Avocado-Onion Slaw, 90, *91*
    Fish Tacos, Soft and Crunchy, *124,*
      125
    Salmon Tacos with Chunky
      Guacamole, 130, *131*
    "Taco" Salad, 9
    Taquitos, Potato and Chive, 158,
      159
    way to use, 23
Tuna Melts, 138, *139*
Tuna-Noodle Skillet Supper, 140, *140*
Turkey
    Black-Eyed Pea and Sausage Soup,
      204, *205*
    Burgers, Breakfast, 252, *253*
    Italian Sausage Soup, 208, *209*
    Lettuce Wraps, Thai, *62, 63*

Meat Loaf, Tastiest, 60, *61*
Sausage, Israeli Couscous Risotto
    with Caramelized Onions and,
    104, 105
Tzatziki Sauce, *72, 73, 126, 127*

U–V

Udon Noodle Bowls, Vegetable-
    Cashew, *172, 173*
Vegetable(s). *See also specific*
      vegetables
    Almond-Crusted Cod with
      Veggies, *122, 123*
    -Cashew Noodle Bowls, *172, 173*
    Cheddar Burger and Veggie
      Packets, Grilled, *74, 75*
    Chicken Packets, Honey-Sriracha,
      50, 51
    cooking chart, 10–11
    Curry with Couscous, 176, *177*
    Fettuccine with Chicken and, *32,*
      32
    Fritters, Oven-Fried Veggie, with
      Ranch-Dill Sauce, 238, *239*
    Pancakes, Veggie, *258, 259*
    Pizza, Root Veggie with Beer Bread
      Crust, 154, *155*
    Pot Pie Stew, Veggie, *186, 187*
    Roasted, *234, 235*
    Soup, Bratwurst and, *206, 207*
    Spaghetti Casserole, Five-
      Vegetable, *182, 183*
    Steak Bibimbap, 84, *85*
Veggie Pot Pie Stew, *186, 187*

W

Waffles, Cornmeal, Spicy, *264, 265*
Waffles, Ham and Swiss, 262, *263*
Wax beans, cooking chart, 10
Wheat Berries, in Three-Grain Salad,
    220, 221
White Bean and Spinach Pizza, 156,
    157

White Spaghetti-Pizza Bake, *40, 41*
Whole Beet Tabbouleh, *166, 167*
Wild Rice and Ham Soup, *212, 213*
Winter squash, cooking chart, 11
Wraps
    Fajita Pulled-Pork, with Avocado-
      Onion Slaw, 90, *91*
    Mediterranean Flatbread, *160, 160*
    rice in, 175
    Turkey Lettuce, Thai, *62, 63*

Y

Yogurt
    Coleslaw, Creamy, 82, *83*
    Lemon Orzo Salad, Creamy, 226,
      227
    Sauce, 116
    Tzatziki Sauce, *72, 73, 126, 127*

Z

Ziti, Parmesan-Chicken, with
      Artichokes and Spinach, *30, 31*
Zucchini
    in Chicken Alfredo with Biscuits,
      Easy, 22, *22*
    Cod, Almond-Crusted, with
      Veggies, *122, 123*
    Frittata, Italian, with Vinaigrette
      Tomatoes, 180, *181*
    Roasted Vegetables, *234, 235*
    Spaghetti Casserole, Five-
      Vegetable, *182, 183*
    Strata, Italian, *178, 179*

HUNGRY FOR MORE
FROM BETTY CROCKER?
YOU'LL LOVE:

BETTY CROCKER
SHEET PAN DESSERTS

ISBN: 978-0-544-81623-7
$19.99
Trade Paperback, 8" X 9"
288 Pages
Full-Color Throughout

BETTY CROCKER
FRESH FROM THE FREEZER

ISBN: 978-0-544-81624-4
$19.99
Trade Paperback, 8" x 9"
304 Pages
Full-Color Throughout